LABOR AND WRITING IN EARLY MODERN ENGLAND, 1567–1667

Labor and Writing in Early Modern England, 1567–1667

LAURIE ELLINGHAUSEN
The University of Missouri-Kansas City, USA

LONDON AND NEW YORK

First published 2008 by Ashgate Publishing

2 Park Square, Milton Park, Abingdon, Oxfordshire OX14 4RN
52 Vanderbilt Avenue, New York, NY 10017

Routledge is an imprint of the Taylor & Francis Group, an informa business

First issued in paperback 2019

A Library of Congress record exists under LC control number: 2007020237

ISBN 13: 978-0-8153-9009-1 (hbk)
ISBN 13: 978-0-367-89301-9 (pbk)

Contents

List of Illustrations

Illustrations 2.1, 4.1 and 5.1 are produced by ProQuest Information and Learning Company as part of Early English Books Online. Inquiries may be made to:

ProQuest Information & Learning
789 E. Eisenhower Parkway
Box 1346
Ann Arbor, MI 48106-1346 USA
Telephone: 734.761.4700
E-mail: info@il.proquest.com
Web page: www.il.proquest.com

Acknowledgments

My first debt is to Richard Helgerson and Patricia Fumerton, who nurtured and encouraged this project in its embryonic stages. For guiding me through these labored beginnings, I thank them. Through a combination of wit and patience, healthy irreverence and impeccable professionalism, they provided the essential guidance without which this project would have never reached printed form. I also thank Mark Rose, who offered incisive responses to my material and suggested readings that productively challenged my developing thinking on authorship and print culture. I would like to thank Claire Busse, Simone Chess, Steven Deng, Tassie Gniady, Soren Hammerschmidt, Roze Hentschell, Jessica Murphy, Anna Viele, and Jessica Winston for taking time from their own work to help with my own.

At the University of Missouri, Kansas City, I have benefited from a rich community of energetic faculty. Their friendship and camaraderie provided a nurturing environment for this project's transition from dissertation to book. Although my thanks go to all, I specifically would like to acknowledge the members of the junior faculty group who read and offered detailed commentary on earlier forms of these chapters: Virginia Blanton, Daniella Mallinick, Jennifer Phegley, Michael Pritchett, Jeff Rydberg-Cox, Lara Vetter, and George Williams. On the conference circuit, I participated in many stimulating scholarly exchanges and forged connections that continue to benefit my work today. In particular, I would like to thank Regina Buccola, Jonathan Walker, and Mark Aune for their enthusiasm and support.

This project could not have been completed without generous funding from several sources. A Faculty Research Grant from UMKC and a Franklin Grant from the American Philosophical Society supported two summers in London, where I was able to focus attention on the primary materials essential to my argument. Additionally, a grant from the University of Missouri Research Board supported a semester's leave from my teaching and administrative duties, permitting me to shape the book into its final form. The brunt of the material here represents the early printed book collections at the Newberry Library, the British Library, the Bodleian Library, and the Guildhall Library. For material on John Taylor "The Water Poet," I am indebted to the Thames River and Rowing Museum in Henley-on-Thames and the Company of Watermen and Lightermen in London. Thanks especially to Colin Middlemiss for a lively and thorough tour of the company's history and headquarters.

Versions of Chapters One and Four appeared in *Studies in English Literature 1500–1900* and *The Ben Jonson Journal*, respectively. They are reprinted here with permission.

Finally, my labors could not have reached their fruition without the ongoing support of my family and friends. In particular, my husband Jeff Callan both challenged my thinking and supplied an atmosphere of love and warmth during this book's final stages. To him goes my deepest gratitude of all.

Introduction

Forging Authorship

One of the most important and enduring developments of what we call the "Renaissance" or "early modern" period is the modern sense of vocation – that is, the sense that one's identity is bound up in one's work. The concept of labor as a calling, which was assisted by early modern experiments in democracy, print, and Protestant religion, had a lasting effect on the history of authorship as a profession – even during a period in which, due to the rise of poverty and the transitory nature of wage labor, a stable occupational identity eluded many people. The English poet, playwright, and erstwhile bricklayer Ben Jonson applied labor to authorship in a literal way when, in his book of literary criticism, *Discoveries*, he likened writing to continuous work in which the poet must "bring all to the forge, and fire, againe; tourne it a newe."[1] This study explores the social and literary context for Jonson's image by examining the texts of non-aristocratic authors who represented their own writing as material work and claimed labor as a positive value for writing: Jonson, the maidservant and poet Isabella Whitney, the journalist and satirist Thomas Nashe, the boatman John Taylor "The Water Poet," and the Puritan radical George Wither. The embrace of writing as work represents a challenge to aristocratic literary culture, which valued decoration, ambiguity, and effortlessness, qualities encapsulated by courtly *sprezzatura*. By contrast, the writers I will discuss differ sharply from reigning modes of authorial self-presentation in their insistence on claiming work, literary and otherwise, as a form of virtue that marks the writer as superior to both the amateur and the typical professional.

When early modern writers claim writing as work, rather than as inspiration or as what courtier Philip Sidney called "this ink-wasting toy,"[2] they summon two closely interrelated kinds of social stigma. First is the "stigma of print," a highly influential term coined half a century ago by J.W. Saunders. Broadly, Saunders's thesis posits that a writer's participation in the burgeoning early modern print market designates him or her as socially inferior, because to write for the market is to write for pay and thus acknowledge that one needs money. The stigma of print is often understood by contrasting the older, manuscript-based form of authorship as a medium of *social* exchange with the newer, market-based form of print production as a medium of *economic* exchange: "whereas for the amateur poets of the Court an avoidance of print was *socially* desirable, for the professional poets outside or only on the edge of Court circles the achievement of print became an *economic* necessity."[3] The

---

[1] *Ben Jonson*, ed. C.H. Hereford and Percy and Evelyn Simpson, 11 vols, Oxford: Clarendon, 1925–52, 8: 638.

[2] *Sir Philip Sidney's Defense of Poesy*, ed. Lewis Soens, Lincoln: U of Nebraska P, 1970, 55.

[3] J.W. Saunders, "The Stigma of Print" A Note on the Social Bases of Tudor Poetry," *Essays in Criticism* I (1951), 139–64.

putative (and false) distinction between the economic and the social partakes of an aristocratic logic that imposes a social hierarchy onto literary cultures, one foreign to our contemporary society in which publication is a mark of authorial legitimacy and success. Yet in practice, the alignment of manuscript culture with aristocracy and print culture with commoners did not always ring true.[4] Furthermore, since Saunders, scholars such as Richard Halpern, Wendy Wall, and Alexandra Halasz have looked at the stigma in more nuanced ways, treating more specific instances of print publication and its social bases.[5] Their richly complex studies demonstrate the different areas in which print could become an opportunity for self-promotion and self-presentation – though always with the probability that print is something for which an author must apologize. In keeping with these lines of inquiry, I too am interested in complicating the "stigma of print" by investigating print's role in fashioning new social and economic identities.

My specific contribution to these discussions comes through an investigation of *labor* and its relationship to writing during the early decades of print capitalism in England. The social liability of print, dependent as it is on class-based discourses, feeds into a much broader liability – what one might call the stigma against labor, a characteristic that scholars have yet to clearly connect to the rise of the early modern print market. As becomes clear from even a cursory glance at the social history of the period, the performance of manual work located a subject on the bottom end of the social scale. Blacksmithing, bricklaying, and rowing, for example, typified the kinds of trade that Richard Mulcaster deemed "manuary" in contradistinction to the "mercantile" trades occupied by the better sort of commoners.[6] Industry – working on raw material with one's hands – was associated with hard labor, sweat, and baseness. Tudor social descriptions, which devote a great deal of attention to exploring the nuances among different grades of nobility, bluntly place laborers and craftsmen into one lump at the very bottom of the hierarchy, denying them the same careful attention as that reserved for "gentlemen." Thomas Smith's *De Republica Anglorum* (1583) begins by comparing writing with metalworking: "Wherefore (gentle Reader) accept in good part my zeale and this honorable mans travaile: assuring thy self that the fame framed by an expert workemaister, and forged of pure and excellent mettall, will not faile in prooving to be a right commodious instrument."[7] Yet later in the book, Smith

[4] Steven May and Peter Burke offer two different examples of ways in which the class-based separation between modes of composition was in fact merely theoretical. Burke, in his *Popular Culture in Early Modern Europe*, argues for a "two-way traffic" between elite and popular culture, London: Maurice Temple Smith, 1978. May presents evidence that aristocrats could, and often did, write for print; see "Tudor Aristocrats and the Mythical 'Stigma of Print'," *Renaissance Papers* (1980), 11–18.

[5] Richard Halpern, *The Poetics of Primitive Acculmulation: English Renaissance Culture and the Genealogy of Capital*, Ithaca: Cornell UP, 1991; Wendy Wall, *The Imprint of Gender: Authorship and Publication in the English Renaissance*, Ithaca: Cornell UP, 1993; Alexandra Halasz, *The Marketplace of Print: Pamphlets and the Public Sphere in Early Modern England*, Cambridge: Cambridge UP, 1997.

[6] Richard Mulcaster, *Positions*, ed. Richard L. DeMolen, New York: Columbia UP, 1971, 162.

[7] Thomas Smith, *De Republica Anglorum*, London, 1583, A4^{v}.

calls laborers and artificers the "fourth sort" among four grades of people; this order merely consists of "lowe and base" persons who "do not rule."[8] On the status of "day labourers, poore husbandmen, yea marchantes or retailers which have no free lande, copyholders, and all artificers, as Taylers, Shoomakers, Carpenters, Brickemakers, Bricklayers, Masons, and c.," Smith writes, "These have no voice nor authoritie in our common wealth, and no account is made of them but onelie to be ruled, not to rule other."[9] Other social descriptions employ similar language. William Harrison's *Description of England* (1576) also nominates craftspeople as the "fourth sort" out of four, while distinguishing gentlemen from non-gentlemen according to the nature of their work – mental or manual, respectively:

> Whosoever studieth the laws of the realm, whoso abideth in the university (giving his mind to his book), or professeth physic and the liberal sciences, or beside his service in the room of a captain in the wars, or good counsel given at home, whereby his commonwealth is benefited, can live without manual labour, and thereto is able and will bear the port, charge, and countenance of a gentleman, he shall for money have a coat and arms bestowed upon him by heralds who in the charter of the same do of custom pretend antiquity and service, and many gay things thereunto, being made so good cheap, be called master (which is the title that men give to esquires and gentlemen), and reputed for a gentleman ever after . . .[10]

Thomas Wilson, writing in 1600, devises more than four categories, but the order is the same: he lists nobles, gentry, citizens, yeomen, artisans and laborers in descending order as the main social groups. William Camden divides the commonwealth into "a King or Monarch, Noblemen or Gentry, Citizens, Free-bourne, whom we call, Yeomen, and Artizans or Handicraftsmen."[11] By 1695, Gregory King uses a ladder of occupations rather than designations of blood or land ownership to distinguish the different levels of gentility.[12] Across these writings, ideas of art and craft are pulled into the service of reinforcing hierarchy. By reading texts by non-aristocratic authors from all over the social spectrum, I will argue that the historical tension between these nominally separate spheres of activity is essential to understanding the development of a sense of modern authorial vocation.

Vocation will be an important term here, as work was a major category that early moderns used to conceptualize social life. While the Elizabethan "great chain of being" represents a fantasy of social harmony, the often strident early modern descriptions that align occupation with social standing offer an accompanying fantasy: that occupation, a category that is gradually assuming the place of land ownership and is undergoing heavy redefinition, can fix a subject into a single, stable social identity. Keith Wrightson describes this impulse as part of an Elizabethan "mental habit" of

---

[8] Ibid., F.

[9] Ibid., F.

[10] William Harrison, *The Description of England*, ed. Georges Edelen, Ithaca, NY: Cornell UP, 1968, 177.

[11] Qtd. in Keith Wrightson, "Estates, Degrees, and Sorts: Changing Perceptions of Society in Tudor and Stuart England," *Language, History, and Class*, ed. Penelope J. Corfield, Oxford: Basil Blackwell, 1991, 30–52, 31.

[12] Qtd. in Anthony Fletcher and John Stevenson, "Introduction," *Order and Disorder in Early Modern England*, New York: Cambridge UP, 1985, 1–40, 1–2.

stratifying people that "bears witness to the fact that the most fundamental structural characteristic of English society was its high degree of stratification, its distinctive and all-pervasive system of social inequality."[13] The idea of vocation can either confirm or put pressure on this stratification. According to Max Weber's influential thesis in *The Protestant Ethic and the Spirit of Capitalism*, the spread of Protestantism in early modern Europe introduced the idea of labor in a "calling" as a way to conceive of the self. By following the role in which they felt themselves "called" by God, subjects could demonstrate personal worth through diligence, thrift, and integrity.[14] Most importantly, the calling was a matter of private revelation between the individual and God – not something dictated by exterior ideologies. In practice, however, the concept of vocation fragmented into two competing ideas. The first takes a calling to be labor in a specific trade that determines one's identity and fortune. This view supports the notion that a person's occupation fixes him or her within a hierarchical order, and it requires consistent affiliation with a trade as evidence of "stability" and obedience to one's "place." The second view of the calling is the one espoused by early modern society's more radical elements: that labor in *any* calling is virtuous. This position challenges the fixity of occupation within the social order by proposing that any work, when approached with diligence, fulfills an individual's duty to God.[15]

Here I will give this interplay between fixed social identity and self-determination a more specific focus by proposing that the development of authorship in early modern England derives much of its energy from the constant up-and-down movements within changing occupational strata. Based on my study of the careers of non-aristocratic authors, a major part of my premise is that positing oneself on the downside of hierarchy, while suggestive of oppression, can result in payoffs for the author as well. Invoking Michel de Certeau's distinction between "strategy" and "tactics" as two different "ways of operating," I will argue that the "tactics" employed by those who claim to be of marginal status (as opposed to the "strategy" that comes from political, scientific, and economic hegemony) allow these writers to "manipulate events in order to turn them into 'opportunities'."[16] According to de Certeau, the "tactic" enjoys "no base where it can capitalize on its advantages, prepare its expansions, and secure independence with respect to circumstances."[17] This baselessness, I propose, compels non-aristocratic authors to *use* their self-professed marginality in ways that actually confer an alternative kind of authority to that of the socially privileged. Throughout, I argue with a distinct awareness that these personae are, to one degree or another, consciously *constructed* modes of self-presentation that may have little basis in the authors' "real" lives. Thus, this study is not restricted to recognizably "working class" figures but treats authors from a

---

[13] Keith Wrightson, *English Society, 1580–1680*, London: Hutchinson, 1982, 17.

[14] Max Weber, *The Protestant Ethic and the Spirit of Capitalism*, trans. Talcott Parsons, London: Routledge, 1992.

[15] I have found the most concise articulation of these two viewpoints in Joseph P. Ward's *Metropolitan Communities: Trade Guilds, Identity, and Change in Early Modern London*, Stanford, CA: Stanford UP, 1997, 47.

[16] Michel de Certeau, *The Practice of Everyday Life*, trans. Steven Rendall, Berkeley: U of California P, 1988, xix.

[17] Ibid.

variety of social positions. We gain the opportunity to explore not only John Taylor's use of his humble profession, but the intriguing paradox of a Cambridge graduate like Nashe deciding to style himself as a "day laborer" in his writing activities.

In Jonson's case, the invocation of labor is strategic as well. His evocation of blacksmithing goes beyond the sense of authorship as a trade of commodities toward the kinds of material, industrial production that located a worker at the bottom – or even outside of – mainstream society. The division between material production and mercantile trade was a very real one in Renaissance culture; this was a distinction rife with potent associations about class and individual character. Despite the derision of the laboring classes that we so often see in Jonson's drama, and the scorn for the mythological blacksmith we see in his poem "Execration Upon Vulcan," it seems as though blacksmithing expresses something *essential* about writing, suggesting a nostalgic longing for an age before print capitalism – after all, blacksmithing, as one of the oldest trades, produces the tools on which all other trades rely. Likewise, no matter what tone the "laboring" authors in this study use to describe their writing, I have found that all of them use labor to evoke marginality, to protest the marginalizing – and yet strangely liberating – effects of social change, and to claim a standard of literary and social evaluation that can correct the perceived *de*-valuation of their authorship within confining occupational and class discourses. Furthermore, despite the fact that all of them produce saleable texts, each identifies with a kind of labor that is *process*-oriented and produces no wealth-generating commodities: Whitney positions herself as a poor maidservant, Nashe styles himself a "day laborer," Jonson chooses blacksmithing as his metaphor, Taylor is a waterman, and Wither redirects the focus from his text as product of his labor to the virtue of his labor itself.

Raymond Williams once suggested a dynamic of "commitment and alignment" for the study of authors' social positions as reflected in their writing. According to Williams, "alignment" represents the social relations that determine who writers are, what genres and voices they choose, and who they try to reach. "Commitment," on the other hand, represents the beliefs to which an author subscribes, which are largely delimited by his or her alignment. In Marxist terms, to fail to recognize one's alignment is to operate under a false apprehension of one's own freedom.[18] But, given the fact that the authors I treat here turn their professed poverty and disenfranchisement into useful rhetorical poses that allow them to negotiate restrictions, it seems that "alignment" is more than merely deterministic – it can become an opportunity to reflect on one's status and to re-frame this status as sardonic reflection, as a platform for authority, or perhaps even as a choice. Thus I explore several key questions. If laborers and artisans indeed represented the lower strata of society (at least in theory, if not always in fact), why does labor become such a common way of imagining writing in this period – in other words, why are non-aristocratic writers identifying with the "fourth sort"? Why do writers in socially complex non-aristocratic positions feel the need to define themselves according to – or *against* – images of labor? Is labor a response to the new fact of the print market, which has made professional authorship possible – but also has called for a new ways to describe texts in terms

[18] Raymond Williams, "The Writer: Commitment and Alignment," *Marxism Today* (June 1980), 22–5.

of their quality, their learning, and their audiences? I am interested especially in how different forms of labor are talked about and what place they occupy within social discourses. How do "types" of laborers help a society think through its social problems? Do their literary representations in particular assist with this? What coincidences might we see between changes in ways of thinking about labor and the development of "literature" as a vocation? By contextualizing writings by five Renaissance authors within the major socioeconomic changes that we have come to identify with the "early modern," I contend that when authors liken themselves to laborers and their writing to labor, this is not to be taken as just a metaphor. Rather, I take it as a sign of historical change that is reflected in changes in literary culture.

Laureates, Possessives, and Others

Key to this study is the issue of self-presentation. Among the ample scholarly literature on this subject, Richard Helgerson's *Self-Crowned Laureates* remains influential. Helgerson groups Jonson with Edmund Spenser and John Milton as "three poets whose ambition preceded and determined their work, three poets who strove to achieve a major literary career and who said so."[19] Important to this striving is the idea that the man and his work are inextricably bound – when they present their works, they are also "presenting themselves,"[20] an important premise to my study as well. Furthermore, like the laureates, the writers I discuss here struggle to articulate a position that has no language of its own yet. They operate within a culture that regards poetry as, at best, a youthful pastime to be cast aside later for more useful, mature enterprises.

But the writers I treat here differ from the "laureates" in two important and unaccounted for ways. First is the notion of expectation. For Helgerson, laureate status hinges on two questions: "What recognition could such a poet hope for? And what position might he expect to fill?"[21] In the case of Spenser, Jonson, and Milton, the poet deems himself the spokesman of the nation; by this means, he makes himself useful to his society and compensates for the view that poets are either leisurely dabblers (the "amateurs") or vulgar hirelings writing for pay (the "professionals"). However, for writers of more decidedly common personae (whether inherited or acquired), the expectation of public service is problematic. Expectation presumes not only access to elite circles, but that the "nation" might be interested in what a particular writer has to say. Helgerson notes: "The laureates began in close association with the amateurs. They attended the same schools, visited the same great houses, wrote poems to the same noble patrons, and sought preferment in the same royal court."[22] Indeed, given this shared characteristic, it is hard to imagine the civic-mindedness of the laureate impressed upon a writer like Isabella Whitney – a woman who claims to have spent her young adulthood as a maidservant, even if it

---

[19] Richard Helgerson, *Self-Crowned Laureates: Spenser, Jonson, Milton and the Literary System*, Berkeley: U of California P, 1982, 1.

[20] Ibid., 2.

[21] Ibid., 6.

[22] Ibid., 28.

were in a well-to-do home. Expectation is equally hard to imagine of John Taylor, who was apprenticed as a waterman at age thirteen, or of Nashe, whose university training nurtured a hope for preferment that would never be fulfilled. These are writers who adopt suspect, marginal identities. And taking up Helgerson's own observation that Jonson is different from Spenser and Milton in the sense that, due to his demographic, he never had quite the same level of expectation, I am placing Jonson in new company. I will acknowledge not only Jonson the servant of James I, but Jonson the bricklayer, whose laboring background – and its influence on his writing – nominates him for a very different style of self-presentation. That group, which I will loosely call "laboring authors," embraces not civic status, but underdog status. This self-conscious marginality becomes a rhetorical pose by which to argue for the virtue of one's own authorial labor as distinct from amateur and professional modes of composition.

The second major difference between these authors and the laureates resides in their attitude toward the materiality of their own writing. Helgerson observes that the laureate resists being tied to the material or the temporal: "A laureate could not be a timeserver. Rather he was the servant of eternity .. . . Truth is one, but times change. The poet who hopes to present a normative self is caught between the two."[23] As Helgerson points out, this is a problem especially for Jonson, who knows that his very visibility depends upon the realm of the material. I will add that, for Jonson and for all the authors I treat here, labor is that specter of material contingency that troubles ambitions toward "eternity." While the laureates may escape materiality somewhat by engaging in the non-manual kinds of work outlined by Harrison, laboring poets find materiality much more difficult to leave behind, particularly those poets who will never gain access to upper social realms.

Laboring writers respond by fashioning laboring status and embracing it, as well as struggling with it. Their embrace of labor is never unequivocal. Their attempts to infuse selfhood into writing for pay thus challenge the notion that professionals are absent from their own writing, which they perform merely to pocket their pay and move on. In each case I treat here, the self is very much present in his or her printed writings, beginning with the awareness that his or her writing is on some level socially compromising. The experience of penury and lack of external appreciation is woven into a story of the self, a phenomenon that supports Jurgen Habermas's observation that the early modern period witnesses a shift toward "representative publicness," from courtly magnificence to everyday concerns.[24] Likewise, Charles Taylor reads the early modern period as entailing "the affirmation of ordinary life," which designates the importance of "those aspects of human life concerned with production and reproduction, that is, labour, the making of the things needed for life."[25] In keeping with this affirmation, the poverty that laboring writers claim,

---

[23] Ibid., 8, 14.

[24] Jurgen Habermas, *The Structural Transformation of the Public Sphere: An Inquiry into a Category of Bourgeois Society*, trans. Thomas Burger, Cambridge: MIT Press, 1996, 5.

[25] Charles Taylor, *Sources of the Self: The Making of Modern Identity*, Cambridge: Harvard UP, 1989, 211.

which moves them toward print, becomes a badge of virtue, leading the writer to morph into a proto-romantic version of what Raymond Williams calls "the unwanted writer, who was soon mythicized as the starving genius."[26] Such is certainly the case with Jonson, who takes his less successful endeavors as proof of his superiority to the masses, making him into "a model of what a serious writer ought to be."[27]

The issue of materiality leads us to the importance of the early modern press. The fact that print capitalism and its agents play important roles in authorial self-presentation is by now impossible to ignore, thanks to the work of Joseph Loewenstein, Martha Woodmansee, and Mark Rose, among others.[28] The emphasis on print culture by no means erases the author's agency. Rather, it situates this agency within its material context, stimulating much scholarly dialogue on the relationship between technologies of print and authorial self-presentation and self-promotion. Loewenstein writes that the press acquires a sort of "alterity" insofar as it conditions "fantasies" of authorship in which authors begin to see their books as commodities over which they have certain rights.[29] The sense of owning one's work is bound up in the way the work is bought and sold. Moreover, print constitutes authors' very senses of themselves *as* authors. This is a more historically specific take on Helgerson's notion of the inextricability of self-presentation and textual product. Print gives rise to what Loewenstein calls the "bibliographical ego, a specifically Early Modern form of authorial identification with printed writing."[30] The idea of the "bibliographical ego" leads Loewenstein to place Jonson in a very different grouping than does Helgerson. Jonson joins Samuel Daniel and George Wither as authors who "would learn to estimate the value of their names and of their writings by the proprietary standards of copyright and commodity."[31] The development of a sense of ownership (or "possessiveness"), as conditioned by broader movements toward commodity culture, represents a major moment in the history of authorship as a vocation.

However, while all of the authors I treat here engage actively in the market for print, not all come away from it with a sense of "possessing" their products. If anything, they feel *dis*possessed, an inversion of the idea that authors ultimately own what they make. This failure once again hearkens back to the problem of expectation or entitlement. Authors who claim marginality not only have restricted access to legal channels that might allow them to lay claim to the production and distribution

---

[26] Williams, p. 24.

[27] Ibid.

[28] Martha Woodmansee, "The Genius and the Copyright: Economic and Legal Conditions of the Emergence of the 'Author'," *Eighteenth Century Studies* 17 (4) (Summer 1984), 425–48; Mark Rose, *Authors and Owners: The Invention of Copyright*, Cambridge: Harvard UP, 1995; and several texts by Joseph Loewenstein, namely "The Script in the Marketplace," *Representations* 12 (1985), 101–14; "Wither and Professional Work," *Print, Manuscript, and Performance: The Changing Relations of the Media in Early Modern England*, ed. Arthur F. Marotti and Michael D. Bristol, Columbus: Ohio State UP, 2000, 103–24; *Ben Jonson and Possessive Authorship*, Cambridge: Cambridge UP, 2002; and *The Author's Due: Printing and the Prehistory of Copyright*, Chicago: U of Chicago P, 2002.

[29] *Ben Jonson and Possessive Authorship*, 14.

[30] *Ben Jonson and Possessive Authorship*, 1.

[31] Ibid., 149.

of their work; it likely would not occur to them to pursue such channels in the first place. Furthermore, the sense of dispossession comes not just from the market for print, but from market culture more generally, including the market for wage labor and, in the case of Whitney, the marriage market. I do not argue against the idea of possession itself, for the feeling of dispossession obviously must be preceded by the sense that one is entitled to what one makes. Rather, I am tying the notion of possession to broader cultural discourses than the legal ones that most directly concern the market for print. Attention to the economics of domestic labor, of education, or of guild politics, for example, widens the category of the possessive to include a more diverse array of authors. These emphases offer a new context for reading Jonson and Wither, whose concerns are tied to the idea of labor generally as well as to the "fantasies" specific to print. I find that poverty and marginality become paradoxically enabling to the authors who claim them, leading them from (in Danielle Clarke's terms) "material dispossession" to "poetic possession."[32] Here, I will show how this bittersweet sense of possession can emerge from a variety of spheres not directly tied to the marketplace for print.

Toward a Non-Aristocratic Poetics: Between Community and Individual

The laureate's dedication to public service through poetry positions him as a servant to the elite or, in the case or Jonson, their servant *and* their teacher. The poet's professed *raison d'etre* is to serve and correct the morals of others. In either case, the poet's sense of himself is bound up in his utility for the upper strata of society, which assumes that he has some hope of access to the court. Scholars have devoted much attention to exploring and defining courtly poetics and its influence on both aristocratic and non-aristocratic writers. Daniel Javitch argues in *Poetry and Courtliness in Renaissance England* that "the court acted virtually as a nursery of English Renaissance poetry" and links courtly values of leisure and play to the flourishing of English vernacular poetry in the Tudor period.[33] However, these remarks posit a "trickle down" model of poetic influence: "Tudor poets could not but benefit from the courtiers' predisposition to play and recreation, especially when, outside the court, influential puritan spokesmen were discrediting poetry as immoral and frivolous."[34] Such is to assume that an ideal of court conduct is not only available, but realistic and desirable; certainly some folklorists and cultural anthropologists have argued along these lines by suggesting that elite culture "sank" down to the masses, rendering "low" culture a mere outdated appropriation of "high." Likewise, despite the numerous products of popular literary culture, like broadsides and ballads composed in rough meter, the "court" is still presumed to be the penultimate influence on poets. Later studies have complicated Javitch's thesis, like Jennifer Richards's *Rhetoric and Courtliness in Early Modern Literature*, which

---

[32] Danielle Clarke, *The Politics of Early Modern Women's Writing*, London: Longman, 2001, 201.

[33] Daniel Javitch, *Poetry and Courtliness in Renaissance England*, Princeton: Princeton UP, 1978, 3.

[34] Ibid.

points out that courtly values were available in public settings, not just in books like Castiglione's *Il Cortegiano*.[35] Nonetheless, such analyses privilege courtliness, leading us to wonder what other influences – less markedly elite ones – might have exerted a positive effect on authorial self-fashioning.

I pose this question with an eye toward Peter Burke's model of a "two-way traffic" between "great" and "little" traditions. While some elite forms *did* "trickle down" – such as architecture, chivalric romances, and some kinds of drama – in other places we see elite culture exhibiting "popular" influences, as in the case of dances and masques.[36] I would take Burke's formulation a step further to suggest that the traffic runs in many more ways than simply two. As Tim Harris argues, if we define "popular culture" as merely that which "elite culture" is not, then we are left with a bi-polar model that is highly limiting; not even the Tudor social commentators I cite above conceived of society in only two layers.[37] Because "low" and "high" are infinitely fragmented and permeable, then, I locate the texts of laboring authors at a crossroads between different class-based cultures, which squares well with the fact that most of them occupied ambiguous class identities themselves.

The wealth of scholarship on "courtly" discourse begs the question of what *non*-courtly discourse might look like, particularly during the cynical 1590s and beyond. By "non-courtly," I mean neither of the court nor visible against it, but a kind of writing that exists in an ambiguous "elsewhere." Is the non-courtly simply an inversion of courtly ideals of leisure and play? Or does it represent an entirely new set of ideals? Do non-courtly poets always seek to integrate themselves within hierarchy despite their social liabilities, or do they sometimes protest, or seek to reform the values of the elite within their own images? This study attempts answers to all of these questions, although the answers frequently appear paradoxical or contradictory. This is to be expected, because a more diverse, capacious account of early modern authorship necessarily shifts our analysis toward unexplored, and sometimes vexing, new territory. Chiefly, this project involves accounting for approaches to authorship that emerge from unstable, vagrant senses of identity that are caught between disappointment and expectation, between a sense of moral and artistic superiority and an intense consciousness of one's own suspect status.

While the laureate finds a way to blend his egotistical investments into service to sovereign and nation, the possessive poet comes across as radically self-interested, a self-promoting economic agent who seeks rights over his own property and profits. One is reminded of Marx's narrative of market relations, which positions the seller of commodities as an autonomous individual who exchanges goods as a "free" agent, meeting other exchangers on theoretically equal terms:

---

[35] Jennifer Richards, *Rhetoric and Courtliness in Early Modern Literature*, Cambridge: Cambridge UP, 2003.

[36] Peter Burke, *Popular Culture in Early Modern Europe*, London: Temple Smith, 1978, 58.

[37] Tim Harris, "Problematising Popular Culture," *Popular Culture in England, c. 1500–1850*, ed. Tim Harris, Hampshire, UK: Macmillan Press Ltd., 1995, 1–27, 14–15. On the fluidity of "elite" and "popular" as specifically literary categories, see also Lori Humphrey Newcomb's *Reading Popular Romance in Early Modern England*, New York: Columbia UP, 2002.

> The juridical moment of the Person enters here . . . No one seizes hold of another's property by force. Each divests himself of his property voluntarily . . . when the economic form, exchange, posits the all-sided equality of its subjects, then the content, the individual as well as the objective material which drives towards the exchange, is *freedom*. Equality and freedom are thus not only respected in exchange based on exchange values but, also, the exchange of exchange values is the productive, real basis of all *equality* and *freedom*.[38]

The sense of freedom, in Marx's view, is a false one that merely testifies to the exchanger's social embeddedness. Such is especially true during the sixteenth century's transition from feudalism to capitalism where, as Karl Polyani observes, "the economic order is merely a function of the social, in which it is contained."[39] Polyani's remarks are especially important to keep in mind, since contemporary theoretical accounts of authorship tend to stress the individual. Roland Barthes locates the birth of the author among Enlightenment discourses that "discovered the prestige of the individual . . . the epitome and culmination of capitalist ideology, which has attached the greatest importance to the 'person' of the author."[40] Likewise, Michel Foucault's influential "What Is An Author?" attributes the privilege of the individual author to notions of literary property, enforced by copyright law in the eighteenth century.[41] But although market-based exchange posits formally free and voluntary agents, late sixteenth and early seventeenth century forms of legal and social control more often than not struggled with this would-be agency.

Certainly, the writers in this study consistently represent themselves as alone and forsaken individuals, unique among others who lack understanding or empathy for their enterprises. They exemplify several manifestations of early modern subjectivity, a term that I approach with due caution. In the early 1980s, practicioners of new historicism and cultural materialism sought to locate ways in which political and cultural discourses determined how individuals came to know themselves. Works like Stephen Greenblatt's *Renaissance Self-Fashioning*, Francis Barker's *The Tremulous Private Body*, Catherine Belsey's *The Subject of Tragedy*, and Jonathan Dollimore's *Radical Tragedy* all sought, albeit in different ways and with different conclusions, to posit the early modern subject in an antagonistic relationship with the social structures that define her or him, thus prompting the appearance of something like modern individualism.[42] Since then, their work has been problematized by medievalists and other scholars who have shown that a seemingly autonomous, antagonistic, and

---

[38] Karl Marx, *Grundrisse*, London: Penguin, 1993, 243–5.

[39] Karl Polanyi, *The Great Transformation*, Boston: Beacon, 1944.

[40] Roland Barthes, "The Death of the Author," *Image, Music, Text*, trans. Stephen Heath, New York: Hill and Wang, 1977, 142–8.

[41] Michel Foucault, "What is an Author?", *The Foucault Reader*, ed. Paul Rabinow, New York: Pantheon, 1984, 101–20.

[42] Stephen Greenblatt, *Renaissance Self-Fashioning: From More to Shakespeare*, Chicago: U of Chicago P, 1980; Francis Barker, *The Tremulous Private Body: Essays on Subjection*, London: Methuen, 1984; Catherine Belsey, *The Subject of Tragedy: Identity and Difference in Renaissance Drama*, London: Methuen, 1985; and Jonathan Dollimore, *Radical Tragedy: Religion, Ideology, and Power in the Drama of Shakespeare and His Contemporaries*, 2nd edn, Durham: Duke UP, 1993.

self-defined individual did exist prior to the early modern period.[43] This challenge requires a rethinking of early modern selfhood, so that we do not forsake the quest to understand the origins of the modern self, but merely the search for some originary moment. The project thus becomes not so much a teleological one, but a matter of noticing where the outlines of a modern sense of individual autonomy exist and why or, as Elizabeth Hanson writes, "*under what conditions* inwardness comes to entail . . . other possibilities."[44] In my search for a more historically specific account of early modern subjectivity, I have come to the conclusion that early modern subjects, particularly those of common status, formed ideas of themselves largely in relation to conventional presumptions about occupation. Furthermore, I suggest that non-aristocratic self-representations threaten occupational hierarchy precisely because they draw so heavily on that hierarchy's contradictions.

Even so, the laboring writer, individualistic as he or she may appear, also possesses a sense of commitment to his or her community. Economic self-interest, figured as loneliness and isolation, and an ideal of civic service can go hand-in-hand, albeit in different ways than that of Helgerson's laureates. Particularly, poets can posit their art as a duty to others on a more local level than that of the "nation" or the monarch. This form of service can work in a variety of ways. In the case of Taylor – a writer active in self-promotion – poetry allows him to vindicate not only himself, but his entire occupation, even allowing him to argue for the interests of watermen to the monarch and to society as a whole. In Whitney's case, although her fundamental aloneness underscores her position as a solitary producer of verse, poetry still serves as a caution for women, more particularly maidservants whose welfare is tied up in precarious social and economic circumstances. The satire of Nashe and the Cambridge dramatists provides comfort and a sense of community for anxious university men and graduates. These poets are like laureates in the sense that they struggle to strike a balance between self and service, but they speak to the interests of smaller, more marginal populations that often get lost within broad notions of "society" or "nation."

Whitney is the subject of my first chapter because her case illustrates several things that will be important throughout this study. She is the most recognizably marginal of the authors I discuss – not only is she a woman, but claims to be single, childless and, by the time she writes her second book, has recently lost her position as a maidservant. I take this persona as I do all the ones I examine here – not necessarily as autobiographical fact, but as a rhetorical pose with certain benefits. Whitney handles her placelessness in a socially risky way for a woman: she turns to publication of her imaginative verse, knowing well that female publication is associated with unchastity and prostitution. I focus on her second miscellany, *A Sweet Nosgay* (1573), where she experiments with such forms as Senecan *sententiae*, the verse epistle, and

---

43 See, for example, David Aers, "A Whisper in the Ear of Early Modernists; or, Reflections on Literary Critics writing the 'History of the Subject'," *Culture and History 1350–1600: Essays on English Communities, Identities, and Writing*, ed. David Aers, Detroir: Wayne State UP, 1992, 177–202.

44 Elizabeth Hanson, *Discovering the Subject in Renaissance England*, Cambridge: Cambridge UP, 1998.

the mock testament in order to compose a narrative that explores the freedom and consequences of mobility. Claiming that her verse is "all I have," she frames her writing as a wage labor. More specifically, Whitney underscores her isolation from family and textual communities as a way of expressing her relationship to the print market which, as part of new capitalist economies, isolates producers and consumers in their own self-interest. Whitney is caught between looking back nostalgically at her mistress's household and looking forward to a future that is both frightening and yet liberating as she explores possibilities for economic independence through publication.

Because the impact of labor discourses on authorship is widespread, not all of the authors I analyze in depth are "working class" figures. In fact, I have chosen authors from a variety of points on the non-aristocratic spectrum whose social positions are made complex by the changes taking place in divisions of labor and in systems of writing and publishing. Thomas Nashe, an upper-middling sort who graduated from Cambridge and become a London pamphleteer, well illustrates the impact of these changes on social identities as well as on literary careers. A Cambridge graduate and ruthless satirist, Nashe wrote prose works that portrayed educated wanderers who turn to a quasi-criminal life. *Pierce Pennilesse his supplication to the Divell* and *The Unfortunate Traveller* contain autobiographical elements in the sense that they satirically reflect on the lot of educated men who fail to find preferment after graduation from university. Nashe's contemporaries at St. John's College were having similar thoughts, as reflected in a series of vernacular comedies known as *The Parnassus Plays*, which depict the struggles of graduates. The plays feature a central character based on Nashe, and he becomes the most eloquent vehicle for resentment and a platform for articulating a new social position for the embittered scholar. The plays frequently describe poetry as a "mystery," as does Nashe – and it is a mystery that is being illicitly practiced by common men with no learning. I argue that erecting writing and learning as a sacred "mystery" essentially amounts to a professional claim. In the case of Nashe and his fellow graduates, a sense of professionalism is borne out of resentment incurred by shifts in the social status of the traditionally privileged.

The role of satire in articulating this position leads to a discussion of Ben Jonson, who is the bedrock figure of this study. I ask how we can make sense of the dissonance between two things: one, Jonson's own non-aristocratic background and two, his own social ambition and disdain for laborers. Jonson's three comical satires – *Every Man Out of His Humour*, *Poetaster*, and *Cynthia's Revels* – were popular at Cambridge in the 1590s; the *Parnassus* plays describe him as the "merriest bricklayer" who ever put pen to paper. If his evident disdain for manuaries and commoners is any indication, the socially and poetically ambitious Jonson would have no doubt bristled at this description – accomplished as he was at writing for the public stage, he put most of his ambition into creating court masques and writing epigrams to nobles. Yet at the same time, Jonson continually returns to metaphors of labor in describing the writing process of the ideal poet and good man; he derives many of these ideas from classical authorities, most particularly Horace in his workmanlike approach to composition and disdain for prosody that shows bad workmanship. I will show that these contradictions play an important role in Jonson's distinguishing himself from other authors (both amateur and professional) and, more specifically, in distinguishing his labor in masque-making from that of his collaborator and rival, Inigo Jones. It is with Jonson that we get a sense of the social and literary uses of erecting "labor" as an abstract ideal separate from – and yet indebted to – the actual workaday labor that takes place on the ground. "Labor" becomes an important link between habits of authorship and individual character, thus feeding into an early sense of authorial identity and its investments.

While much of London's trade and production took place outside of official guild structures, the study of guilds and company politics provides ample opportunity to view how the individualistic nature of print authorship and publishing might intersect with labor-based notions of community. John Taylor "The Water Poet," a contemporary and admirer of Jonson, was a member of the London Watermen's Company while he simultaneously carried on a career as a writer of approximately 200 works of popular literature. As a Thames waterman, Taylor interacted with a broad cross-section of the population, which is reflected in the fact that he wrote something in nearly every genre: jest books, verse encomia, political prose, and English history, to name just a few. Like many writers around the time of the civil war, Taylor also seized the opportunity to use political prose to promote the interests of his company and his own Royalist, Anglican sympathies. Yet, despite his conservative politics and his disgust at the "radical" elements that eventually ousted the officers of the Watermen's Company, Taylor embraced a democratic approach to authorship by likening his books to a boat in which everyone can travel. This strategy legitimated Taylor's own status as an author of humble origins. But it went even farther than this: it legitimated Taylor's work, both writing and scullery. While books – like all commodities – are saturated with potential for commercial deceit, Taylor's writing is "honest" and transparent because, like his rowing, it is "seen and known." This rhetorical move draws a distinct connection, one that I am charting throughout this study, between individual character and text. Taylor uses his non-literary reputation to build a sense of personal "credit" in a literary market that can and often does deceive those who purchase from it.

My final chapter treats the poet and Puritan radical George Wither, who has recently attracted interest due to his legal battles with the London Stationers' Company. Loewenstein in particular has written extensively about Wither, calling his legal struggles a major milestone in the formation of a sense of intellectual property and the vocational privileges that this property confers. I will use these observations as a springboard to note what characteristics Wither shares with the other authors in my study. I wish to show that, while legal property debates do represent a major moment in the history of modern authorship, other cultural discourses are equally important in delineating a sense of authorial labor, and that Wither is not the first to employ them toward this end. For example, Wither's militant Puritanism lends the Protestant idea of the "calling" to his sense of authorial vocation – a characteristic he shares with Taylor, his religious and political opponent. Also like Taylor, Wither employs the idea of "credit" in dealing with the Stationers, drawing upon notions of individual intent and personal character as the justification for seeking profit from one's own work.

By this logic, Wither drives home the idea that labor shapes the laborer as much as it does the material world, but his argument also represents how the justification of self-interest becomes important in early capitalist England. The authors I will treat here are all situated within a broad and complicated transition from pseudo-feudal custom to systems of social organization that support and are supported by capitalism. Indeed, they are not the only writers deserving of the questions I raise here, since for the sake of brevity I have had to omit (or give very brief attention to) figures such as Thomas Deloney, Thomas Dekker, Margaret Tyler, Joseph Hall, Robert Greene and, in anticipation of the next century, Mary Collier and Steven Duck. Their contradictions in these writers' stories point toward the fact that they felt and thought deeply about these changes. Their careers are important indices of cultural transition in process. This transition, I argue here, has much to tell us about the forging of modern authorial vocation.

Chapter 1

"Tis all I have": Print Authorship and Occupational Identity in Isabella Whitney's *A Sweet Nosgay*

The relationships that early modern writers established between labor and the act of writing were conditioned not only by the print market and its commodity culture, but by the relationship between print and other discourses of labor with which they came into contact. Throughout this study, an individual writer's awareness of his or her text as print commodity is expressed through metaphors of labor that were in close proximity to the writer in question – domestic labor, scholarly labor, or blacksmithing, to name a few. Nascent print capitalism, along with the increasingly widespread presence of wage labor, leads authors who adopt the persona of the laborer to express a sense that not only is their text a commodity, but they *themselves* are commodities in a socioeconomic landscape where everyone fits in according to his or her usefulness, or lack of it. Furthermore, the markets for print and labor prompt these authors to experience themselves as detached from their own texts. Reclaiming one's own textual labor, then, represents an attempt to reclaim the virtues and the content of the text itself – that is to say, the *process* by which the text came into being.

Perhaps the feeling of separation from one's own product comes most easily for the early modern woman writer, whose experience of the print market accompanies an awareness of patriarchal cultural discourses that condition social and economic disempowerment. The mid-Tudor poet and maidservant Isabella Whitney (fl. 1567–1573) published her second book of verse, *A Sweet Nosgay* (1573), from a stance perhaps surprising to readers of Renaissance women's writing – as a poor single woman who explicitly claims to write for money. Describing herself as "Harvestlesse, / and servicelesse also," Whitney bases her volume on a dynamic tension between the penury of the single life and the elusive comforts of domesticity. An epistle to her married sister, Anne Barron, compares their respective situations:

> Had I a Husband, or a house,
> and all that longes therto
> My selfe could frame about to rouse,
> as other women doo:
> But til some houshold cares mee tye,
> My bookes and Pen I wyll apply.

Whitney frames her writing as pure necessity. In the interim between service and marriage, her writing is her companion and her property, but paradoxically, this writing is predicated on her isolation from service, family, and textual communities. In contradistinction to recent scholarship that locates the birth of literary property within copyright debates,[1] Whitney's relationship to her literary labor suggests that a notion of professional authorship could also be formulated by deploying cultural discourses – not only those concerning print, but discourses of marriage and domesticity – and locating oneself in the spaces in between.

Whitney has attracted critical attention in recent years because she is the first English woman to publish a substantial body of original poetry on secular subjects. However, she is rarely put into dialogue with male writers – critics tend to treat her as "woman writer" first and foremost, privileging her gender identity over the other important characteristics that she imparts in her poetry, like occupational displacement, poverty, and isolation from community. This is not to say that her gender is separable from these traits, but to point out that she shares these instrumental facets of her persona with the growing class of sixteenth century professional writers, female and male, who wrote to maintain themselves financially.[2] Outside of what she tells us in her own writing, information on her life is scarce: no one has definitively identified the dates of her birth and death, nor do we know if she ever married. She seems to have originated from an upper middle class family in Coole Pilate, Cheshire, and might have been the sister of Geoffrey Whitney, author of the first emblem book in England. Due to sparse external evidence on her life, the poetry itself has supplied most of our information on her life and career. Her first book, *The Copy of a Letter . . . by a Yonge Gentilwoman: to her Unconstant Lover* (1567), explores abandonment by lovers from both female and male perspectives: it contains two poems by Whitney and two by anonymous bachelors in what amounts to a literary debate between the sexes. The addition of a female voice might have been intended to provoke interest in the nature of women, since Jones's verse introduction, "The Printer to the Reader," markets the work as something new: "What lack you, Maister mine? / some trifle that is trew? / Why? Then this same wil serve your turne / the which is also new"

[1] See Martha Woodmansee, "The Genius and the Copyright: Economic and Legal Conditions of the Emergence of the 'Author'," *Eighteenth-Century Studies* 17, 4 (Summer 1984), 425–8; Mark Rose, "The Author as Proprietor: *Donaldson v. Becket* and the Genealogy of Modern Authorship," *Representations* 23 (Winter 1988), 51–85; Roger Chartier, *The Order of Books*, Stanford: Stanford Univ. Press, 1992, 24–59; Joseph Loewenstein, "Wither and Professional Work," *Print, Manuscript, and Performance: The Changing Relations of the Media in Early Modern England*, ed. Arthur F. Marotti and Michael D. Bristol, Columbus: Ohio State Univ. Press, 2000, 103–23.

[2] It may be objected that Whitney scarcely could have supported herself on only two books, but several scholars present evidence that Whitney contributed at least a few anonymous poems to miscellanies as well. See, for example, Robert J. Fehrenbach, "Isabella Whitney (fl. 1565–75) and the Popular Miscellanies of Richard Jones," *Cahiers elisabethains* (April 1981), 85–7; and Raphael Lyne, "A Case for Isabella Whitney," Cambridge University CERES Project, http://www.english.cam.ac.uk/ceres/aeneas/attrib.htm, last retrieved March 10, 2006.

(ll. 1–4). Jones's intervening voice deploys the rhetoric of novelty to package the authors' lines in the most saleable way possible.

The tripartite *Nosgay* also caters to readers' tastes by experimenting with popular mid-Tudor genres: Senecan *sententiae* in the first part, verse epistles in the second, and the mock testament in the third.[3] But while *Copy* offers the conventional voice of a woman abandoned by a lover, *Nosgay* presents readers with the less familiar viewpoint of a woman forsaken *economically*. This emphasis highlights the need to complicate gendered authorial identity with questions of economic and occupational discourse. When Whitney presents herself as a subject who must write to live, she participates in a shifting notion of what it means to have an occupation – from fulfilling a social role to sustaining oneself by producing a useful product. The speaker of *Nosgay* longs not for a lover, but for the employment of a mistress whose "losse I had of service hers / I languish for it still." Louise Schleiner sees *Nosgay* as aimed at the lady of lost service and argues that the now-solitary Whitney longs for a "reading formation" represented by the mistress and her household circle.[4] Ann Rosalind Jones reads Whitney's pining for community in a slightly different vein by calling attention to how Whitney's epistles build in responses to friends and family, and thus "demonstrate[s] the networks of need and appeal, of creative accommodation and subtle critique" – in short, the collective writing processes crucial to our understanding of Renaissance literary culture.[5]

The stress on the ways in which Whitney creates the appearance of connection is a just one, considering the social danger inherent in her position as a woman in print. However, when highlighting *Nosgay*'s attempts to soften this position, critics have given scant attention to the other side of the equation: the *aloneness* evident in Whitney's self-presentation as a woman without "a Husband, or a house." This fundamental aloneness, accompanied by the sense of being a forsaken victim and often leading to an insistence on one's own unique virtue, is a major characteristic of the "laboring writers" I seek to define here. It is a stance that enables the laboring writer to negotiate the social discourses of print in a way that justifies his or her own engagement.

If we associate the woman writer's longing for companionship with desire for the relatively safe space of manuscript circulation, then it seems to me that Whitney's isolation from support networks underscores her position as a writer who hopes to profit from the sale of her work. Given the persistence with which she reminds us of her single state, I begin with the hypothesis that this isolation is at least as important as her allusions to past and present communities. Thus, self-interest and community become an important and complicated dialectic within which laboring writers struggle to define themselves. Specific to Whitney's case, this chapter seeks to uncover the strategic value of the single stance by arguing that *Nosgay*'s narrative of loss permits

[3] Citations from the first and second parts of *Nosgay* are from Richard Panofsky's facsimile edition, New York: Scholars' Facsimiles and Reprints, 1982.

[4] Louise Schleiner, *Tudor and Stuart Women Writers*, Bloomington: Indiana Univ. Press, 1994, 4, 17.

[5] Ann Rosalind Jones, *The Currency of Eros: Women's Love Lyric in Europe*, 1540–1620, Bloomington: Indiana Univ. Press, 1990, 51–2.

an investigation of economic independence through the sale of textual labor. Thus we can add to the individual/community dialectic one that concerns mobility – the advantages and disadvantages of being "masterless" in a culture that still stresses hierarchies of order and obedience. The strategic use of masterlessness registers itself in several ways: making personal misfortune into the occasion for productive labor, a sense of inwardness (enforced by aloneness and isolation in misfortune), and a sense of the self as alienated (and different) from the rest of society.

Taking up Richard Panofsky's recommendation that *Nosgay* be read "in order from cover to cover,"[6] I will trace my first example of such a narrative throughout the text's three parts. I do not aim to dismiss scholarship that highlights Whitney's strategies of connection; rather, I wish to complicate these conversations by noting that, more often, Whitney imagines herself as a solitary producer of imaginative poetry. These self-representations raise important questions as to the value of her text as *labor* in a socioeconomic climate that tended to deny many people, but especially women, ownership of their work and property.

Freedom and Necessity: Maidservants in Early Modern England

If Whitney wished to establish herself as a credible poet worthy of remuneration, her choice of persona – as a single woman of the lower orders – seems counterproductive indeed. Among the scholars who apply the "stigma of print" to women's writing, Kim Walker suggests a helpful model for considering the social consequences of female publication: "If writing for a public audience could be interpreted as unchaste, then writing for financial gain could be read as a form of prostitution."[7] Writing for an audience defied codes of modesty; furthermore, the idea of paying a lady for her services suggested the trade of sex. These associations meet a particular challenge in *Nosgay*, because when Whitney fashions herself as an unemployed maidservant, she specifically aligns herself with a group that was prone to prostitution in cultural imagination as well as in fact. Prostitutes are an extreme example of how sexuality becomes a commodity. Likewise, Whitney will come to experience herself as a commodity detached from the market because she is no longer useful; her text becomes an extension of this experience, as she expresses both cynicism about its status and an insistence on telling the story of its creative production, the process by which it came to be.

The marginal, vagrant status she adopts for *Nosgay* is a major departure from the more conventional voice she uses in *The Copy*. This new voice places her in the company of later writers like Nashe who, as we shall see, uses his mobility as a way to position himself as unmoored, unfortunate, yet nonetheless free. With respect to the work of the woman writer, historians of women's work have shown that early modern women had few opportunities to fashion a stable, independent occupational

---

[6] Op. cit. xii.

[7] Kim Walker, *Women Writers of the English Renaissance*, New York: Twayne Publishers, 1996, 146.

identity outside of marriage.[8] The 1563 Statute of Artificers led to the arrest of masterless women (and men) "living at their own hand" and ordered them into service. By 1589, no single woman could trade, sell ale, or keep a house or chamber.[9] With a dearth of sanctioned options for the exercise of independent industry, single women in economic straits often resorted to prostitution. Unemployed maidservants contributed high numbers to this group since the swelling population of Elizabethan London made it difficult for a released domestic to find a new position. The category of the "vagrant nightwalker" captured the common female urban experience of movement in and out of service and households.[10]

Yet even maidservants in service raised anxiety over the permeability of the domestic sphere. The lawyer and moralist Edward Hake exploited perceptions of maidservants as dishonest by attacking the "light" behavior of domestics in *Newes out of Paules Churchyard* (1567). Hake's pamphlet invited a "Letter sent by Maydens of London" (1567) that defended the chastity and loyalty of maidservants. The authors, who identify themselves as "Rose, Jane, Rachell, Sara, Philumias and Dorothie," answer such charges as one in which Hake "accuseth Rachel to occupie for hir selfe" through commercial sex.[11] While the "Letter" takes offended employers as its chief audience, its publication suggests that the wider public recognized common stereotypes of maidservants as would-be prostitutes and thieves. Furthermore, the letter counters the ideology of the household as enclosed space, like the bodies of the women who inhabit it, by suggesting that both the household and its women are deeply embedded in public life.

Several critics have drawn parallels between Whitney's writing and the concerns expressed in the "Letter."[12] While such studies shed valuable light on Whitney's lines, they tend to posit the "real" Whitney as a maidservant. Given the lack of biographical information on her life, we must be careful in assuming this; the maidservant Margaret Tyler, translator of Diego Ortunez de Calahorra's *A mirrour of princely deedes and knighthood* (1578), did not announce her occupation, and

---

[8] See, for example, Alice Clark, *Working Life of Women in the Seventeenth Century*, London: Routledge, 1919; *Women and Work in Pre-Industrial England*, ed. Lindsey Charles and Lorna Duffin, London: Croom Helm, 1985; Susan Cahn, *Industry of Devotion: The Transformation of Women's Work in England, 1500–1660*, New York: Columbia Univ. Press, 1987; Sara Mendelson and Patricia Crawford, *Women in Early Modern England, 1550–1720*, Oxford: Oxford Univ. Press, 1998.

[9] Generally, widows inheriting brewing businesses or tippling houses from their husbands provided an exception to this rule. See Peter Clark, *The English Alehouse, A Social History, 1200–1830*, New York: Longman, 1983, 79–80.

[10] Paul Griffiths, "The Structure of Prostitution in Elizabethan London," *Continuity and Change* 8, 1 (1993), 39–63, 51.

[11] All quotes from the "Letter" are from R. J. Fehrenbach's edition, "A Letter sent by Maydens of London," *English Literary Renaissance* 14, 3 (Autumn 1984), 285–304, 299.

[12] See Ann Rosalind Jones, 'Maidservants of London: Sisterhoods of Kinship and Labor," *Maids and Mistresses, Cousins and Queens*, ed. Susan Frye and Karen Robertson, New York: Oxford Univ. Press, 1999, 21–32; Patricia Phillippy, "The Maid's Lawful Liberty: Service, the Household, and 'Mother B' in Isabella Whitney's A Sweet Nosgay," *Modern Philology* 95 (1998), 439–62.

there is no reason why Whitney would have either unless it served her somehow. I propose that Whitney, "real" maidservant or not, *chose* this persona as a means of expressing her tenuous relationship to her own literary property. The strategic use of discourses surrounding maidservants – more specifically, the anxieties that maidservants raised concerning sexuality and property – helps her explore the issues of gender and ownership that her status as a professional author raised. For the woman author facing the social consequences of print publication, the pose of the dismissed maidservant becomes a savvy means by which to explore her own socially tenuous position as print author.

Because women's capacity to earn independently was sharply regulated by the ideology of the household, and because prostitution conflated sexuality and profit, chastity and earning tended to cancel one another out. As Constance Jordan suggests, "a woman may have propriety (as honestly in service or married) without property, or property (as a prostitute) without propriety."[13] Hake's indictments and the maidservants' defenses wrestle within this double-bind. To his alarm at "Our great costes and charges in good chere and banketting," the maidservants respond that they have spent little of their wages on their own enjoyment. On a day in which "Rose" and "Jane" went to the tavern, they bought "a quart of the best beere" for only a penny: "*Summa totalis* of all that was spent that daie betwene them two at the costely banket, was a peny. . . . Thus have you a quicke reckening and a slow payment, a marvellous expence and a mischevous charge."[14] This spirit of thrift and moderation also extends to their judicious handling of their mistresses' goods. While they deny pilfering, they also trust their own judgment in giving alms to beggars, even the poor procuress "Mother B." The maidservants transform Mother B from a tempting bawd to a piteous pauper, remarking that "a candles ende is not so costly, that giving it to a poore woman to light hir home in a dark night for breaking hir face or shinnes, would undoe you, or greatly hinder you." The procuress threatens both the sexual virtue of the household and the security of its property, and when she lurks at the door, the maidservants handle this double threat by demonstrating virtuous charity. But their defense quickly slips into a vindication of servants' own right to earn by asking, "when is [Hake] thus offended that poore women should have their hire for their paynes, a few scraps of broken breade meete for their toyle and travaile?"[15] The slippage between the speaking subjects (the maidservants) and the subject of whom they speak (the poor woman) suggests two things: one, that maidservants could never consider the fate of paupers far from their own destiny; and two, that maidservants, with no goods of their own, were considered ripe for both prostitution and theft of others' property.

"What would not one do pinched with penury?" ask the maidservants, as they construct a defense that concerns all of London's female domestics, "under those

---

[13] Constance Jordan, "Renaissance Women and the Question of Class," *Sexuality and Gender in Early Modern Europe: Institutions, Texts, Images*, ed. James Grantham Turner, Cambridge: Cambridge Univ. Press, 1993, 90–106, 101.

[14] Fehrenbach, 301–2.

[15] Fehrenbach, 302–3.

sixte names above sixe thousand of us."[16] The category of necessity expands the bounds of justifiable behavior to allow for basic survival. Yet the "necessity" defense does not stop at this negative determination but goes further, to enable the surviving subject to find a new set of terms perhaps unavailable to her before. Necessity gives birth to a new perspective and indeed, a new kind of creative subject. Ilana Ben-Amos notes that the lack of opportunities for independent trade required female servants to "use their initiative when they were fired" and, if they eventually married, bring "the experience of long years during which they learnt to cope with many tasks, and to switch between different skills, masters and working environments."[17] The maid whose working conditions have forced her into a perilous "freedom" acquires a certain resourcefulness as she learns to create opportunities from prohibitions and, in the terms of de Certeau, positively "make do."[18]

By adopting the voice of a forsaken former domestic and turning it to creative use, Whitney harnesses the questions of sexuality and property that maidservants raised to compose her own narrative of intellectual labor. While the text contains rhetorical moves familiar to readers of Renaissance women's writing – transgressions balanced by apologies and pleas for male protection – her position as a single, unemployed woman permits her to explore the productive potential of her newfound lack of enclosure. The first part of the volume, a collection of pseudo-Senecan verse *sententiae* modeled on Hugh Plat's *The Floures of Philosophie* (1572), offers moral counsel on such subjects as fortune, friendship, and love. Whitney adapts Plat's work to one hundred and ten stanzas that reflect her own interest in these topics and translates them into ballad meter for a wider audience. The material that introduces and concludes the collection attempts to deflect suspicions of literary theft by expressing anxiety about borrowing from Plat. Whitney playfully imagines him fuming, "were she a man, / that with my Flowers doth brag, / She well should pay the price, I wolde / not leave her worth a rag." In more sober passages, she describes her verses as "slips" grafted from another's garden. The dedication to her childhood friend George Mainwaring asks that he accept her verses "although so little of my labour was in them." In these instances, Whitney downplays her own labor in order to disclaim any idea that she might think of the stanzas as her own creation.

Yet these apologies also assume that she *might* claim her verses as her own, should she decide to link her labor in "gathering" with a sense of her "flowers" as textual property. This possibility receives ample enough exploration to compete with her initial deference. In the dedication to Mainwaring, she compares herself to a laborer in Plutarch's "Life of Artaxerxes" who, "having no goods, came with his hands full of water to meete the Persian Prince [Artaxerxes] withal, who respecting the good wyll of the man: did not disdayne his simple Guift." She also likens herself to a pauper who trespasses on others' property, "not havyng of mine owne to discharg[e] that I go about (like to that poore Fellow which wente into an others ground for his water) did step into an others garden for these Flowers." The figure that ties these

---

16 Fehrenbach, 297.

17 Ilana Krausman Ben-Amos, *Adolescence and Youth in Early Modern England*, New Haven: Yale UP, 1994, 153–4.

18 *The Practice of Everyday Life*, xv.

stories together is the impoverished and well-meaning laborer. Like him, Whitney is a giver with nothing "of mine owne to discharg[e]."

But despite her initial self-deprecation, Whitney beseeches Mainwaring to accept her flowers on the basis of her own work in gathering and ordering, reasoning that this labor still makes them a sufficient gift: "though they be of an others growing, yet considering they be of *my owne* gathering and making up: *respect my labour* and regard my good wil" (emphasis added). Whitney closes by repeating her assertion:

> Yf you take pleasure in them, I shal not only be occasioned to endeavour my selfe to make a further viage for a more dayntier thing (then Flowers are) to present you withall: but also have good hope that you wil *accept this my labour*, for recompence of al that which you are unrecompenced for, as knoweth god. (emphasis added)

The poverty of the poor laborer results in her marginalization; labor becomes the basis for restoring her place in society. While Whitney will not go so far as to own the "flowers" as her original creation, she proposes that "growing," "gathering," and "making up" are themselves industrious acts that give her some claim over her text. These gestures demonstrate one way in which a sense of textual ownership can be tied to discourses not explicitly associated with the marketplace for print.

Noting how Whitney describes her flowers as healthful herbs, some critics detect an attempt to legitimate her labor by making it look like "housekeeping," that form of female industry by which she, in Jones's words, "appropriated bourgeois gender discourse for her own profit."[19] By producing salutary bits of usable wisdom, Whitney serves her readers through her own industry. What precedes this service, however, is a story of solitary intellectual labor that serves only the self. Following the dedication to Mainwaring with "The Auctor to the Reader," Whitney describes how she spent her time upon finding herself newly unemployed – by plunging into undirected study and taking pleasure in what she finds:

> This Harvest tyme, I Harvestlesse,
> and servicelesse also:
> And subject unto sicknesse, that
> abrode I could not go.
> Had leasure good, (though learning lackt)
> some study to apply:
> To reade such Bookes, wherby I thought
> my selfe to edyfye.

In contrast to the "reading formation" of Whitney's former household, this speaker staves off idleness through solitary scholarship. Later, she tests the dangers of wandering outside; she adopts the pose of the "vagrant nightwalker" and yet rejects the notion that walking outside alone can cause her moral or physical harm. When a "friend" advises her to "have regard unto your health," she responds: "I'le neither

---

[19] Ann Rosalind Jones, "Nets and Bridles: Early Modern Conduct Books and Sixteenth-Century Women's Lyrics," *The Ideology of Conduct: Essays on Literature and the History of Sexuality*, ed. Nancy Armstrong and Leonard Tennenhouse, New York: Methuen, 1987, 39–72, 64.

shun, nor seeke for death, / yet oft the same I crave." Eschewing the counsel of friends, she wanders home "all sole alone" and faces study with renewed energy. Fortune now favors her and "made mee pleasures feel" by bringing her to "*Plat* his Plot," where she makes the gratification of reading into a basis for industry: "I mee reposde one howre. / And longer wolde, but leasure lackt, / and businesse bad mee hye: / And come agayne some other time, / to fill my gasing eye." The blending of pleasure and industry in the moment of aloneness provides a stark contrast to the other-oriented service we see in the dedication to Mainwaring. Her encounter with Plat's text provides a "defence" for wandering "In stynking streetes, or lothsome Lanes / which els might mee infect." Just as the maxims may preserve readers from moral harm, so her own reading has "kept mee free."

While Whitney purports to serve others by offering them salutary maxims, she makes the story of their creation autobiographical by building it upon her own struggles to keep "free" while "all sole alone." Her story, if it may serve as an example to her readers, encourages nurturing the mind in solitude and employing oneself in scholarly industry. "The Auctor to the Reader" thus describes the writer's labor as an individual struggle with the dangers of freedom and mobility. One the one hand, her position enables her to conceive of a kind of literary invention that affirms and makes use of her newly "masterless" position and all its attendant misfortunes. Yet paradoxically, she also finds that her status as a marketplace producer ultimately conditions a sense of alienation from the community and even from her own public. The putatively "free" solitary laborer persists into the next section, where her isolated state faces harder tests.

The Maidservant's Epistles: Community and Isolation

The second section, a series of thirteen "familier Epistles," imitates manuscript circulation more closely than any other portion of the miscellany. Here Whitney complains of her own losses and draws responses from several male friends: "An answer to comfort her" from one "T. B.," another answer by one "C. B.," and "An other Letter sent to IS. W." from her cousin "G. W." The dynamic of solicitation and response demonstrates the "networks of need and appeal" that Jones sees in *Nosgay* as a whole. The appearance of manuscript exchange in print enables this non-aristocratic writer to present herself as part of a protective coterie, exchanging private thoughts and experiences that, in the end, get printed for a wide readership.

But this sense of community, I suggest, is countered by the figure of a woman economically and socially forsaken, who endures increasing isolation through internal torment. The sense of connection that Whitney strives to achieve actually underlines her alienation from family and service, exposes this network of dependencies as insufficient for her maintenance, and creates a solitary, reflective figure who wrestles with her bad fortune alone. Letters are, after all, a form of communication predicated on distance. They are a genre particularly suitable to the situation of maidservants, who typically migrated to London to work away from their connections at home.[20]

[20] In a recent article, Susan Whyman notes that, for single women, letter writing was "crucial for survival," as letters "were used instrumentally to preserve social networks, obtain financial support and to maintain a place of residence" (177). Whyman contextualizes

The first five epistles capture Whitney's estrangement from her immediate family. Business takes precedence over letter-writing for all of these family members; none of them writes back, despite Whitney's evident longing to hear from them. Her oldest brother, Geoffrey, is occupied with his own affairs and cannot find a "vacanttime" to ride to the city or even write. Isabella wonders, "cannot I once from you heare / nor know I how to send: / Or where to harken of your health / and al this would be kend." To her brother Brooke, she "often looke[s] / to heare of your return" and surmises that he "must with Maister bee." Her sisters in service do not respond either, and as we have seen, the married Anne is busy with "huswyfery." Isabella emerges as the sole writer who keeps the family bonds, straining to reassert connection in a socioeconomic arrangement conducive to alienation. The family members' work keeps them atomized in business while "I to writing fall."

The "fall" to writing points out the difference in respectability between a woman in "huswyfery" and an unmarried writer – Anne's business is culturally approved, while Isabella's writing represents a "fall." But the "fall" also more generally places Whitney's writing as her sole resource after the loss of her goods, earnings, and connections; that is to say, she makes it clear that she writes because she must. Thus, necessity becomes an occasion for writing a narrative of the self. Furthermore, writing becomes a substitute for community, an effort by the writer to re-create what she misses. This substitution becomes evident as the letters regularly describe writing and the physical proximity of intimates as mutually exclusive. When she hints at her misfortune to Brooke, she promises, "I wyll show / you more when we doo speake," while in the meantime, "wyll I wryt, or yet resyte, / within this Paper weake." The "weake" paper mirrors the physical and emotional fragility that she displays throughout the letters, and the paper – both its material and its content – is the closest her addressees can get to her. The absence of relations becomes the occasion for writing her misfortune; it is to be undertaken, she claims, only *until* she sees them again. In like fashion, she tells her sisters, "when I / shal further from you dwell: / Peruse these lines." The lines register her presence, but they depend upon her absence to do so. The "bookes and Pen," as we have seen, also stand in for the husband and house that Whitney lacks. The series' final letter, to her cousin "G. W.," recalls the language of the dedication to George Mainwaring by describing the poems as paltry goods, but goods nonetheless. Asking her cousin to accept her letter, she renders it as her only gift: "though it be a Beggers bare rewarde / Accept the same . . . Tis all I have." She writes because she has nothing else to give; presumably, the possession of other kinds of gifts would render the letters unnecessary. The sorrow of isolation thus becomes an occasion for producing verse.

---

these letters by noting how "the fragile threads of kinship were being stretched thin in an increasingly market-based society" and that single women in isolation "had letters to keep them company" (190–1). I apply the dynamic between community and isolation that Whyman sees in single women's letter writing practices to note how Whitney uses the genre to capture her own isolated state. See "Gentle Companions: Single Women and their Letters in Late Stuart England," *Early Modern Women's Letter Writing, 1450–1700*, ed. James Daybell, London: Palgrave, 2001, 177–93.

As the letters move from one-sided communication to exchanges between friends, Whitney delves further into her sorrow and uses the responses to define its nature. Despite the dependence upon others that she professes to Geoffrey, who will be her "chiefest staffe" in time of need, the letters to friends take on a strange dynamic: they solicit feedback and advice, yet at the same time they resist the categories that friends use to describe her suffering. Readers are left with the impression that the medium of exchange ultimately cannot mitigate Whitney's situation, because the conventional literary tropes that her interlocutors offer for female suffering insufficiently represent her experience. While Whitney's first publication depicted female suffering as the result of faithless men, her second discusses suffering as the result of economic losses. In *Nosgay*, these losses become a subject for extended philosophical exploration.

The shift from conventional modes of female abandonment to this more abstract form of suffering is registered as resistance to the usual occasion for literary female complaints: faithless men. The classical figures of suffering that *Copy* enlists are denied as fitting models in *Nosgay*. Whereas the speaker of *Copy* looks to Dido as an exemplary figure of feminine despair, the writer of the "familiar Epistles" eschews such identification, arguing that her own misery is worse than anything wrought by lovers. Despite T. B.'s admonishment that she "with silly DIDO be content," Whitney insists that "greater cause of griefe" compels her own sorrow. Dido's own "fickle fancie," Whitney reasons, caused her attachment in the first place, but now that Aeneas is gone, "His absence might well salve the sore, / that earst his presence wrought." By comparison, Whitney's own mourning stems from "endles griefes" as "heapes of deadly harmes, / styll threaten my decay." She compares her case with Dido's by noting that, while Dido's sadness can be healed in time, her own state is continual. She describes herself as one of the "Mourner's trade," suggesting that mourning has become an occupation. Rather than choosing Dido as her model, the mourner elects a Biblical male: Job, who shows her how "I may take with quietnesse, / whatsoever is [God's] wyll." Like Job's counselors, Whitney's interlocutors fail to satisfy her on the causes of her suffering. Like Job himself, Whitney perceives her current situation as a matter between self and God, not as one resolved by earthly relations. In doing so, she casts herself as the agent of self-representation and the author of her own tropes of suffering, rather than adhering to a model in which she becomes the *object* of representation.

The author of the "familier Epistles," then, distances herself from traditional modes of female sorrow and suffering. This denial of literary tradition distances the speaker from others' representations of her situation, and thus paradoxically enforces the very isolation of which she complains. The letters contain two contradictory, and yet mutually constitutive, personae: that of the woman who finds relief and safety in connection, and that of the woman who finds connection (at least in written form) insufficient to abate her sorrow. The letters impart the sense of a speaker who yearns to share the burden of her misfortune. On this level, writing is a process of maintaining relationships; the letters, as an entire series, depict the deterioration of textual communities as an effective medium for representing the author's experience.

The last letter finalizes this process by portraying an inward turn in which the speaker's aloneness establishes itself as the fundamental fact of her current existence. A final letter to her cousin, entitled "IS. W. beyng wery of writyng," expresses resignation at her interlocutors' advice as she decides to write no more letters. With two stanzas and fourteen total lines, the letter is the shortest of the series and this relative brevity parallels the writer's exhaustion. She vows to abandon her writing until Fortune's wheel turns again; in the meantime, she asks her cousin not to reply but to accept her verse because "Tis all I have":

> This simple verce: content you for to take
> for answer of your loving letter lardge,
> For now I wyll my writing cleane forsake
> till of my griefes, my stomack I discharg:
> and tyll I row, in Ladie Fortunes barge.
> Good Cosin write not nor any more replye,
> But geve mee leave, more quietnes to trye.

Thus, the end of communication across geographical distances is weariness, frustration over insufficient help from her associations, and disappearance from the page. This withdrawal would undermine my argument – that solitude produces her writing – if it were the last poem in the volume. But when the spirited "Maner of her Wyll" follows, one senses from its placement that the speaker has derived creative benefits, and perhaps spiritual maturity, from this implied inward turn. The solitary "I" will dominate "Maner" and, as the poem that most closely resembles a print commodity, it captures the final stage of her movement from communal authorship to the individual agency of the professional writer.

Commodity Logic and the "Wylling" Mind

The next section offers an example of one way in which the personal experience of poverty can be linked, however problematically, with a more general sense of community. Just as the "familiar Epistles" put absent relations at the forefront of a narrative of loss, so the satirical "The Maner of her Wyll" uses the genre of the testament to highlight the speaker's relationship to money and other material goods. Punning on the term "wyll," she imagines her impending disappearance from the city of London, presumably due to financial straits. Although poor, she bequeaths – or "wylls" – London's own commodities to itself by directing its denizens to the city's diverse marketplaces. This show of charity, which she undertakes even though the city "never yet, woldst credit geve / to boord me for a yeare: / Nor with Apparell me releve / except thou payed weare" (lines 32–5),[21] accompanies a description of the criminals, debtors, and lunatics that marketplace bounty has left behind. As she gives away goods that are not her own, the speaker repeatedly suggests that, like the criminal runoff of the system, she herself is outside of the market-driven cycle of

---

[21] All citations from "Maner" are by line number from Betty Travitsky's edition, *English Literary Renaissance* 10, 4 (Winter 1980), 6–95.

mutual benefit. But even as the author's body disappears, her text enters the system of exchange as both an agent of distribution and a commodity in its own right. In Danielle Clarke's terms, which I invoke with respect to all the authors in this study, the speaker balances between "material dispossession" and "poetic possession."[22] These polarities, I wish to add, make visible the contradiction inherent in Whitney's position as a professional author who owns her text (in the sense that it is a product of her labor), and yet does not own the means of its production and distribution. While she, impoverished, must leave the city where she was "bred" (line 76), it is the printer and bookseller who stand to profit from the sale of her work.[23] The poem thematizes this irony by locating its speaker outside the socioeconomic system that stands to benefit from her literary labor.

Generically, "Maner" captures the possession/dispossession dynamic through two common types of mid-Tudor literary testament. The first is the "female tradition" of advice from dying women to their children, exemplified by Dorothy Leigh's *The Mother's Blessing* (1616) and Elizabeth Richardson's *A ladies legacie to her Daughters* (1645). Wendy Wall situates "Maner" alongside these texts to show how testaments commonly contain "a strangely performative and self-constituting gesture dependent on the erasure of the subject at the very moment of powerful self-assertion"[24] – that is to say, testaments permit a kind of speech that is predicated on the speaking subject's extinction. While the testamentary form specifically aligns Whitney with these particular conditions of women's writing, the poem also partakes of the popular tradition of testamentary ballads.[25] "Maner" is written in ballad meter and contains the voice of the dying protagonist that we see in such ballads as "The testament of the hawthorne," "The Cruel Brother: or, the Bride's Testament," and "The Child's Last Will." At times, the testamentary ballad speaker bids a sorrowful goodbye, while still maintaining that his or her mind remains strong as the body expires. The anonymous "The testament of the hawthorne," which appears in the second edition of *Tottel's Miscellany*, presents the first person declaration of a dying man who, "In faithfull true and fixed minde," resigns his past joy to a lady "whom that I served last." The speaker describes their relationship as one of "service" to "the

[22] Danielle Clarke, *The Politics of Early Modern Women's Writing*, London: Longman, 2001, 201.

[23] Before copyright, printers paid a small, flat fee for a manuscript – a short-term solution for impoverished authors. Margaret Ferguson surmises that, given the scarcity of women in the book trade, the power imbalance would have been even greater for female professional writers. See "Renaissance Concepts of the 'Woman Writer'," *Women and Literature in Britain*, ed. Helen Wilcox, Cambridge: Cambridge Univ. Press, 1996, 143–68, 162.

[24] Wendy Wall, *The Imprint of Gender: Authorship and Publication in the English Renaissance*, Ithaca, NY: Cornell Univ. Press, 1993, 286.

[25] Peter Burke notes that "mock" religious rituals and legal forms were a staple of popular culture all over early modern Europe. He notes that while these appropriations sometimes were purely for the purpose of poking fun, they were more often "not a mockery of religious or legal forms but the taking over of these forms for a new purpose," a way of "taking over the forms of official culture." The fact that this could be a serious kind of play was evident in the fact that these mock forms usually did not use the word "mock." See Burke's *Popular Culture in Early Modern Europe*, London: Temple Smith, 1978, 123.

fayrest that ever was"; that Whitney might have applied the term "service" to capture her own longing for her mistress presents an intriguing possibility. "The testament of the hawthorne" presents impending death as isolation, in contradistinction to the enjoyment of earlier social connections. Alternatively, "The Cruel Brother" and "The Child's Last Will" put the testament into the voices of murder victims.[26] In the first, the protagonist's brother stabs her for not getting his consent for a marriage. The piece expresses a sense of eye-for-an-eye justice, as the dying bride answers the question, "What will ye leave to your brother John?" with "The gallows-tree to hang him on." In "The Child's Last Will," a child poisoned by her nurse and her stepmother wishes them "some pangs" and "bitter sorrow." Such ballads expose fantastic tales of cruelty and enact justice through the last words of a dying victim.

The female testamentary tradition, the anonymity of the "Hawthorne" speaker, and the vulnerability of ballads' victimized brides and children all indicate that the testament was a genre in which the will of an ordinary subject could find a final moment of assertion prior to its extinction. Clearly, Whitney found something in these traditions that suited her aim. True to testamentary convention, "Maner" juxtaposes the strength of the mind to the dying body: "I trust you all wyll witnes beare, I have a stedfast brayne" (lines 69–70). The speaker's death provides the occasion for an otherwise marginal individual to occupy the page as an "I." Furthermore, her erasure permits her to speak critically of whomever or whatever brings about her destruction. But "Maner" also departs from convention by making it clear that the speaker's losses are economic, rather than sexual or familial. Casting the struggle in this way stresses her status as a woman without "a Husband or a house" and underscores her claim to be writing professionally for lack of other options.

Whitney opens by substituting her purse for her body as the mark of her material presence: "I Whole in body, and in minde, / but very weake in Purse: / Doo make, and write my Testament / for feare it wyll be wurse" (lines 51–4). As we learn when she castigates London's lack of charity, she links her departure to the city's unwillingness to extend her board, credit, and clothing. Financial solvency and material comfort would have continued her presence in the city; conversely, her lack of wealth conditions her disappearance. The association of bodily presence and material possessions provides the terms by which she designates who is "in" (merchants, purchasers) and who is "out" (debtors, lunatics, other prisoners) in contemporary London. The "wyll" that persists in spite of material want creatively links the well-fed and the wretched of the city; moreover, it mediates between comfort and despair by registering the speaker's own experience with these two disparate states.

Whitney frames her bequeathment as an act of selfless charity that starkly contrasts with the city's indifference. But upon closer examination, we see that she implicates the city's denizens in the socioeconomic system in the same terms by which she herself has been excluded. Just as the city refused her help "unless thou payed weare," London's people may only partake of the city's bounty if they can pay for it. Those who do not pay cannot leisurely roam the city like their solvent counterparts, but remain confined in Ludgate prison, which Whitney confesses she

[26] "The Cruel Brother" and "The Child's Last Will" are cited from Francis James Child's *English and Scottish Ballads*, London: Sampson Low, 1861.

"dyd reserve . . . for my selfe . . . [if I] ever came in credit so / a debtor for to be. / When dayes of paiment did approch, / I thither ment to flee" (lines 229–34). In a society increasingly driven by market relations, charity wanes as an old ideal and freedom to participate in social life depends upon a person's ability to command economic resources. She warns the city that its people's "keeping craveth cost" (line 81), just as did her own keeping. In a gesture that benefits producers as well as buyers, Whitney advertises for the markets – wool in Watling and Canwick streets, linen in Friday street, mercers in Cheap, and so forth – and points readers to a boy by the stocks who "wil aske you what you lack" (line 118). But the mutually beneficial exchange between buyers and sellers depends upon money, to which Whitney directs them as well: "Yf they that keepe what I you leave, / aske Mony: when they sell it: / At Mint, there is such store, it is / unpossible to tell it" (lines 159–62). Of course, casting the mint as an unlimited store of means is ridiculously disingenuous, particularly from a speaker who claims to suffer from *lack* of means: if money is so readily available, one might ask why she has not helped herself. Furthermore, if merchants who "aske Mony" were merely exercising an option rather than acting on a necessary condition, then the entire system of commodity exchange would fall apart. The humor of Whitney's imaginings – her fantasy of unlimited bounty in a system that necessarily limits the participation of some people – contains bite when we realize how this fantasy delineates her own status as economic victim. If we can detect a ballad speaker's revenge here, it resides in the way she involves her supposed beneficiaries in the same harsh system that has marginalized her. Moreover, despite some critics who locate *Nosgay*'s claim to authority within the bourgeois gender discourse of "housekeeping,"[27] "Maner" mocks the bourgeois ideal of thrift. The speaker asks to be buried "in oblivyon" and tells the city, "Ringings nor other Ceremonies, use you not for cost: / Nor at my buriall, make no feast, / your mony were but lost" (lines 317, 319–322). The very fact that Whitney put her own name to published original poetry counters this request for "oblivyon." Her wish here seems to parody women's rhetorical gestures that strenuously denied the writer's desire for fame.[28]

It may be objected that my reading of "Maner" is overly cynical; perhaps we are meant to take Whitney's "perfect love and charitye" (line 40) at face value. Comparing "Maner" to the tone of most testamentary ballads, Michael Felker writes, "the irony of Whitney's 'Wyll' is gentle rather than bitter," which "indicates that she had, indeed, found a way to overcome much of her self-pity and sorrow."[29] While I would agree that the placement of "Maner" as last in the miscellany suggests a triumph of the "wyll," readings that privilege the speaker's "perfect love" overlook the fact that

[27] See Jones, "Nets and Bridles," on Whitney's use of "bourgeois gender discourse" (op. cit.) and Walker's characterization of Whitney's work as "model housewifery" (op.cit., 162).

[28] On the opposition between poetic fame and the sober, useful work of the bourgeois woman, see Ann Rosalind Jones, "Surprising Fame: Renaissance Gender Ideologies and Women's Lyric," *The Poetics of Gender*, ed. Nancy K. Miller, New York: Columbia Univ. Press, 1986, 74–95.

[29] Michael Felker, "The Poems of Isabella Whitney: A Critical Edition," diss. Texas Tech Univ., xii, xc.

this triumph comes at great cost. Furthermore, such readings shortchange Whitney's skill as a satirist, for she frequently describes social abuses in deceptively benign terms. In addition to the patients and prisoners that linger in London's disciplinary institutions, Whitney finds women who are not criminals, but who occupy potentially dangerous positions. These figures recall her own struggles with singlehood and the stigma on female independent industry. Toward the end of the poem, after her description of the criminalized underclass, she notes the plight of "Maydens poore," to whom she leaves rich widowers who "shal mary them, / to set the Girles afloate" (lines 251, 253–4). In order not to sink, poor women face rich widowers as their only respectable option for survival. In turn, Whitney leaves "wealthy Widdowes" to young men who, she assumes, will know how to put their new wives' riches to use: "see their Plate and Jewells eake / may not be mard with rust. / Nor let their Bags too long be full, / for feare that they doo burst" (lines 255, 259–62). Lone widows cannot or will not handle their own riches; marriage is needed to allow these goods to circulate actively as exchange value, and this, Whitney suggests, is their proper use. In both cases, marriage secures economic functioning, although achieving full citizenship in this regard first means entering the marriage market as a commodity oneself. Immediately following this commentary, Whitney notes the "Fruit wives" – bawds – who "compas" the city walls. These border creatures entertain "such as come in and out," bawdily suggesting prostitution. The fruit wives signify the trade of sex as an alternative to marriage for keeping a girl "afloate." Haunting the outskirts of the city, as Mother B does the back door to the household, the bawd provides the relay point between sanctioned and unsanctioned female economic activity. Just as the maids in service found themselves meeting Mother B, so does Whitney's choice to place the fruit wife after her remarks on the marriage market suggest close proximity between the two putatively separate spheres of domesticity and prostitution.

Although Whitney claims intimate familiarity with the city, her inability to remain there on its terms casts her outside of it. On the one hand, the testament attempts to re-enact a sense of community that has been lost to the speaker, who affects goodwill to the city "and to all those in it" (line 50). But the testamentary author's contact with readers will take place only when the author is gone. As both a print commodity and a guide to the purchase of further commodities, "Maner" represents the author's bid for permanence in a city where market success ensures survival: "I whole in body, and in minde, / but very weake in Purse: / Doo make, and write my Testament / for feare it wyll be wurse" (lines 51–4). When Whitney leaves the city a "Treasurye" (line 42), it is unclear whether she refers to the goods or to the poem itself. But the poem's status as print commodity is marked in several ways. Whitney's use of ballad meter calls attention to the text as a product of the print market. Furthermore, the poem includes print culture's agents in its beneficiaries. In the lines immediately following Whitney's allusions to her own troubles with debt and before her commentary on the marriage market and on prostitution, she wishes continued success to "all the Bookebinders by Paulles," hoping that "They evry weeke shal mony have, / when they from Bookes departe" (lines 244, 245–6). Books are numbered here among the city's other commodities, although this is the first spot in the poem where Whitney directs her good will to the *merchant's* benefit rather than to that of the consumer. She personalizes this wish by leaving money to her own printer: "Amongst them all, my Printer must, / have somwhat to his share: / I wyll my friends these Bookes to bye / of him, with other ware" (lines 247–50). The printer serves as a reminder that others will benefit from the labors of the author, who can claim no profits from her text other than a small, flat fee for a manuscript. Additionally, the printer's profit underscores the rift between the author as outsider and the text as a circulating commodity within a marketplace society. The "friends" to whom the poem is directed can only access the speaker's "wyll" by *purchasing* the poem. Paradoxically then, the speaker's selfless "charitye" can only be enacted by self-interested agents. This irony adumbrates the situation of the professional author as a laborer with a low level of command over the circulation and distribution of her text. The permanence that Whitney achieves, then, comes at the cost of the text's separation from its author's person, thematized by the author's "death."

Finally, the poem depicts the site of writing as one in which the author is alone with "Paper, Pen and Standish" (line 371) as her sole witnesses. Even if the "familier Epistles" succeeded as an imitation of collective writing practices, this last image of "Maner" – which is also the concluding image of the miscellany – reinforces the author's self-representation as a woman forsaken and alone.[30] The writing materials that witness her "wyll" remind readers of this fact. They also testify to the poem's status as a material artifact that purports to speak for her after her disappearance. These final lines encapsulate both the permanence that Whitney has invested in her commodity-poem and the alienation that has conditioned its creation. In between the old ideals of charity and patronage and the new order of market exchange, we find the figure of the non-aristocratic woman writer, who imagines professional independence before legal practices – not to mention cultural practices – have made it fully possible.

Furthermore, by subordinating the fate of London's people to the acquisition and exchange of money and goods, Whitney's vision is in many ways a prescient one: she describes a society saturated with markets, in which the social is contained within the economic. Placing markets everywhere as the sole providers of necessities for a dependent public, Whitney's vision looks something like the "historical shift" that Jean-Christophe Agnew attributes to early modern proto-capitalism: "[The market moves] from a place to a process to a principle of power . . . a gradual displacement of concreteness in the governing concept of commodity exchange. The attributes of materiality, reality, and agency ordinarily assigned to the sphere of social relations (or to God) were implicitly reassigned to the sphere of commodity relations, as supply and demand took on a putative life of their own."[31] In "Maner," Whitney sees commerce as finally dominant; it is the inescapable reality that conditions the agency of the will, the creative imagination, and the capacity for survival. Markets

[30] The poignancy of the speaker's solitary death is reinforced by the fact that the deathbed was an important site of community for women, who commonly gathered around a dying friend or relation to offer prayers, care, and comfort. See Lucinda M. Becker, *Death and the Early Modern Englishwoman*, Aldershot, UK: Ashgate, 2003, 29–33.

[31] Jean-Christophe Agnew, *Worlds Apart: The Market and the Theater in Anglo-American Thought, 1550–1750*, Cambridge: Cambridge UP, 1986, 56.

are everywhere, but they do not support everyone. As she dramatically quits the struggle to find charity in the market landscape, the only action left to take is to make her statement, and depart.

Conclusion: Formally Free

The unusual stance that Whitney adopts as the narrative occasion for her book is, I believe, to be taken seriously as a governing theme for her work and a major clue to its reception – namely, that the position of the single, impoverished maidservant raises provocative questions not only about the dangerous and problematic relationship between a lady and her pen, but about the gendered discourses surrounding property ownership and the problems that these pose for professional writers in the age before copyright. A sequential reading of the *Nosgay* reveals aspects of her approach to authorship that anthologized excerpts cannot. While *Nosgay* showcases Whitney's hand at literary forms characteristic of the moment, it is also unique among miscellanies of the mid-Tudor period in that it offers a sustained narrative conditioned by the social and economic losses of one otherwise unremarkable person – the author herself, registered in the persistence of the "I" throughout all three sections. *Nosgay*'s distinct autobiographical strain – with its emphasis on personal authority, the possibility of ownership, the uses of experience, and the search for occupation – provides an early glimpse of how alienating social and economic relations could in fact be deployed to enable a sense of literary professionalism. Throughout her book, Whitney insists that she writes only because she must. But this concession to propriety meets with ironic commentary on economic conditions, made apparent by Whitney's quest to provide herself with a fitting maintenance through the sale of her literary labor. The figure of the solitary author, which runs throughout the text, allows this exploration of the contradictory discourses that govern professional authorship. As we will see in subsequent chapters, laboring authors' senses that they are maligned and alone always have deep ties to their senses that their texts are both detached from their creation and yet a stand-in for their place in the world, like avatars of themselves that are both false (because they are compromised by their very materiality) and true (because despite their materiality, they purport to bear the authors' life and soul to a reading public).

When Ann Rosalind Jones notes the gestures at community present in the "familier Epistles," she maintains that reading Whitney as a self-consciously solitary writer involves "postromantic" assumptions that run contrary to common writing practice in the Renaissance. This charge merits re-examination in light of solitary "I" that persists throughout the entirety of *Nosgay*. The point is not whether a community figures in the text, but how that community is represented in relation to the speaker. The tension from the individual and the community will figure in different ways in the chapters to follow, always problematized by the fact that authors feel compelled to designate themselves as individual and unique without compromising their intelligibility. Community is certainly present in *Nosgay*, as it will be in the writings of the other authors I survey here. But the more persistent isolation inherent in Whitney's inward turn, made dramatic by her alienation from family, service, and the whole of London, shows that the trope of the writer as forsaken by society need not be specific to the post-romantic period. Whitney may indeed have had a network of support in actual fact, but the text works through these connections finally to position her as alone in her misfortune, with "Paper, Pen and Standish" as the sole witnesses to her invention. This fact necessitates a further look at what textual communities actually signified for writers who looked to anonymous consumers as their primary source of monetary support. Whitney may have had well-intentioned friends, but in the final statement of her "wyll," it is the unbridgeable distance of these friends, the city's lack of support and, most importantly, her low status relative to her own labor that brings her to see herself as an outsider. The contradiction between her avowed "charytie" and demands of marketplace exchange suggests that, while Whitney may be no postromantic figure, perhaps she – and the laboring authors that follow her – deserves a place in the history of the idea.

Chapter 2

The Uses of Resentment: Nashe, *Parnassus*, and the Poet's Mystery

In the previous chapter, I note several features of Isabella Whitney's authorial self-presentation that help her turn misfortune into professional opportunity. First, as we see in "The Maner of Her Wyll," satire becomes a means by which to reflect on her own marginalization in a way that appears playful, but actually indicts the social and economic forces that have made it necessary for her to leave London. By locating herself outside the life of the city – suffused by the very market system that renders her unable to participate – she becomes a sardonic observer who centralizes her own "wyll" and represents society in her own verse. Outsider status is frightening but also becomes an opportunity to represent oneself in fresh, less traditional terms. Moreover, the aloneness she experiences as a woman without marriage or service helps to underscore her rhetorical pose as a writer without community, who must sell her verse for her own survival.

With Cambridge graduate and satirist Thomas Nashe, we shift to a very different context, one that features nominally elite men. While universities often produced men who went on to administrative positions and perhaps wrote amateur verse in their leisure time, the changing economic conditions and shifting cultural conceptions of learning during the late Tudor period witnessed graduates who became colorful and controversial London literary figures, like Nashe, Christopher Marlowe, and Robert Greene. As in the case of Whitney, concrete external evidence on Nashe's life is frustratingly scarce and inconclusive. Despite his claim that he sprung "from the Nashes of Hereford," it appears that his father, William Nashe, was a minister. Virtually nothing is known of Thomas's upbringing until his father sent him to St. John's College, Cambridge, around 1582, where he matriculated as a sizar. After taking a B.A., he left before completing an M.A. degree, most likely due to lack of money – his father, who had been financially supporting him, died in 1587.[1] He moved to London shortly thereafter to write works for the print market, most notably the semiautographical *Pierce Pennilesse his supplication to the divell* (1592), which voices a poor, embittered learned man who makes a bargain with the devil. What we know about Nashe, combined with what he indicates in his writings, presents the

[1] *The Works of Thomas Nashe*, ed. Ronald B. McKerrow, 5 vols, Oxford: Basil Blackwell, 1958, V: 1–12. All quotes from Nashe's works are taken from McKerrow's edition.

story of a frustrated scholar *cum* writer for pay – one who is compelled to adjust to a new socioeconomic reality.

In the introduction to this study, I sketch the issue of *expectation* with respect to authorial ambition. A "laureate" author, in Helgerson's sense of the term, expects to be able to speak to and to serve the monarch and the nation through his poetry. With the "laboring" authors I treat here, however, the social position from which an author speaks cannot be so easily taken for granted. Sometimes, an author might begin with very little expectation, as in the case of Whitney, due to her gender, the occupation she claims to have, and her status without a family. But the case of Nashe shows how one can begin with expectation and become frustrated later, only to turn that frustration into a position from which to engage the market for print. Nashe's works are driven by a dynamic that Michael McKeon calls "status inconsistency."[2] The traditional discourse of nobility posits that ascribed and achieved status are one and the same: at a purely theoretical level, noble blood is reflected in noble virtue and actions, and vice versa. Literature of the Tudor and Jacobean period does much to trouble this elision – for example, the prose tales of Thomas Deloney, like *Jack of Newberry* and *The Gentle Craft*, which suggest that gentle virtue can exist in an artisan of the common orders. We cannot always assume that such texts work toward revisionary ends, but the discourse of upward mobility attends the possibility of *downward* mobility as well. "Status inconsistency" describes the sense that one's social expectation, or early sense of one's social identity, is at odds with the actual reality that one lives. In early capitalist Britain, the idea of the market places the inherent value of things – and people – on their uses, rather than on inactive, inherent qualities. As many learned graduates of Cambridge and other institutions will discover, the discourse of "use" works to their disadvantage because learning is no longer taken as an automatic badge of entitlement, thus forcing many of them to engage in forms of labor that "gentlemen" are meant to disdain.

The writings of Nashe and his other learned contemporaries capture this struggle. The *Parnassus* plays refer to numerous poets and playwrights in their attempt to vindicate learned authors, but only Nashe merits adoption as a central character. In a scene in which two characters compare the relative merits of the poets of their age, they name Nashe last as a fellow who "carried the deadly stock [ado] in his pen" (2 *Returne* l. 314).[3] Some university-educated authors serve as examples of unrewarded learning, such as Spenser, who died "Denying maintenance for his deare releife" (l. 228). Others stand out for personal characteristics that shortened their careers, like Marlowe, who had "wit lent from heaven, but vices sent from hell" (l. 293). But the graduate Judicio names Nashe with sympathy and admiration as a satirist whose skill makes one forgive his faults: "Let all his faultes sleepe with his mournfull chest, / And [there] for ever with his ashes rest. / His style was wittie, though [it] had some gal[l], / Something[s] he might have mended, so may all. / Yet this I say, that for a

---

2 Michael McKeon, *The Origins of the English Novel, 1600–1740*, Baltimore: Johns Hopkins UP, 1987. The term is used throughout the text, beginning at xxii.

3 All quotes from the plays are from William Dunn Macray's edition, *The Pilgrimage to Parnassus: with the two parts of The Return from Parnassus; Three Comedies Performed in St. John's College, Cambridge*, Oxford: Clarendon, 1886.

mother witt, / Few men have ever seene the like of it" (ll. 318–23). In short, the plays describe Nashe as both typical and singular, embedded in the world and above it.

By paying tribute to Nashe's life and his perceived originality, the plays present him as a poet who maintains skill and integrity even as he imperfectly navigates a corrupt world. It is useful here to recall Clifford Siskin's definition of professionalization as the "authority to convert knowledge of the deep self into prescriptive expertise" as "a central form of modern power."[4] Even if Nashe never constructs himself as a "deep self" in the postromantic sense, the *Parnassus* plays allow him a "mournfull chest" full of sorrows that lurks underneath, and indeed informs, his acerbic wit. His potency as a satirist is tied to this brooding, a mood created by the experience of unemployment, penury, and lack of recognition. Thus, in a very different demographic than the one Isabella Whitney occupied, we find a similar strategy for linking the labor of authorship to non-aristocratic social identity: the conversion of displacement and poverty into a professional opportunity as well as a virtue. This conversion attends the construction of a deep self who creates in isolation and occupies an ambivalent relationship to the literary market. While this transformation of bitterness into mastery may not yet signify full "professional identity," it does provide an early means to envision professional possibilities beyond service and patronage.

Here, I will trace the idea of professionalism as power into Nashe's writings and the very site that produced learned men of his class – the late Tudor university. The *Parnassus* plays provide an ideal occasion for studying early figurations of mastery over the literary field. These comedies, performed as Christmas plays between 1597 and 1601, are connected with Nashe in several ways. First, they were performed in his own former college, St. John's. Second they contain a central character named Ingenioso, whose experiences with patrons and the market mirror those of Nashe. Within the plays' central theme, which is the economic tribulations of scholars after graduation, Ingenioso represents the man who turns to print as a means of emancipating himself from the humiliating positions in which he and the other characters find themselves – as servants to patrons, as tutors, as vicars, as cony-catchers, and as balladeers. Third, the plays contain lines, either paraphrased or directly copied, from Nashe's popular writings, especially *Pierce Pennilesse*.

The anonymous author(s) of the *Parnassus* plays clearly viewed Nashe as an important and recognizable figure in a narrative of scholars' displacement within marketplace culture. The plays use Nashe's example to stage a collective consideration of the place of scholarly labor in the late Tudor commonwealth – a crucial issue for a group who feared the loss of status traditionally conferred on graduates. While the plays offer no clear resolution, they respond to these losses by allowing the poet-scholar critical distance not only from the world outside of the university, but from the university itself as a site of humanist discourses concerning the privileged role of learned men in the commonwealth.

---

[4] Clifford Siskin, *The Work of Writing: Literature and Social Change in Britain, 1700–1830*, Baltimore: Johns Hopkins UP, 1998.

Wandering as Social Strategy

The *Parnassus* trilogy as a whole charts a progression from hope to disillusionment. The first play, *The Pilgrimage to Parnassus*, contains five short acts in which two students, Philomusus and his cousin Studioso, ascend Parnassus to drink "Of Hellicons pure stream" (l. 195). They set out on a rough, craggy path under the counsel of Philomusus's elderly father, Consiliodorus, who advises them to eschew riches and flattery and to expect poverty, for "Learninge and povertie will ever kiss" (l. 76). On the way, the young men encounter obstacles in a drunk reader of Horace named Madido, in a Puritan and Ramist named Stupido, and in Amoretto, a devotee of Ovid who tempts them to venery through love poetry. Having emerged successfully from the lands of logic, rhetoric, and philosophy, they finally meet the Nashe-like Ingenioso, who warns them not to ascend the hill because "Parnassus is out of silver pitifullie" (ll. 583–4). Nonetheless, the cousins complete their journey in four years. At the end, they declare their devotion to the muses and their scorn for the "common songes" that "vulgar witts" admire (l. 726). While the play does not present its heroes as always steadfast in temptation, it affirms the path of study as a sacred pilgrimage; those who faithfully adhere to it will reap conference with the muses as their reward.

The last two plays, *The Returne from Parnassus Part I* and *Part II*, abandon allegory in favor of satire, a decision that suits the shift in focus from the holy mission of study to the humiliating penury of graduates. These plays cast a wider thematic net than the first and contain more scenes and characters. Here Philomusus and Studioso find Consiliodorus's characterization of the scholar's life far more difficult to accept as they discover the truth of Ingenioso's warning. In *Pilgrimage*, Ingenioso cautions, "take heede I take youe not napping twentie years henc in a viccar's seate . . . or else interpretinge *pueriles confabulations* to a companie of seaven-yeare-olde- apes" (ll. 659–63). In the *Returne* plays, the two young men find themselves in exactly these positions, with Philomusus as a vicar and Studioso as a tutor to a commoner's child. Both get ignominiously dismissed from their positions and leave the country for Europe's seats of Catholicism. When they return they try their hands at cozening citizens by posing as French doctors; then they try acting, and then fiddling. More friends join them in their struggles: Luxurioso becomes a London ballad-rhymer; Academico tries to obtain a benefice but is told he can succeed only by resorting to simony. Ingenioso, who is now a central character, serves foolish young noblemen before turning to the printing house. His companions are Furor Poeticus, a railer, and Phantasma, who speaks in borrowed Latin phrases. In the final scene of *Part II*, Philomusus and Studioso retreat to the countryside to become shepherds; Furor and Phantasma depart for the "Ile of dogs" (l. 2106) with Ingenioso, who has been exiled for writing seditious plays;[5] Academico takes to a cell in Cambridge.

---

[5] The reference to the Isle of Dogs provides the most explicit link to Nashe, alluding to a play by the same name on which he probably collaborated with Jonson and for which Nashe was exiled to Yarmouth. Nashe's *Lenten Stuffe* (1599) responds to this situation with a critique of the power relations that resulted in his exile.

The fate of each character represents a different response to social dislocation. But while the other scholars make it clear that they are escaping from the world and its denigration of learning, Ingenioso imagines his own position as a place in which he may inhabit the world and yet still maintain enough distance and comment on it:

> Faith we are fully bent to be Lord of misrule in the worlds wide [hall]; our voyage is to the Ile of Dogges, there where the blattant beast doth rule and raigne renting the credit of whom it please.
> Where serpents tongs the pen men are to write,
> Where cats do waule by day, dogges barke by night:
> There shall engoared venom be my inke,
> My pen a sharper quill of porcupine,
> My stayned paper, this sin loaden earth:
> There will I write in lines shall never die. (ll. 2146–55)

Whereas Philomusus and Studioso resort to a pastoral setting as a way of evading the contradictions of labor and gentility, Ingenioso turns back upon the world – "this sin loaden earth" – and makes it into his "paper." Philomusus and Studioso will constrain their wandering to a single conceptual space. Alternatively, Ingenioso plans to live in the "wide world" and rule it through his pen.

Several of Nashe's most popular writings reveal an interest in these exact themes: occupational displacement, the degradation of learning by both amateurism and by the vulgar literary market, and the embrace of satire as a means of vindication. In his address to "Gentlemen Students of Both Universities" which serves as the preface to Robert Greene's *Menaphon*, Nashe homes in on the proliferation of poets in print, a phenomenon he takes as cause for alarm among the learned. Styling himself "your Scholler-like Shepheard" (III.311) for a group that he hopes will remember him from his days at St. John's, he launches a sharp critique of unlearned writers. Nashe explicitly identifies these "thredbare wits" according to their lack of university education, "having no more learning in their skull then will serve to take up a commoditie, nor Art in their braine then was nourished in a serving mans idlenesse" (312). Unaware of true eloquence, these undiscerning individuals rush to publish their own folly. Nonetheless, Nashe assures his audience, "God and Poetrie doth know they are the simplest of all" (312). By invoking "God and Poetrie" as an exclusive realm, Nashe constructs poetry as a calling that only men of sufficient learning may rightfully claim. Unlearned poets have plundered the store of the literate elite, and Nashe promises to "persecute those idiots and their heires unto the third generation, that have made Art bankerout of her ornaments, and sent Poetry a begging up and downe the Countrey" (324). Referring readers to his own *Anatomie of Absurditie* (1589), he vows to meet the usurpers on their own turf by besting them in print and exposing their lack of learning.

Nashe's remarks exhibit several themes important to the satirist's construction of himself as a learned, "true" author among pretenders. He claims poetry as an exclusive vocation for trained individuals by aligning it with God; it thus becomes a sacred mystery in the medieval sense, to suggest a special body of knowledge that only a licensed few may rightfully practice. This claim serves a self-promoting end, as we see in his reference to *Anatomie*, where readers may go if they wish to savor more of his pointed wit. Furthermore, Nashe adopts a pastoral persona when addressing those whom he deems "pure" as himself. The pastoral, as we know from both period and contemporary literary criticism, represents an idealized landscape that, to use an oft-invoked quote from George Puttenham, allegorically "glaunce[s] at greater matters."[6] This "glancing" has been taken by Louis Montrose and others to refer to frustration at court.[7] In Nashe's case, however, the idealized space of the pastoral represents a retreat from the discrepancy that learned men of his generation feel between entitlement and socioeconomic reality. This conflict will become present again in a more detailed reading of the *Parnassus* plays below.

More specific to the issue of professionalization, the relationship that Nashe draws between poetry and divinity represents an attempt to extricate "true" poetry, and "true" poets, from their imitators in the marketplace. If the market for print threatens to obfuscate all social distinctions, then Nashe responds by asserting university education as a credential for writing, a ticket to poetry's upper realms. His claim represents an early form of the "professionalization" of authorship as identified by Siskin, where "technicality" and "indetermination"[8] combine to designate a specialized, exclusive body of knowledge. The language of Nashe's preface fits the model to the extent that Nashe designates poetry as something divine and accessible only to the initiated few. However, Siskin's analysis centers on the late eighteenth and early nineteenth centuries. Prior to the changes in mode of production witnessed by this period, "Both work and desire had to be rewritten before they could naturally come together."[9] Two centuries prior to this "rewriting," Nashe's works show him struggling to transform writing for the market, which he often describes as his "day-labor", into something less ignominious for a learned man than other kinds of labor. By doing so, he strains against traditional definitions of work that confined intellectual activity to the elite and manual labor to commoners. The incompatibility of writing verse and selling it presents a contradiction not only for Nashe, but for the university literary culture that nurtured him.

This awareness exists also in *The Anatomie of Absurditie*, which appears to have been written near Nashe's departure from the university. Fittingly, it captures the prejudices of the learned man who seeks to claim some gentility. In the prefatory epistle to Sir Charles Blunt, Nashe reports overhearing a conversation among highly ranked gentlemen, one of whom advances the opinion that "the onely adjuncts of a Courtier were schollership and courage, returning picked curiosity to paultry Scriveners and such like" (I.7). The alignment of "schollership" with the more traditional knightly virtue of "courage" assumes that the two go hand-in-hand as a mark of gentle status. Nashe takes the elision of scholarship and gentility a step further by positing that learning actually *stands in for* traditional markers of elite status: "It is learning and knowledge which are the onely ornaments of a man, which furnisheth the tongue

---

6 George Puttenham, *The Arte of English Poesie*, ed. G.D. Wilcock and A. Walker, Cambridge: Cambridge UP, 1936, 38.

7 See, for example, Louis Montrose, "Of Gentlemen and Shepherds: The Politics of Elizabethan Pastoral Form," *ELH* 50 (1983), 432.

8 These terms are used throughout Siskin's *The Work of Writing*.

9 *Ibid.*, 113.

with wisedome, and the hart with understanding, which maketh the children of the needy poore to become noble Peeres, and men of obscure parentage to be equall with Princes in possessions" (34). Nashe's insistence that learning makes one equal to the peerage re-orients traditional discourses of nobility from inherent qualities (like "blood") toward individual achievement. At the same time, he rejects the idea that learning can be something merely to show, as when he argues with certain moralistic pamphleteers: "Thy knowledge boots thee not a button, except another knowes that thou hast this knowledge. . . . . so these men seeme learned to none but to Idiots, whom with a coloured shew of sezle, they allure unto them to their illusion, and not to the learned in like sort" (21). In a formulation similar to one we will see with Ben Jonson, Nashe suggests that learning *can* function as merely an outward show, but the *correct* use of learning proceeds from an inward, ineffable quality that keeps learned shows from functioning as empty signs. The possibility that learning *might* function as an empty sign, however, raises anxiety for the man who wishes to distinguish himself socially on the basis of his education, if only because he lacks other claims to gentility.

Although *Anatomie* purports to be an explication of the inherent evil of women, it roams over a variety of topics and is informed by Nashe's sense of belonging to a community of learned superiors. He excoriates print authors and laments the way their lack of learning adversely affects public morality (9–11); he decries those who make poetry an "occupation" as he paraphrases a classical author: "lying is their lyving, and fables are their mooveables: if thou takest away trifles, sillie soules, they will famish for hunger" (24). "Occupation," in this negative sense, means treating poetry as hire-and-salary, as a means to earn money. Although this is exactly what Nashe seems to have been doing after leaving Cambridge, his insistence on the preeminence of learning creates the distinction he needs. As with the preface to *Menaphon*, he calls poetry "a more hidden & divine kinde of Philosophy, enwrapped in blinde Fables and darke stories, whrein the principles of more excellent Arts and morrall precepts of manners, illustrated with divers examples of other Kingdomes and Countries, are contained" (25). The sentiment here – that poetry presents the truth in more alluring form than philosophy, and can lead the soul toward truth – is certainly a conventional one in Renaissance literary criticism. But Nashe deploys it in the specific context of concern for the fate of learning itself in a culture that leads learned men to ignominious labor. He rehearses graduates' common grudges, as in one passage where he describes the fate of sons released from the university at an early age:

> Wheneas wits of more towardness shall have spent some time in the university and have as it were tasted the elements of art and laid the foundation of knowledge, if by the death of some friend they should be withdrawn from their studies, as yet altogether raw and so consequently unfit for any calling in the Commonwealth, where should they find a friend to be unto them instead of a father, or one to perfect that which their deceased parents began? Nay, they may well betake themselves to some trade of husbandry for any maintenance they get in the way of alms at the university, or else take upon them to teach, being more fit to be taught, and perch into the pulpit, their knowledge being yet unperfect, very zealously preaching, being as yet scarce grounded in religious principles. How can those men call home the lost sheep that are gone astray, coming into the ministry before their wits be staid? This green fruit, being gathered before it be ripe, is rotten before it

> be mellow, and infected with schisms before they have learnt to bridle their affections, affecting innovations as newfangled, and enterprising alterations whereby the Church is mangled. (37)

Nashe points out the problem of replacing a lost "father" with new guidance for youths incapable of navigating the world. In the absence of mentors or nurturers, they ineptly take up husbandry, teaching, or preaching. These young men lack judgment and thus become susceptible to "newfangled innovations" and "enterprising alterations" that threaten church and state. They are potential dangers to society.

Pierce Pennilesse was written later, after Nashe arrived in London and began his stint as a writer for the print market, which was quite possibly his sole source of income. While *Anatomie* contains no topical references to London and very little of the gritty satire of the 1590s (largely because very little of it is original), *Pierce* is rife with the kind of grotesque, scathing humor characteristic of prose writing during the economically troubled decade. The persona of Pierce, which inspires the Ingenioso character of the *Parnassus* plays, ironically embraces his dislocation.[10] Unlike *Anatomie*, which begins with an address to a patron, the opening epistle of *Pierce* is addressed to Nashe's printer. Underscoring the text's status as a free commodity on the market for print, Nashe cautions the printer to look after the text in the absence of its writer:

> I heare say there bee obscure imitators, that goe about to frame a second part to it, and offer it to sell in Paules Church-yard, and elsewhere, as from mee. Let mee request you (as ever you will expect any favour at my hands) to get some body to write an Epistle before it, ere you set it to sale againe, importing thus much; that if any such lewde devise intrude it selfe to their hands, it is a coseanage and plaine knavery of him that sels it to get mony, and that I have no manner of interest or acquaintance with it. (I.154)

As does Whitney in "Maner," Nashe betrays a clear understanding that the market entails a rift between the producer and his product – the book, like Pierce himself, becomes a wanderer. Also like Whitney, Pierce envisions himself all alone with his pen after a period of economic frustration:

> Having spent many yeeres in studying how to live, and liv'de a long time without mony: having tired my youth with follie, and surfetted my minde with vanitie, I began at length to looke backe to repentaunce, & addresse my endeavors to prosperitie: But all in vaine, I sate up late, and rose earely, contended with the colde, and conversed with scarcitie: for all my labour turns to losse, my vulgar Muse was despised & neglected, my paines not regarded, or slightly rewarded, and I my selfe (in prime of my best wit) laid open to povertie. Whereupon (in a malecontent humor) I accused my fortune, raild upon my patrones, bit my pen, rent my papers, and ragde in all points like a mad man. In which

[10] McKerrow speculates on the origin of Pierce's name. He suggests that the character of "Piers" might come from *Piers Plowman*, with Langland's Piers being known for his plain-spokenness. This possible inspiration helps make sense of Pierce's prophetic, warning voice as well as his propensity to speak "plainly" which, in civil discourse, often coded as "roughly" or "rudely." See IV.86, n. 1.

> agony tormenting my selfe a long time, I grew by degrees to a milder discontent: and pausing a while over my Standish, I resolved in verse to paint forth my passion . . . (157)

This introduction reads like a parody of the first sonnet of Philip Sidney's *Astrophil and Stella*, where the speaker frets with his muse over how to best express himself in verse to his lady. (In fact, Nashe mentions Sidney as the most "vertuous, witty, [and] learned" of poets – 159.) But Pierce's version of the poet's struggle is not inspired by courtly love, but by poverty. The cruel mistress he addresses is England itself: "Adieu unkinde, where skill is nothing worth" (158). Poverty, representing a different kind of frustrated desire, becomes the occasion for producing verse – with great difficulty, yet nonetheless with eloquence, as a four-stanza poem on his misery proceeds from Pierce's pen. While Sidney's version of authorial "labor" takes childbirth as its metaphor, "labor" for Pierce will mean the kind of gritty, difficult toil that he needs to maintain himself.

Pierce looks with disdain upon tinkers and scriveners who earn comfortable livings while he dines "with Duke Humphrey," that is, not at all. He regards this state of affairs as a confusion of proper social categories, asking, "have I more wit than all these? . . . Am I better born? Am I better brought up? Yea, and better favoured? And yet am I a beggar?" (158). "Wit" and "better" birth together should entitle him to rule over his inferiors. Yet despite his conclusion that "the world was uncharitable, and I ordained to be miserable," he regards himself as free of responsibilities and goods: "I live secure from all such perturbations; for thanks be to God, I am *vacuus viator* [one who travels light], and care not, though I meet the Commissioners of Newmarket Heath at high midnight, for any crosses, images, or picture that I carry about me, more than needs" (160–61). As a man unburdened by troublesome coins, he moves more freely than men of wealth and place. This remark would be purely ironic if it did not lend itself so well to Pierce's position as an observer and exposer of vice, which he inhabits in his survey of sins throughout the rest of the book. Mobility means masterlessness, but it also means traveling light – without investment, and without fear of loss. This attitude may appear nonchalant, as when he declares, "The worse for me . . . if my destinie be such, to lose my labour every where, but I meane to take my chance, be it good or bad" (217). But diminished social status meets with compensatory gains as Pierce authorizes himself to exploit the very system that has led to a general demise of "honor" in society. Pierce presents his audience with a frightening and yet exhilarating possibility – that the loss of status ultimately can help create a new basis for identity, freeing one up to laugh at the world even as one profits from its audiences. By all means, this new identity is an occupational one. Comparing poets to preachers, he nominates poets as the true divines, those with access to truth and who have the ability to manifest truth in language, rather than the falsehood in language that he accuses preachers of practicing (192).

Some critics identify Nashe as a figure who manipulated the social susceptibility of print to approach something like professional independence, albeit at great cost to his identity as a man of learning. According to Alexandra Halasz, Nashe handled his position in the marketplace by "encoding it in terms that allowed [learned men] other kinds of authorization."[11] In other words, the emphasis on scholarly skill that we see in texts like the preface to *Menaphon* represents an attempt to impose hierarchy onto a plane that appears level, alarmingly so to those heavily invested in social distinctions. By referring to his writing as "day-labor," he "exploits artisanal metaphors to define his vocation and thereby acquires a means of asserting control" over "a discursive field no longer delimited by institutional sites of high literacy and audience whose rank and status could be predicted."[12] At the heart of such a strategy, I would add, is *mastery* as compensation for authority lost in the marketplace. Jennifer Turner identifies Nashe's frequent antagonism toward patronage as a critique of the learned man's role as a servant to the commonwealth; Nashe becomes an anti-humanist who "substitutes a decentered subjectivity for the professional author who is *not* an employee of the state, or in the service of one of her lords."[13] Nashe deliberately flouts the ideal of service to state and master in order to "lend machismo to his professional identity as a masterless mind."[14] The association between "professional identity" and "masterlessness" casts professionalism as economic and social independence – a means by which to embrace mobility and to play at being one's own master.[15] The challenge, then, is to rewrite masterlessness as an embrace of power over the economic field. However, this power is not strictly individual, as the idea of the radically masterless and untethered scholar might suggest. Rather, it is an experience felt by other learned writers who imagined, like Nashe did, a kind of bittersweet vindication.

Useful Young Men: The Ideology of Humanist Education

To historically situate how wandering figures as a way to handle issues of occupational identity, it is necessary to outline more specifically the discourses to which Nashe responds. Peter Holbrook dissents from critical opinion that positions Nashe as antithetical to elite culture, reminding us that Nashe, as a university man, was aligned with the elite and that his status as print author need not constitute an outright rejection of elite culture: "Nashe's works reveal discontent, but this does not issue in a fundamental, subversive alienation."[16] Certainly, Nashe retained affection for his alma mater and, if the plays borrow from him so liberally, then university

[11] *Marketplace of Print*, 88.

[12] Ibid., 99, 87.

[13] Jennifer Turner, "Jack Wilton and the Art of Travel," in *Critical Approaches to English Prose Fiction 1520–1640*, ed. Donald Beecher, Ottawa: Dovehouse, 1998, 123–56, 126.

[14] Ibid., 152.

[15] Siskin points to changes in modes of production during the early nineteenth century as leading to the closing of "the established gap between master-worker and apprentice-laborer" (144). During Nashe's lifetime, such distinctions were, at least in theory, still in place; yet Nashe nonetheless conceives of the possibility of being one's own master with the help of the market. Joseph Loewenstein has argued the same of Nashe's contemporary and probable collaborator, Jonson; see "The Script in the Marketplace."

[16] Peter Holbrook, *Literature and Degree in Renaissance England: Nashe, Bourgeois Tragedy, Shakespeare*, Newark: U of Delaware P, 1994, 45.

men must not have regarded him as wholly alien either.[17] But this does not mean that learned men, including Nashe, did not feel deep frustration over the discrepancy between their nominative status and their lived reality; Nashe's parody of Latinate academic drama in *The Unfortunate Traveller* shows a willingness to satirize university culture and its pretensions (2: 246–7). When the *Parnassus* plays present Nashe as a dangerous satirist revenging himself on a corrupt world, they draw on concerns present to many late Tudor graduates: social displacement, occupational ambiguity, primogeniture, vagrancy, and a popular literary culture they regarded as both repulsive and potentially liberating. The roots of this experience largely reside in the ideology of humanist education, which during the Tudor period stressed young men's "use" in a way that led to a commodification of the learned self within an increasingly market-driven society.

In theory, university education signified genteel status. William Harrison classed graduates with members of the lower nobility because they performed intellectual activity; it was supposed that any man who engaged in such activity need not "work" in a material sense. That passage from *Description of England*, which contemporary scholars take to be a standard definition of the Tudor gentleman, draws an intimate connection between learning and gentility.[18] Men who devote their minds to their books acquire enough knowledge to be of service to the commonwealth. Furthermore, such service precludes manual labor and entitles them to a coat of arms "for money." Men of learning do not merely study for its own sake – they make their learning into the foundation for an occupation and way of life. Like bearing arms, learning distinguishes a man from the commonality and invests him with the right to rule. In 1600, Thomas Wilson built upon Harrison's terms by ranking all university graduates with knights, esquires, gentlemen, lawyers, professors, ministers, archdeacons, prebends, and vicars in the *nobilitas minor*.[19] Writers of humanist educational treatises operated under similar assumptions: that the purpose of learning was to prepare a man for state service, because a public role was the natural lot of a gentleman. Early humanists such as Tiptoft, Elyot, Smith, More and Colet rejected the Aristotelian idea of sequestered contemplation in favor of what Rosemary O'Day calls "Social Humanism," an educational approach based on "the concept of honesty, which was to be achieved only by fulfilling the duties of one's position."[20] Genteel status, with its implied social obligation, needed proper

---

[17] Whatever his bitterness toward life after graduation, Nashe maintained consistent reverence for Cambridge, "that most famous and fortunate Nurse of all Learning" ("Preface" 317).

[18] See my pg. 4.

[19] Joan Thirsk and J.P. Cooper, eds., *Seventeenth Century Economic Documents*, Oxford: Clarendon, 1972, 753. The status of learning in the social order, like the status of wealth, did not go uncontested. But these descriptions show that, like wealth, learning represented a significant enough form of social power to force older notions of ascribed status (based largely on birth) to accommodate it. See Ruth Kelso, *The Institution of the Gentleman in English Literature of the Sixteenth Century: A Study in Renaissance Ideals*, Urbana, IL, 1926, 26–8.

[20] Rosemary O'Day, *The Professions in Early Modern England, 1450–1800: Servants of the Commonweal*, Harlow, UK: Pearson, 2000, 26.

training to develop. Richard Mulcaster opined that "young gentlemen should be public, because of their use,"[21] stressing the outcomes and products of learning as those things which give purpose to the educational process. Mulcaster's theories betray a distinct awareness, if not a veiled contempt, for the lower orders' role in a marketplace society, as he separates gentlemen from the commonality on the basis not of blood nor of riches, but according to the nature of their work: "The common is divided into *merchants* and *manuaries* . . . *Merchandise* containeth under it all those which live anyway by buying or selling; *manuary*, those whose handiwork is their ware and labor, their living."[22] Pointing out the qualitative difference between the commoner's role and that of the gentleman, Mulcaster asks, "which be gentlemanly qualities, if these be not: to *read*, to *write*, to *draw*, to *sing*, to *play*, to have *language*, to have *learning*, to have *health* and *activity*, nay even to profess *divinity*, *law*, *physic* and any trade, else commendable for cunning?" [23] This inventory of gentlemanly qualities de-mystifies elite status, breaking down its mystery into a list of attainable qualities. Furthermore, it posits that class-based virtue finds its ultimate culmination in a person's achievements as they are used and perceived by the outside world. The ability to deploy language and learning is both the gentleman's privilege and proof of his status, for "to be a *gentleman*, [is] to have excellent virtue to show."[24] By showing this virtue, gentlemen prove themselves "so excellently qualified as they may honest their country and honor themselves."[25] The purpose of a gentleman's education, then, is to make him "useful" for the nation, which guarantees his superiority over commoners because it may be seen in action. Learning should not be confined to a cloister, but put to a purpose.

The emphasis on "use" suited the expanding state, which required large numbers of men to fill professional posts. While the late medieval university had been primarily a place where the sons of poor men could prepare for entry into the church, the demand for administrative talent in the mid-sixteenth century led to an influx of gentlemen's sons into Cambridge, Oxford, and the Inns of Court.[26] O'Day reads the sharp increase in matriculation as a sign that "some of the upper classes were rejecting the old idea that learning was an attribute of clerks and accepting that there was a place for learning in preparing lay persons for an active role in society."[27] While some graduates took posts in the central government, some joined other

---

[21] Richard Mulcaster, *Positions*, ed. Richard L. DeMolen, New York: Columbia UP, 1971, 146.

[22] Ibid., 162.

[23] Ibid., 174.

[24] Ibid., 165.

[25] bid., 166.

[26] Mark Curtis, *Oxford and Cambridge in Transition, 1558*–1642, Oxford: Clarendon, 1959, 56; Lawrence Stone, "The Educational Revolution in England, 1560–1640," *Past and Present* 28 (1964), 41–80, 47–57; O'Day, *Professions*, 28. Elizabeth Russell has contested this thesis by noting that Oxford did not begin keeping accurate matriculation records until the mid-sixteenth century. However, no evidence shows that such was the case at Cambridge or at the Inns. See "The Influx of Commoners into the University of Oxford Before 1581: An Optical Illusion?", *English Historical Review* 92 (1977), 721–45.

[27] *Professions*, 29.

learned professions such as law or medicine. Because the custom of primogeniture persisted well into the latter half of the century, education was especially important for second sons – the oldest son could live as a landed gentleman, while the younger could take his learning as a means to a comfortable life.[28] Certainly, some men still trained for the church; others had no real need to earn a living but were educated to "practice the art of being a gentleman."[29] Nonetheless, the combination of learning and gentility implied "governmental responsibilities at local and national levels."[30]

However, the real value of a university education as a sustainer of wealth and status was challenged by the fact that, due to high matriculation, universities turned out graduates that exceeded available posts. Those on the lower end of the elite, like Nashe, found it difficult to obtain preferment. The result was a surplus that alarmed some observers. Mulcaster writes:

> To[o] many [learned men] burdens any state to[o] farre: for want of provision. For the rowmes which are to be supplied by learning being within number, if they that are to supply them, grow on beyound number, how can it be but too great a burden for any state to beare? To have so many gaping for preferment, as no goulfe hath stoore enough to suffise, and to let them rome helples, whom nothing else can helpe, how can it be but that such shifters must needes shake the verie strongest piller in that state where they live, and loyter without living?[31]

In keeping with the view that learned men should be put to "use," Mulcaster imagines young men without place as at best a drain on the state, at worst, a danger. Learning should be contained in "rowmes" rather than deployed in free, indeterminate ways. Learned men, unequipped for other kinds of labor, "rome helples" without position or master. In such a condition, they threaten to become "shifters" – both cunning and changeable – who "loyter without living" and, for lack of a better occupation, might "shake the verie strongest piller" of the state. Graduates without position are masterless men, and thus hazardous men. Notably, despite their very different social positions, masterless graduates such as Nashe experience a market-driven society in a similar way to Whitney in "Maner" – they feel themselves to be the runoff of the system, unemployed and thus without "use" within the terms of commodity logic. As I will describe more fully below, the masterless position becomes a rhetorical occasion for satire, as well as a means to redefine one's labor.

Members of the university surplus often did find occupations as schoolmasters, lower church officials, and hack writers, among other kinds of work. But men in such positions were regarded as virtual vagabonds nonetheless. Due to low pay and high turnover, schoolmastering was distinctly associated with wandering, displacement, and lack of commitment to a stable occupation. For this reason, those who hired schoolmasters were typically more concerned with a candidate's

---

28 Siskin, *The Work of Writing*, 115.

29 O'Day, *Professions*, 28.

30 Ibid.

31 Qtd. in Halasz, *Marketplace*, 82.

age and moral standing than with his learning.[32] The lack of prestige attached to the schoolmaster is evident in his wages – an average of ten pounds a year in the late sixteenth century, the same average wage as two centuries before.[33] Despite the pleas of John Brinsley and Marchamount Nedham, who argued that more pay and security could give schoolmasters prestige and "professional" standing, attempts at making the job seem like a kind of preferment never succeeded. With no one to rule over but children, schoolmasters continued to regard their lot as a "moiling and drudging life," a "fruitless, wearisome and unthankful office," the "most laborious calling," and other descriptions suggestive of drudgery. Nedham himself compared schoolmastering to laboring in the galleys.[34]

Graduates who entered the church fared little better. By the 1630s, low church officials in nearly every parish had university degrees. Curates typically earned ten pounds a year and had no security of tenure, since they could be discharged without the legal proceedings needed to dismiss vicars and rectors. Mark Curtis presents evidence that such instability could and did cause disruptive behavior and sedition, mentioning an exemplary case in which a curate converted to Catholicism and spread libels about his superiors.[35] Men who could not obtain even curacies became lecturers – stipendiary preachers who did not hold regular church livings and were not under the same control as parish clergy. Lecturers, by reputation, were physically, morally, and ideologically restive. Like schoolmasters, curates and lecturers were viewed as occupational transients, as is clear in the concern of early Stuart church leaders moving from job to job or holding several at once.[36] These cases show that formal occupations did not necessarily afford sufficient "rowmes" in which to contain less successful graduates.

Depictions of the frustrated scholar as fundamentally useless and occupationally vagrant found their way into literary representations. In his *Characters* (1615), Thomas Overbury portrayed "A Meere Scholler" as an overblown pedant with "much in profession, nothing in practise."[37] The Overburian graduate has a great store of unused experience because he has no competence with practical affairs: "That learning which he hath, was as in his Non-age put in backward like a Clister, and 'tis now like Ware mislaid in a Pedlers packe; a ha's it, but knowes not where

[32] David Cressy, "A Drudgery of Schoolmasters: The Teaching Profession in Elizabethan and Early Stuart England," in *The Professions in Early Modern England*, ed. Wilfrid Prest, London: Croom Helm, 1987, 129–53, 139–40.

[33] Cressy, "Drudgery," 145, Nicholas Orme, "Schoolmasters, 1307–1509," in *Profession, Vocation, and Culture in Later Medieval England: Essays Dedicated to the Memroy of A.R. Myers*, ed. Cecil H. Clough, Liverpool: Liverpool UP, 1982, 218–41, 224. Normally, schoolmasters could expect their incomes to be augmented by small admiision fees collected from pupils. Benevolence could also be given by parents or friends, but on a voluntary basis. The hope for gifts of this kind must have been, in David Cressy's words, "no way to build up professional self-respect" (145).

[34] Qtd. in Cressy, 129–30.

[35] Mark Curtis, "The Alienated Intellectuals of Early Stuart England," *Past and Present* 23 (1962), 25–43, 34.

[36] Curtis, "Alienated," 32–3, 35–7.

[37] *The Overburian Characters*, ed. W.J. Paylor, Oxford: Basil Blackwell, 1936, 34.

it is."[38] Overbury likens the scholar to a merchant who cannot sell his own goods because he cannot even find them. Flouting the supposed separation between the scholar's work and that of the merchant, Overbury holds the scholar up to mercantile standards and finds him wanting. More sympathetic representations explicitly reacted against the ideology of "use" by viewing it as too easily adaptable to a mercantile model. Joseph Hall, another Cambridge graduate, devoted the second book of his *Virgidemiarum* [*Satires*] (1597) to exploring "Academicall" abuses from a frustrated scholar's point of view. He disdains the imperative to sell one's verse as a betrayal of the proper spirit of scholarship: "Let them that meane by bookish businesse / To earne their bread, or hopen to professe / Their hard got skill; let them alone for mee, / Busie their braines with deeper bookerie" (Satire II, ll. 25–8).[39] In contradistinction to mercantilism, Hall erects an ideal of otherworldly asceticism for the scholar: "For thred-bare clearks, and for the ragged muse, / Whom better fit some cotes of sad secluse?" (ll. 3–4). The scholar's withdrawal permits him to disdain the money system that governs the rest of the world: "We scorne that wealth should be the finall end, / Whereto the heavenly Muse her course doth bend; / And rather had be pale with learned carees, / Then paunched with thy choyce of changed fares" (ll. 59–62). Here the clerkly ideal, rejected by the new social humanism in favor of "use," gets reasserted as a "rowme" – an identity and a place – for those men who have been rendered useless in the capitalist marketplace. Hall further promotes the ascetic model by portraying the thankless labors of graduates who are out in the world. Satire VI presents a scene in which a scholar is hired as a tutor under a demeaning set of conditions: he must "lie upon the trucke-bed" under his young master and never beat him, "rise and wait" at mealtimes while never "presum[ing] to sit above the salt," and be content with "five markes and winter liverie" as compensation (ll. 5, 8, 16).[40] The demotion of the scholar to a position of servility runs counter to the scholar's actual superiority: "Here may you, *Muses*, or deare *soveraignes*, / Scorne each base *lordling* ever you disdaines" (Satire II, ll. 11–12). Hall's remarks attempt to reverse the new social order by pointing out its absurd logic. While treatments such as Hall's view the scholar's degradation as a transgression of proper social hierarchy, others portray him as a wanderer who could easily turn his knowledge to treason. In the ballad "Alas poore Scholler, whither wilt thou goe" (1641), Robert Wild describes the graduate as "fit to beg / In Hebrew, Greek and Latin," drifting from town to town, taking up demeaning and low-paying posts, and finally going overseas to "Turne Jew or Atheist / Turke or Papist." [41] The three illustrations that accompany the ballad

---

[38] Ibid.

[39] Joseph Hall, *Viridemiarum*, Edinburgh: Tait, 1824.

[40] Scholars of university drama nominate Hall as a possible author of the last two *Parnassus* plays, which draw heavily upon satire, including Hall's own. See J.B. Leishmann's introduction to *The Three Parnassus Plays (1598–1601)*, London: Ivor Nicholson and Watson Ltd., 1949, 26–34; and also Frank Livingstone Huntley's "Joseph Hall, John Marston, and *The Returne from Parnassus*," in *Illustrious Evidence: Approaches to English Literature of the Early Seventeenth Century*, ed. Earl Miner, Berkeley: U of California P, 1975, 3–22.

[41] Robert Wild, *Alas poore scholler, wither wilt thou goe: or Strange altrations which at this time be; there's many did thinke they never should see. To the tune of, Halloo my fancy, &c*, London, 1641.

first show a fatigued scholar huddling to warm himself at a fire, and then depict him wandering into a town, wearing a priest's robes, and carrying a rosary. The final illustration pictures a ship sailing east, perhaps carrying the scholar to Rome (Figure 2.1). These representations, sympathetic or otherwise, highlight the displacement of the learned man within a culture that viewed education as preparation for service to society and they call attention to the social consequences of this displacement. An emphasis on the "use" of a learned man commodifies his learning, thus rendering those who cannot be "used" as placeless.

The *Parnassus* plays make use of these kinds of representations in their satirical treatment of the socioeconomic plight of their characters. But while the plays assign ample space to rehearse these common stereotypes, they also offer an alternative to Hall's reassertion of asceticism in the figure of Ingenioso, who participates fully in the corrupt world even as he attempts to expose its vices. In my reading of the plays, I shall return to Nashe's intervention in the connection between learning and status, for it is in these plays that one can detect how university men used Nashe in their consideration of the changing role of learning. The discourses concerning learned men raise several issues that would have been present to Nashe, the play's author(s), and their contemporaries. First, the humanist emphasis on virtuous action required the virtue be performed in a specified role – one that served the commonwealth, rather than one that stood to undermine it. Men who could not find such a role were considered a problem for the state, and concerns about the moral effects of displaced learned men were expressed in descriptions that recalled vagrancy – wandering, isolation from society, masterlessness, and unbridled cunning. Second because of the lack of sufficient posts, many men without preferment identified with the elite in their expectations, but with commoners in their daily lives, thus promoting the sense of inconsistency in social status. Third, learning was intended as a store of wealth and status for second sons whose older brothers inherited the traditional store: land. The *Parnassus* plays, like Nashe's writings, utilize the figure of the father both to highlight the deteriorating effectiveness of learning as inheritance and to emphasize the characters' increasing distance from the university as parental nurturer.

From Parnassus Hill to Shoreditch Street

The critical distance that the Nashe/Ingenioso character embraces is undergirded by a sense of wandering – that is, an involuntary distance from the nurturing influence of the university. Scholars find themselves literally outside the walls. The *Parnassus* plays draw generously on common representations of displaced learned men as wanderers or vagrants. The occupations that the characters take up – as schoolmasters, as low church officials, hack writers and players – were distinctly associated with occupational itinerancy; men who adopted such posts were virtually vagrant. The plays present a variety of different responses to itinerant status. Among these alternatives, Ingenioso represents a fantasy of revenge on a market-driven society by deploying resentment as a rhetorical tool and the basis for a new identity. This deployment critiques the promise of a university education for wealth and status while at the same time preserves the cultural capital of learning for the displaced

Alas poore Scholler,
whither wilt thou goe:
OR
Strange altrations which at this time be;
There's many did thinke they never should see.
To the tune of, *Halloo my Fancy, &c.*

Alas poore Scholler whither wilt thou goe?

Alas poore Scholler, whither wilt thou goe?

Alas poore Scholler whither wilt thou goe?

Alas poore Scholler whither wilt thou goe?

The second part, to the same Tune.

Alas poore Scholler whither wilt thou goe?

Alas poore Scholler whither wilt thou goe?

Alas poore Scholler whither wilt thou goe?

FINIS.

Figure 2.1 Robert Wild. *Alas poore Scholler, Whither wilt thou goe: or – Strange altrations which at this time be, There's many did thinke they never should see. (1640?)*

graduate. In order to succeed in this re-definition of his identity, he must position his scholarly and authorial labor in a way that makes status inconsistency into an occasion for superior skill and virtue.

The differences in tone and attitude between the first play and the last two announce themselves in the respective prologues. Each prologue frames the audience according to the play's treatment of scholarly labor. The short prologue of *Pilgrimage* addresses the spectators in a self-deprecating fashion and asks the audience to think of spectatorship as a kind of study: "If youle take three daies studie in good cheare, / Our muse is blest that ever shee came here. / If not, wele eare noe more the barren sande, / But let our pen seeke a more fertile lande" (ll. 3–6). In the first *Returne*, the unspecified speaker of the *Pilgrimage* prologue is replaced by a stagekeeper who begins to address the audience as "gentle," and then thinks better of it: "Howe gentle? Saye, youe cringinge parasite, / That scarpinge legg, that droppinge curtisie, / That fawninge bowe, those sycophant's smoothe tearmes, / Gained our stage muche favour, did they not?" (ll. 1–4). In these lines, the stagekeeper addresses the hollow pretensions of university men who style themselves gentlemen; furthermore, the fact that they watch plays at all calls their true gentility into question: "Call noe rude hearer *gentle, debonaire*" (l. 15). The prologue also hints at the identity of the author, suggesting that he came from Cheshire and calling him "a staide man . . . [who] had like to have made him a senior sophister" (ll. 5, 7). This "sophister," who peddles words without understanding them, is a shadowy figure with dubious academic credentials: "He was faine to take his course by Germanie / Ere he coulde gett a silie poore degree" (ll. 8–9). This portrait of the author makes a mockery of degrees and fine speaking as exterior markers of elite status. Yet despite this debasement of the author, the stagekeeper still protects him from the crowd in a hostile dismissal of critics and a defiance of flattery: "We'le spende no flatteringe on this carpinge croude, / Nor with gold tearmes make each rude dullard proude. / A Christmas toy thou haste; carpe till thy deathe! / Our Muse's praise depends not on thy breathe!" (ll. 16–19). In this speech, the trilogy moves from courting its audience to a mixture of courting and repudiation. Moreover, the outline of an individual author is visible – subject to criticism and yet distant and whole unto himself – presenting the play less as a collective project and more as the product of individual invention. A satirist has taken the stage.

The prologue of *Part II* continues in this vein by adding a boy, a critic, and a defensor. The critic, "Momus," informs the audience, "What is presented here, is an old musty show, that hath laine this twelve moneth in the bottome of a coalehouse amongst broomes and old shooes, an invension that we are ashamed of, and therefore we have promised the Copies to the Chandlers to wrappe his candles in" (ll. 25–9). While the play is being staged for a select group within the university walls, Momus presents it as a cheap work whose pages are fit for the basest uses. The predilection for describing written pages as liners for drawers and coal bins, wrapping paper for wares, and toilet paper is a strategy that Nashe frequently employed; Ingenioso describes his work in the same terms: "I have indeede a pamphlet here that none is privie unto but a pinte of wine and a pipe of tobacco. It pleased my witt yesternighte to make water, and to use this goutie patron instead of an urinall, whom I make the subject and content of my whole speache" (1 *Returne* ll. 219–23). In a scene from the second *Returne*, Ingenioso bargains with his printer, who offers him forty shillings for a pamphlet: "40 Shillings? a fit reward for one of you reumatick poets, that beslavers all the paper he comes by, and furnishes the Chaundlers with wast paper to wrap candles in" (ll. 351–4). Descriptions of pages as "waste paper" and "privy tokens" can both debase writing on the basis of its materiality and, ironically, argue for its value – after all, it has multiple uses. In any case, these descriptions help "identify the author who embraces print instead of patronage as an unfortunate traveller and anti-humanist subject."[42] In like fashion, the prologue enables the playwright to situate himself and his labor among the work of so many scholars who turn from patronage to print. Exhorting the audience not to expect a noble story of love or a romance tale of lost gentle sons, the defensor warns, "If the Catastrophe please you not, impute it to the unpleasing fortunes of discontented schollers" (ll. 52–3). If the words and the delivery of the play cause offense due to their resemblance to popular forms, then the audience must remember that the form suits the subject matter: the degradation of scholarly labor in the marketplace.

The *Returne* plays complete the story of Philomusus's and Studioso's sojourn in a way that make the *Pilgrimage* seem wistful and naïve. The *Pilgrimage* stages confrontations between the holy mission of study and several threatening influences: drink (as the mother of invention), Puritanism, courtly love poetry and its implied concupiscence, and finally, the gritty and penurious reality of the graduate's lot, as presented by Ingenioso. A long opening speech by Consiliodorus releases them to their mission. Consiliodorus intends his words as a bequest, as he predicts that he soon will die: "Eare youe return from greene Parnassus' hill / My corps shall lie within some senceless urne, / Some litel grave my ashes shall inclose . . . Ile therefore consel youe while I have time, / For feare youre faire youth wither in her prime" (ll. 17–19, 24–5). His speech sets a standard of purity for the scholar as he counsels the youth to avoid the worldly devices that entrap weaker souls. Money presents a particular threat to the scholar's integrity: "Though I foreknewe that gold runns to the boore / ile be a scholler, though I live but poore" (ll. 63–4). Consiliodorus's speech makes poverty a virtue, a mark of fortitude against the baseness of working and earning.

Even when Philomusus and Studioso give in to temptation, they always revert to this ascetic ideal before they go too far. After the young men return from a visit to Amoretto, who sways them from their path through love poetry, Studioso exclaims, "Howe sourelie sweete is meltinge venerie! . . . I'le nere hereafter counsell chaster thoughtes / To travell through this lande of poetrie" (ll. 516, 518–19). Calling Catullus, Ovid, and Martial "entisinge pandars, subtile baudes," Studioso regards love poetry as a pollution of true study and a threat to virtue: "Heare them whilest a lascivious tale they tell, / Theile make thee fitt in Shorditche for to dwell, / Here had wee nighe made shipwracke of our youthe, / And nipte the blossomes of our buddinge springe!" (ll. 520–25). Philomusus objects by arguing that a soul who is truly pure can withstand temptation anywhere: "who reades poets with a chaster minde / shall nere infected be by poesie. / An honest man that here did stande in sheete / Maye chastlie dwell in unchaste Shordiche streete" (ll. 544–7). The error in Studioso's thought, according

[42] Turner, "Jack Wilton," 126.

to Philomusus, is the belief that true virtue can be shaken by outside influences. In response, Philomusus constructs a fantasy of a strong, subjective center as the antidote to worldly corruption. His steadfast belief in a centered self that retains its integrity in all places and at all times resembles humanist counsel to travelers abroad. As Turner shows in a survey of advice manuals for diplomats, "evidence of fortunate and judicious travel was a way of demonstrating their capacity as centered, humanist subjects, and therefore of advertising their fitness for patronage and employment by the centralized state."[43] While Philomusus makes no reference to state service or patronage, his belief regarding travel to "Shorediche streete" presumes a centered self that maintains composure and equanimity. Thus, Philomusus's naivete sets up a target for the anti-humanist impulses that the next two plays present.

As we witnessed in Mulcaster's account of the learned gentleman, the humanist ideal assumes non-dependence on work for survival; in *Pilgrimage*, non-dependence figures as a rejection of money. This prejudice meets its challenge in Ingenioso, the only figure who retains his original characterization in the next two plays. In the final scene of *Pilgrimage*, Ingenioso chides Philomusus and Studioso for going "to Parnassus to converse with ragged innocents" (ll. 581–2), portraying those who live there as immature and foolish in their poverty: "they coulde scarce get enoughe to apparell there heade in an unlined hatt, there bodie in a frize jerkin, and there feet in clouted paire of shoes" (ll. 597–9). Philomusus and Studioso, still fresh from Consiliodorus's counsel, reject this fixation on basic material necessities. When Studioso tells him, "Within Parnassus dwells all sweete contente, / Nor care I for those excrements of earthe" (ll. 604–5), Ingenioso retorts with a grotesque brand of wit typical of Nashe: "Call you gold and silver the excrements of earthe? If those be excrements, I am the cleanest man upon the earth, for I seldome sweate goulde" (ll. 606–9). While Philomusus and Studioso eschew the physical body in favor of poetry and philosophy, Ingenioso taunts them with grotesque bodily metaphors. Eschewing delicate and refined speech, he speaks vulgarly and "plain."

The characters' increased distance from the seat of learning is paralleled by their estrangement from the paternal figure that nurtured their ideals in the past. Consiliodorus gradually disappears; he appears twice in the first *Returne* and not at all in the second. The first scene of *Part I* also opens with Consiliodorus, but here we find him disillusioned with his son and nephew. Seven winters have passed since he went with the young men to Parnassus, but Consiliodorus now sees that where the youth once "Promised a plenteous harvest," there are now "nought but thornes and thistles to be mowne" (ll. 68, 70). Consiliodous suspects that Philomusus and Studioso have become prodigals, having foolishly spent their store. When he later learns that the boys have in fact become a teacher and a country vicar, he abandons hope: "Hencforthe let none be sent by carefull syres, / Nor sonns nor kindred, to Parnassus hill, / Since waywarde fortune thus rewardes our coste / With discontent, theire paines with povertie" (ll. 1088–91). He views the men's occupations as a

[43] Turner, "Jack Wilton," 125–6. Turner discusses humanist ideas on travel within the context of Nashe's *The Unfortunate Traveller*, which she reads as a rejection of humanist ideals in favor of a decentered subject (in the character of Jack Wilton) who not only reacts to his foreign surroundings, but is changed by them.

lamentable triumph of the "Mechanicke arts" over "liberall arts" (ll. 1092–3). The death of Consiliodorus thematically enlarges the distance between the young men and the idealized seat of learning – in the end, voluntary poverty proves to be a source of ignominy rather than pride.

Despite Consiliodorus's unwillingness to blame himself, the characters curse their father for sending them to university in the first place. Their lamentations echo Hall's *Virdigemiarum*, which addresses the bitter lot of second sons relative to their older brothers in the primogeniture system:

> Have not I lands of faire inheritance,
> Deriv'd by right of long continuance
> To first-borne males? so list the law to grace
> Natures first fruits in an eternall race.
> Let second brothers, and poore nestlings,
> Whom more iniurious Nature later brings
> Into the naked world, let them assaine
> To get hard peny-worths with so bootlesse paine. (ll. 39–46)

The second son's fate is to use his learning as his inheritance and to employ his wit as, in Ingenioso's words, "my revenues, my land, my money, and whatsoever I have" (2 *Returne* ll. 1547–8). But barring the proper post, the learned son is condemned to "bootlesse paine." The attitude of Philomusus and Studioso toward their "store" gradually becomes more bitter as they descend the occupational hierarchy, but Ingenioso has been past the point of hope from the beginning. Early in *Part I*, Pihlomusus exclaims to Ingenioso, "I am glad, y'faith, thy father hath lefte thee such a good stock of witt to set up withall! Why, thou cariest store of landes in livinges in thy heade!" (ll. 165–7), to which Ingenioso replies, "But the'le scarse pay for the cariage! I had rather have more in my purse and less in my heade!" (ll. 168–9). Studioso persists in counseling him to "husbande thy witt, if thou beest wise; it's all the goods and cattels thy father lefte thee" (ll. 184–5). But a store of learning yields nothing, as Luxurio, the scholar turned ballad-rhymer, exclaims, "my father's sonne might have had a better trade if it had pleased Fortune" (ll. 837–9). Just as Nashe's Pierce feels the discrepancy between expectation and lived reality, so do the characters maintain a memory of gentle beginnings that sharpens the discrepancy between past and present. In recognition of this change, Philomusus sighs, "We have the words, they the possession have" (l. 408).

Philomusus and Studioso describe their situation as hopeless not only because learning allows no living, but because the university did not prepare them to cope with the world outside. Here, as in Nashe's writings, the university figures as mother whose attentions have been torn away from her children before they have been fully weaned. Philomusus bitterly remarks, "In our first gamesome age, our doting sires / Carked and cared to have us lettered: / Sent us to Cambrdige where our oyle is spent: / Us our kind Colledge from the teate did teare: / And for'st us walke before we weaned weare, / From that time since [y]wandered have we still / In the wide world, urg'd by our forced will" (ll. 1451–7). The implication is that learning can in no way prepare a young man for an occupation and a place. Without 'parents," they become wanderers.

In contrast to the humanist ideal that a man should retain his "place" not only literally but by behaving as though he were a centered "self," the scholars of the two *Returne* plays are affected by the social and economic lots. They have begun to resemble unfortunate travelers, as Philomusus's former confidence in his incorruptible virtuous self has devolved into a self who reacts and is transformed by his situation: "see [how] a little vermine poverty altereth a whole milkie disposition" (2 *Returne* ll. 443–4).[44] The scholars now closely conform to Mulcaster's description of learned men without place. Trying different jobs and abandoning them quickly, they are "Running through every trade, yet thrive by none" (l. 567), suggesting the impermanence and lack of vocational skill that contemporaries often attributed to graduates in lowly occupations. The prologue to *Part II* promises a tale in which Philomusus and Studioso "have beene followed with a whip, and a verse like a Couple of Vagabonds through *England* and *Italy*" (ll. 38–40). This process in fact begins early in *Part I*, where the young men see themselves as "ordained to be beggars" and resolve "to wander in the worlde" (l. 132). Ingenioso, who intends to "shifte for [his] livinge" in the printing house, takes Philomusus and Studioso with him to London so that they can either get a living of "dye learned beggars" (l. 391).

Philomusus and Studioso keep clear of the printing house, preferring to wander among other trades. Throughout, their inferiors (who have become their betters in the new economic order) view them as beggars and vagrants, and indeed, they fit this perception despite their claims to superiority. When a boor of the parish that employs Philomusus as a vicar acquires the title of "Mr. Warden" through the death of his father, he releases Philomusus from his post, citing failure to keep the chancel in proper order. As a final insult, the new warden gives Philomusus a passport, "least the clarigols att some town's ende catche you" and arrest him as a vagabond (ll. 1268–9). The nobility and the governing figures of the town echo this perception and intensify it with a hatred of scholars. In *Part II*, Amoretto reappears in the form of a nobleman who cares nothing for learning and favors hunting instead. Also a former Cambridge student, Amoretto once inhabited the same house as the scholars, but now differentiates himself from men whom he regards as beggars in need of control by statute: "is it not a shame that a gallant cannot walke the streete for [these] needy fellowes, and that, after there is a statute come out against begging?" (ll. 1683–5). The scholars' style of life contrasts with that of the nobleman with whom they are nominally classed by virtue of education. Rather than living a settled existence on an estate, practicing hunting as one of what Amoretto calls "the mysteries of my art" (ll. 924–5), their own art makes a life of begging inescapable. In recognition of this fate, Luxurio leaves for the country to take up ballad-peddling: "Farewell, thou impecunious clyme! Luxurio and his page / Will beggars prove elsewheare, and run

[44] Mark Curtis, responding to contemporaneous views that study at the university nurtured rebellion, attributes graduates' treasonous tendencies to "alienation" – defined as a common experience of frustration at meager opportunities for preferment: "The universities were dangerous – through not the 'core of rebellion' – because they were, paradoxical as it may seem, too successful in carrying out the primary task of training men for service to Church and State" ("Alienated" 27). This argument supports the idea that social and economic frustration could turn "gentle dispositions" into vagrant and criminal ones.

from thee in rage" (1 *Returne* ll. 1555–6). Philomusus and Studioso, upon returning from the continent, become peddlers of false medical expertise, using technical jargon and foreign terms to cheat a burgess. By this point, their vagrancy has led to a life of cony-catching, expertly cunning dissembling. Furthermore, as will become a concern for Jonson as well, they mimic the learned language and labor well enough to become that which they are not – in this case, physicians.

There is a difference in the way that Philomusus and Studioso handle their "wandering" and the use that Ingenioso makes of his own dislocation. Philomusus and Studioso closely follow the pattern for the oversupply of learned men that I outline above – physically roaming from place to place, taking up ignominious occupations, and finally becoming criminals. *Part II* ends with them choosing a shepherd's life over the printing house: "So shall we shun the company of men, / That growes more hatefull as the world growes old, / weel teach the murmering brookes in tears to flow: / and steepy rocke to wayle our passed wo" (ll. 2196–9). Like Nashe's "schollar-like shepheard" move, the turn to the pastoral landscape represents an attempt to preserve scholarly dignity and to live in purity. As shepherds, they resolve to spend their days "Turning a Cambridge apple by the fire," and teaching each tree "To keepe our woefull name within their rinde . . . The woods and rockes with our shrill songs weele blesse, / Let them prove kind since men prove pittilesse" (ll. 2138, 2142–3). But when Studioso asks Ingenioso about his own plans, Ingenioso expresses a resolution to become one of the "Lords of misrule in the worlds wide [hall]." Whereas Philomusus and Studioso resort to a pastoral setting as a way to evade social contradiction, Ingenioso turns his back upon the world – "this sin loaden earth" – and makes it into his "paper."[45] Philomusus and Studioso will constrain their

[45] In a discussion of eighteenth-century Georgic, Siskin historically situates the trope of "laboring on the land," which among English poets "has varied considerably depending on how the connection with laboring on the land was interpreted. When the emphasis was on the base nature of that laboring, as during the Tudor and Stuart reigns, it was displaced by an idealized pastoral" (119). I read Philomusus and Studioso's final decision to become shepherds as a way to suture over these rough contradictions by retreating into an idealized pastoral landscape that, unlike "work-in-the-world," will pose no challenge to the worth of their labor or their gentility. Yet prior to Philomusus's and Studioso's decision, the plays have already done the work of distancing from the pastoral mode. In a parody of the echo scene from Sidney's *Arcadia*, an echo answers Academico's questions with terms that encourage simony and enforce his dependence on the money system:

> *Acad.* Faine would I have a living, if I could tel how to come by it.
> *Eccho.* Buy it.
> *Acad.* Buy it fond Ecc[ho]? why thou dost greatly mistake it.
> *Ecc.* stake it.
> *Acad.* stake it? What should I stake at this game of simony?
> *Ecc.* mony.
> *Acad.* What is the world a game, are livings gotten by playing?
> *Eccho.* Paying. (1 *Returne* ll. 589–97)

This parody of Sidney's tale numbers pastoral among the elite literary modes that the play holds up to satirical treatment.

wandering to a single conceptual space; alternatively, Ingenioso plans to live in the world and rule its "wide hall" through his pen. The pastoral is coded as a place of oratory and song; the "world" is a space to be mastered through writing. For Ingenioso, the contradictions of learning and earning will find their resolution in the pages of the satirist who masters the socioeconomic field through his rhetorical skill.

The difference between the resolution of Philomusus and Studioso and that of Ingenioso is essentially the difference between the *Pilgrimage* and the two *Returne* plays. The *Pilgrimage* strains to preserve the scholars' purity by positing a centered self who withstands the temptations of his journey; the retreat to the pastoral at the end of *Part II* recognizes the impossibility of doing so as long as scholars are in touch with the "wide world," its humiliations, and its demands. The *Returne* plays, on the other hand, also present satire as a new alternative to handling this world. Throughout the plays, Philomusus and Studioso deliver numerous speeches that bespeak their woe and bemoan the state of a bad world. By doing so, they turn sorrow inward and leave the world untouched. In one scene, when they visit Richard Burbage and Will Kemp to ask about becoming actors – and thus stooping to what they call "the basest trade" (l. 1886) – a smug Kemp calls the scholars proud slaves and asks, "is it not better to make a foole of the world as I have done, then to be fooled of the world, as you schollers are?" (ll. 1826–8). To Ingenioso, this is sound advice; he urges his friends to reassert autonomy by adopting a critical point of view through satire: "Nay, sighe not, men! laughe at the foolish world; / They have the shame, though wee the miserie" (ll. 1557–8). In spite of this advice, Philomusus and Studioso elect to turn away from the world, doing their best to symbolically re-erect the university walls.

Ingenioso's advice could just as well be aimed at the audience itself, for in other scenes, he directly enlists their laughter as part of his own project. Gullio, his patron in *Part I*, represents the kind of dishonorable patron that Nashe excoriates in *Pierce Pennilesse* and other works.[46] When Gullio first approaches, Ingenioso speaks aside to the audience, "Nowe, gentlemen, youe may laugh if you will, for here comes a gull" (ll. 854–5). Gullio fancies himself a soldier, a lover, a poet, and a court favorite – in short, "a complet gentleman" (ll. 950–1). His taste in poetry favors Shakespeare over Spenser and Chaucer, prompting another aside from Ingenioso: "We shall have nothinge but pure Shakespeare and shreds of poetrie that he hath gathered at the theators! . . . Take heed, my maisters! he'le kill you with tediousness ere I can ridd him of the stage!" (ll. 1009–10, 1056–7). Through these asides, Ingenioso enlists the

[46] For example, in *Pierce Pennilesse*, a critique of illiberal patrons helps frame the pamphlet's focus on lack of "honor" in the contemporary world: "Believe me gentlemen (for some cross mishaps have taught me experience), there is not that strict observation of honour, which hath been heretofore. Men of great calling take it of merit to have their names eternized by poets; and whatsoever pamphlet or dedication encounters them, they put it up their sleeves, and scarce give him thanks that presents it. Much better is it for those golden pens to raise such ungrateful peasants from the dunghill of obscurity, and make them equal in fame to the worthies of old, when their doting self-love shall challenge it of duty, and not only give them nothing themselves, but impoverish liberality in others" (I.159).

"maisters" of the audience in his point of view, prompting a critique of the nobility that allows for the superior virtue and judgment of scholars.

When Gullio finally dismisses Ingenioso from his service, Ingenioso responds with words intended to expose the lack of honor lurking under the noble habit: "Farewell, base carle clothed in a sattin sute, / Farewell, guilte ass, farewell, base broker's poste!" (ll. 1479–80). Determining to "goe to the press" rather than "be tormented with the tedious talks / Of Gullio's wench and of his luxuries" (ll. 1499, 1484–5), he promises, "For Gullio's sake I'le prove a Satyrist" (l. 1493). This statement of independence from service embraces print as an instrument of emancipation, as well as of vindication against the perceived usurpers of professional privilege. When Ingenioso breaks from Gullio, he asks, "thinkest thou a man of art can endure thy base usage?" (l. 1471) and responds to Gullio's poetic pretensions by calling him "the scorne of all good witts" who "never spokest wittie thinge but out of a play" (ll. 1465–7). In *Part II*, Ingenioso's "revenge" on Amoretto takes place on the same grounds: "you Maister *Amoretto*, that art the chiefe Carpenter of Sonets, a privileged Vicar for the lawlesse marriage of Inke and Paper, you that are good for nothing but to commend in a sette speech, [the colour and quantitie] of your Mistresses stoole, and sweare it is most sweete Civet . . . . Base worme must thou needes discharge thy craboun to batter downe the walles of learning" (ll. 1721–6, 1764–6). Just as Nashe railed against pretenders to learning in his preface to *Menaphon*, here we see that luxurious aristocrats are subject to the same scorn, as Ingenioso employs occupational language – "Carpenter," "Vicar" – to satirize the amateur's aspirations. The end result of this critique of both higher and lower degrees is an elevation of the scholar as "man of art" – one whose learning qualifies him as the only authentic writer of verse in a world of mere pretenders.

The anti-aristocratic bent of the last two plays sharpen the distance between wandering scholars and the elite culture with which they were customarily categorized. Men without place can claim no legitimate role within the polity, but Ingenioso's propensity for satire as social criticism anticipates a new public role for the scholar – as a corrector of morals, an exposer of vice, and a commentator on everyday life. Yet paradoxically, the satirist must inhabit the world as well as transcend it. Ingenioso's impending banishment from London only physically removes him from society, for he intends to maintain conference with "the blattant beast [who] doth rule and raigne Renting the credit of whom it please" (ll. 2148–9). Furthermore, he envisions his difficult task as continual toil – the price of life and work outside of the university walls. He addresses Acadmico in terms that evoke the contrast between ascetic and worldly activity: "thou still happy *Academico*, / That still maist rest upon the muses bed, / Injoying there a quiet slumbering, / when thou repay[r]est unto the Grantaes streame, / Wonder at thine owne blisse, pitty our case, / That still [doe] tread ill fortunes endless maze" (ll. 2209–14). The fate of Ingenioso, the play proposes, is the fate of St. John's most notorious graduate and of scholarly labor itself in the "wide world": marginal, wandering, toiling, and yet possibly free enough to write its own redemption.

Conclusion: Scholarly Labor in the "Wide World"

During the period in which Nashe and his university contemporaries wrote, the idea of labor for a wage was still largely incompatible with the idea of a positive vocational identity. I have taken Nashe as a focus because, due to the discrepancy between graduates' social origins and the actual situations of many, the contradictions between work and desire become more clearly demarcated than perhaps in any other social group. The plays' attempt to bridge this contradiction shows the extent to which, as in Whitney's case, social and economic change attended new possibilities as well as losses for non-aristocratic authors who turned to the market for print. More particularly, the ambivalent attitude that these authors take toward print testifies to their claims that they need it for their own maintenance. The question, then, is not whether or not one participates in the market, but what one does with it.

The inconsistencies between work and positive vocational identity are never seamlessly resolved – not for Nashe, nor for the authors of the *Parnassus* plays, who drew on him so heavily as an example of what a displaced scholar can become. Rather, it is the friction between the two that opens the field for new ways of imagining authorship. In this case, the plays' predilection for satire as a means of cultivating critical distance marks an ideological break with older forms of authorization into at least a consideration of the possibilities of print for independence from service and patronage. The fact that this break occurs in a work by and for learned men shows that a desire for something like professional independence could be envisioned not only by Whitney's humble maidservant persona, but by those orders who normally disdained "work." Although the plays court learned audiences – even at the end, when the scholars solicit applause from "none but" those who understand scholars' struggles (l. 2263) – they also allow reflection on the institution and its unfulfilled promises. The result is a command of a variety of genres and styles that highlight wit as well as the critical capacity of the satirist, and through satire, writers may construct themselves as subjects who see and speak rightly, even when they unappreciated and marginalized.

Chapter 3

"laborious, yet not base": Jonson, Vulcan, and Poetic Labor

Isabella Whitney and Thomas Nashe present two cases of "labored" authorship in very different contexts. With each of these authors, I have posited labor as a new way to understand how they negotiate their respective roles in the burgeoning market for print. But to the minds of many readers, Ben Jonson exemplifies labored authorship better than any other figure in the early modern English canon. I state this first with a wealth of criticism in mind that characterizes his writing as "labored," learned, solid art in comparison to Shakespeare's "natural" wit and fancy. Bruce Boehrer invokes this well known contrast when he identifies Jonson as "one of early modern England's first self-conscious representatives of literature as vocation." Boehrer locates Jonson between patriarchal absolutism (patronage relations) and early capitalism (relations with audience popularity), noting that Jonson's sense of vocation depends in large part on his insistence on labor. What Boehrer calls "the Jonsonian conundrum" is that Jonson must claim to be unique or he melts into the crowd – and his uniqueness resides in his labor.[1] But this "proletarianization" would make his art available to others, particularly members of the lower orders whom we find him scorning in some places, but embracing in others. What is missing in this account, which is important to understanding the "conundrum," is that labor itself is a social discourse fraught with hierarchy. The complexity of the term thus calls for a fuller definition of what Jonsonian labor actually *is* and what it is not. If Jonson appears at war with himself – as Richard Helgerson and others have observed – this is largely because, as we have seen with the previous two authors, labor itself signifies complex discourses about vocation, mobility, and change.

A closer look at early modern labor adds deeper dimensions to the anti-materialist bias present in Jonson's texts. According to Jonas A. Barish, Jonson's scorn for the realm of material, mechanical production results in an anti-theatrical attitude toward the very kind of work that sustains him:

> When we turn to the plays we find that in them Jonson does not shed his antitheatrical bias. Rather, he builds it in; he makes the plays critiques of the instability they incarnate… despite his persistent and at times vehement antitheatricalism, Jonson was nevertheless able to create so many masterpieces for both the public stage and that of the court.[2]

---

[1] Bruce Boehrer, "The Poet of Labor: Authorship and Property in the Work of Ben Jonson," *Philological Quarterly* 72 (1993), 289–312.

[2] Jonas A. Barish, "Jonson and the Loathed Stage," *A Celebration of Ben Jonson*, ed. William Blisset, Julian Patrick, and R.W. Van Fossen Toronto: U of Toronto P, 1973, 27–53, 42, 50.

The question of material labor deserves attention, because it represents an important component of the general agon that many critics have noted in Jonson. Barish attributes the conflict to Jonson's ambivalence about "art," in which "it is precisely the uneasy synthesis between a formal antitheatricalism, which condemns the arts of show and illusion on the one hand, and a subversive hankering after them on the other."[3] Certainly, the multiple significations of "art" – from divinely inspired creativity to the deception of "craft" – trouble Jonson throughout his career. What should be added to the problem of "art," however, is the fact that Jonson's attitude toward theater runs parallel to his attitude toward material labor in general – an outlook especially agonistic given Jonson's own lowly background and his higher aspirations.[4] The fact that Jonson's stepfather was a bricklayer is not, in and of itself, remarkable: Christopher Marlowe's father was a cobbler; Robert Herrick's was a goldsmith; George Peele's was a salter; and Gabriel Harvey's was a ropemaker; to name just a few examples of widely read authors with family connections to a trade.[5] However, Jonson worked in his stepfather's trade at one time himself, and in no other canonical author's writings do we see "mechanicals" and their realm repudiated so sharply. I propose placing discourses of writing and theater and of labor into dialogue with one another as a means of locating Jonson's anti-materialism within a broader social context.

To begin accounting for Jonsonian labor in this way, I wish to highlight his stint as a bricklayer and status as a bricklayer's stepson. Even though Jonson operated in a courtly context for much of his career, his lowly background was widely known and remains so. His bricklaying was derided by his detractors, but it also provokes whimsical anecdotes from his admirers, as Walter George Bell tells of this most famous "Citizen and Bricklayer" in *A Short History of the Worshipful Company of Tylers and Bricklayers of the City of London*:

> None is more persistent, perhaps, than that which sets Ben Jonson working as a bricklayer upon the great turret gateway in Chancery Lane of Lincoln's Inn, bearing a trowel in one hand and a Horace in the other.[6]

We do not get to linger over this image for long: "That excellent piece of brickwork bears arms of Henry VII, and Ben was born *circa* 1572–3."[7] To some imaginations, Jonson's embrace of Horatian workmanlike composition dovetails naturally with

---

3 Barish, "Jonson," 52.

4 This is a kind of question frequently asked of Shakespeare, but far less often of Jonson, despite the fact that both Jonson's lowly origins and his contempt for the working classes are highly visible. Thus the impetus for this chapter is derived from studies like Annabel Patterson's *Shakespeare and the Popular Voice*, which asks "what were Shakespeare's social assumptions and, in particular, what was his attitude to the ordinary working people inside and outside his plays?" Cambridge, Mass.: Basil Blackwell, 1989, 1. The question may revealingly be applied to Jonson as well, albeit with very different results.

5 Louis B. Wright, *Middle-Class Culture in Elizabethan England*, Chapel Hill: U of North Carolina P, 1935, 17–8.

6 Walter George Bell, *A Short History of the Worshipful Company of Tylers and Bricklayers of the City of London*, London: H.G. Montgomery, 1938, 21.

7 Ibid.

his engagement in the building trades. Yet readers of the ambitious Jonson know that he would have scorned to embrace his lowly roots as the stepson of a bricklayer and a bricklayer himself. He spent his career disassociating himself from the very degree of people in which he once worked. His derision is such that the diversity of craftspeople in early modern England, who in fact occupied all different levels of the social scale, are collapsed into one lowly degree.

Jonson's attitudes, which appear at odds with one another, intersect with changing early modern discourses concerning social mobility, vocation, and authorship. Here I will extend my examination of the deep cultural ambivalence toward labor – and its relation to writing, as laboring authors variously express it – into the puzzling relationship between Jonson's reliance on metaphors of labor and the disdain for laborers that so frequently emerges in his writing. Jonson both disparages labor and uses it as his vocabulary for defining a new profession of authorship. In keeping with the body/soul division noted by Barish and others, Jonson's representations of labor take two forms: one, as part of the earthly realm, which he aligns with the business of theater and printing house; and two, as an abstract ideal that becomes the locus for virtuous, diligent composition from the ideal poet. This Platonic duality appears in the public dramas, in the poetry, and in the court masques, where his quarrel with Inigo Jones concerning the relationship of poetry to spectacle becomes manifest as a struggle to hierarchize kinds of artistic creation. Particularly in the masques, it becomes clear exactly what Jonson does when he embraces labor as a principle for authorship: as a means of distinguishing his own poetry as that of the "soul," he claims "labor" as a kind of privileged knowledge that eludes the material trappings of literary and theatrical culture, thus positioning the poet as one whose art transcends the material realm. Whether he does so successfully is a matter of debate. But however much texts like the masques and the epigrams serve power, they are still rife with Jonson's personal and professional struggles to distinguish his labor as more than just hire and salary.

Jonson's attempts to both denigrate labor and adopt its terms take on a distinctly vocational dimension. D.J. Gordon writes that the dispute between Jones and Jonson was more than just a clash of two irascible personalities; it was part of a serious debate concerning the respective status of the liberal and mechanical arts:

> From Alberti and Leonardo on, arguments in defence of the visual arts had been brought forward and their claims had been by tacit consent, at any rate admitted. … Theorists like Scamozzi and Lomazzo still apparently find it necessary to defend their claims. They were defending themselves against the charge that Jonson liked to bring against Inigo: that he is a craftsman only – a joiner in this case. And it had been of considerable importance to do so, for till well on in the sixteenth century the legal position of the artist had been that of member of a craft guild.[8]

The English word "architect" does not even appear until the mid-sixteenth century, for buildings were usually designed by the carpenters, bricklayers, and stonemasons who built them. Jones's brand of architecture in England, which combined aesthetics and design, originated with him and associations with material craft were not far

[8] D.J. Gordon, "Poet and Architect: The Intellectual Setting of the Quarrel Between Ben Jonson and Inigo Jones," *Journal of the Warburg and Courtauld Institutes* 12 (1949), 152–78, 166.

behind. Stephen Orgel and Roy Strong note that neither Jonson nor Jones wants to eradicate poetry or spectacle – rather, the two artists argue about which is *dependent* on the other, according to which one is meant to *express* the other.[9] Such arguments, as Loewenstein suggests with respect to Jonson's publishing activities, constitute proprietary claims.[10]

But when we chart the social dynamics of Jonson's sense of ownership, we see that labor discourses reveal nuances that legal discourses do not. Labor is an essential part of the "proprietary" because, in an economic landscape increasingly defined by wage labor, labor too becomes something one might claim to own, as will be clear in the later case of George Wither. While Loewenstein argues that Jonson "does not denigrate spectacle so much as put it in its place,"[11] it is difficult to clear Jonson from imposing value judgments, given the frequency with which he attaches negative representations of material labor to Jones's work. In tracing such representations, I will show that a claim about the work of oneself respective to that another person *always* imposes a hierarchy of entitlements, intentionally or not, because occupation is an essential part of the language of social stratification in early modern England. Jonson's approach to labor provides a powerful point from which to investigate how this language is inflected in literary culture. I will examine these representations in two contexts: first, within Jonson's varying treatments of the mythological blacksmith Vulcan as a figure of both artistic creation and destruction; second, in the masques, where the anxieties that Vulcan represents become theatricalized as part of the Jonson/Jones quarrel.

Representations of Labor and Laborers

Material labor supplies Jonson with a store of metaphors. In his book of literary criticism, *Discoveries*, he draws an analogy between writing and blacksmithing in which the poet must revise his work continually, maintaining the discipline to "bring all to the forge, and fire, againe; tourne it a newe."[12] Jonson's commonplace book invokes labor to elevate the work of the mind:

> *Arts* that respect the mind, were ever reputed nobler, then those that serve the body: though wee lesse can bee without them. As *Tillage*, *Spinning*, *Weaving*, *Building*, & c. without which, wee could scarce sustaine life a day. But these were the workes of every hand; the other of the braine only, and those the most generous, and exalted wits, and spirits that cannot rest, or *acquiesce*. The mind of man is still fed with labour: *Opere pascitur*.[13]

---

[9] Stephen Orgel and Roy Strong, *Inigo Jones: The Theatre of the Stuart Court, Including the complete designs for productions at court for the most part in the collection of the Duke of Devonshire together with their texts and historical documentation*, 2 vols, Sotheby Parke Bernet for University of California Press, 1973, 1: 4.

[10] Joseph Loewenstein, *Ben Jonson and Possessive Authorship*, Cambridge: Cambridge UP, 2002, 177.

[11] Ibid.

[12] 8: 638. Except for the masque texts, all citations of Jonson are from *Ben Jonson*, ed. C.H. Hereford and Percy and Evelyn Simpson, 11 vols, Oxford: Clarendon, 1925–52.

[13] 8: 568.

This passage plays on standard occupational hierarchies by, on the one hand, reaffirming the superiority of intellectual to manual work, yet on the other hand insisting that intellectual work is still "labour," equally beneficial and necessary to "the mind of man." Further, labor becomes an index by which Jonson values the worth of other authors. "To the Memory of My Beloved, The Author Mr. William Shakespeare" utilizes blacksmithing imagery to describe the kind of composition that makes one worthy of the name of poet:

> [. . .] he,
> Who casts to write a living line, must sweat,
> (Such as thine are) and strike the second heat
> Upon the *Muses* anvile: turne the same,
> (And himselfe with it) that he thinkes to frame;
> Or for the lawrell, he may gaine a scorne,
> For a good *Poet's* made, as well as borne.[14]

Accordingly, Jonson presents himself as a writer who labors intensely at his product. Unlike the courtly amateur Crispinus and the vulgar upstart Demetrius in *Poetaster*, Jonson's avatar "Horace" presents himself as "I, that spend halfe my nights, and all my dayes, / Here in a cell, to get a darke, pale face, / To come forth worth the ivy, or the bayes."[15] The masque *Neptune's Triumph* (1624) opens with a dialogue between a Poet (Jonson) and a Cook (Jones), who addresses the Poet as "Creature of diligence, and businesse!"[16] As if to defy the *sprezzatura*-like ideals of composition that reigned in the Tudor period, Jonson describes the best lines as "well torned" and "true-filed."[17] The sense of artist as craftsman is as old as Jonson's beloved classical authors. But in a departure from his amateur contemporaries, Jonson wants his audiences to know that what they see and read from him is the result of laborious *process*, not of fancy, accident, or sudden inspiration. "*A Poeme*," he writes in *Discoveries*, "as I have told you is the worke of the Poet; the end, and fruit of his labour, and studye."[18]

Yet his texts consistently betray contempt toward those who perform actual, material labor. Bumbling mechanics provide comic relief on public and private stages alike as Jonson attaches specific occupational labels to each character. Judith K. Gardiner and Susanna S. Epp record negative representations of commoners (89% negative), and positive characterizations of the gentry (64.1% positive) and the titled class (67.9% positive) in Jonson's work, with the common characters appearing disproportionately in the poems and in the comedies for the public stage (60% of the characters). Jonson's attitude toward these characters emerges as overwhelmingly negative (74% "negative attitudes"). While these classifications are certainly subject to scrutiny, they do show that characters from the working orders provide fodder

---

[14] 8: ll. 58–64.

[15] 4: ll. 233–5.

[16] Citations of Jonson and Jones's masques are from *The Complete Masques*, ed. Stephen Orgel, New Haven and London: Yale UP, 1975.

[17] "To the Memory of . . . Mr. William Shakespeare," 8: l. 68.

[18] 8: 636.

for Jonsonian derision.[19] This low regard extends to the "groundlings" of the public theater audience, to whom the prologue of *The Magnetick Lady* refers as "Faeces, or grounds of your people, that sit in the oblique caves and wedges of your house, your sinfull sixe-penny Mechanicks." [20] Simply to call someone "mechanic," regardless of his or her actual social status, designates an audience member as low, thus eliding important occupational distinctions among craftspeople themselves.

Laborers also appear in antimasques, where they compete with the main masque in their own rustic music and dance. These antimasques truly are "rude" in the sense that they comically confront hierarchy.[21] *The Masque of Augurs* (1622) opens with a group of mechanicals who try to intrude and see the spectacle: Notch the brewer's clerk, Slug the lighterman, Vangoose the Rare Artist (also a satirization of Inigo Jones), Lady Alewife and her two women; three dancing bears; and Urson the bear ward. Disregarding the Groom of the Revels's censure, they put on a masque of their own. *Pan's Anniversary, or the Shepherds' Holiday* (1620), presents a competing antimasque led by a "tooth-drawer" (also the late medieval title for a blacksmith), a tinker with a kettle drum who is "a master of music and a man of mettle,"[22] a juggler, a corn-cutter, a bellows-mender with splayed feet, a tinder box man, a clock-keeper, a former politician who now makes mousetraps, a tailor, and a clerk "who (they say) can write, and it is shrewdly suspected he can read too."[23] In *Pleasure Reconciled to Virtue* (1618), the grotesque Comus invokes images of mechanical work as he uses drink to tempt Hercules away from virtuous labor:

> Room, room, make room for the bouncing belly,
> First father of sauce, and deviser of jelly;
> Prime master of arts, and the giver of wit,
> That found out the excellent engine, the spit,
> The plough and the flail, the mill and the hopper,
> The hutch and the bolter, the furnace and copper,
> The oven, the bavin, the mawkin, the peel,
> The hearth and the range, the dog and the wheel.[24]

While mechanicals also appear in masques by other artists, such as the anonymous *Masque of Flowers* (1614), Francis Beaumont's *The Masque of the Inner Temple and Gray's Inn* (1613), and James Shirley's *The Triumph of Peace* (1634), none are repudiated with the force that issues from the Shepherd of *Pan's Anniversary*, who

---

[19] Judith K. Gardiner and Susanna S. Epp, "Ben Jonson's Social Attitudes: A Statistical Analysis," *Drama in the Renaissance: Comparative and Critical Essays*, ed. Clifford Davidson, C.J. Gianakaris, and John H. Stroupe, New York: AMS Press, 1986, 84–102, 91, 99.

[20] 6: ll. 32–4.

[21] See Parker's discussion of "rude" and its cognates, which she associates with vulgarity and rebelliousness, in *Shakespeare from the Margins: Language, Culture, Context*, Chicago: U of Chicago P, 1996, 83–4.

[22] Orgel, *Complete Masques*, ll. 86–7.

[23] Orgel, *Complete Masques*, ll. 123–4.

[24] Orgel, *Complete Masques*, ll. 10–7. For a study that treats the Rabelaisian influences on masques, see Anne Lake Prescott's *Imagining Rabelais in Renaissance England*, New Haven and London: Yale UP, 1998.

exclaims, "Now let them return with their solid heads, and carry their stupidity into Boeotia, whence they brought it, with an emblem of themselves and their country. This is too pure an air for so gross brains."[25]

Further, *Mercury Vindicated* (1616), *The Gypsies Metamorphos'd* (1621), and *Love's Welcome at Bolsover* (1634, written after Jonson's collaboration with Jones ended in 1631) all use labor or figures associated with labor as foils for defending Jonson's own poetic enterprise. In an expression of what Barish calls Jonson's "deeply rooted antitheatricalism,"[26] Jonson aligns the working orders specifically with *theatrical* labor and machinery that, in the quarrel with Inigo Jones and in the face of Jones's own rising importance at court, he strenuously wished to show was dependent on poetry and song. This tension becomes detectible even in the earliest masques, *The Masque of Blackness* (1605) and *The Masque of Queens* (1609), whose dazzling theatrical displays Jonson knows are integral to the masque's success, but also are framed in a way that erects barriers between Jonson's and Jones's respective kinds of creation. Moreover, in the masques, Vulcan appears three times, but with very different consequences. The figure of Vulcan the divine laborer is worth some attention, because Vulcan becomes both a foil for Jonson's authorship and his alter ego.

Bricklayer and Blacksmith: Jonson, Vulcan, and the Horatian Aesthetic

When applied to authorship, the courtly notion of *sprezzatura* represents a fantasy that the composition of poetry, like the ideal courtly self, needs no process. In these terms, the opposite of *sprezzatura* would be art that *calls attention to* this process. In an important analysis of Shakespeare's *Midsummer Night's Dream*, Patricia Parker notes that what makes the player-mechanicals "rude" is the way their bungling play shows that art *is* work:

> The proclaimed order and harmony of this *Dream*'s end involves, I would argue, something like Frank Whigham's sense of the contradictions inherent in the representation of aristocratic *sprezzatura* as spontaneous and natural when, like the professed natural order of discourse, it was offered as a product for reproduction, mastery of whose rudiments (cognate of rude) was part of the construction of new elites whose power depended not just on this edification but on concealing its joints and seams.[27]

This "disjoinery," as an alternative form of artistry, begs for further application. While Shakespeare's ego arguably is absent from his plays, Jonson's treatments of theatrical labor are inextricably bound up in his own ego-driven self-promotion. Yet he does not merely repudiate the "seams." He strains for a way to reconfigure them

---

[25] Orgel, *Complete Masques*, ll. 217–21.

[26] Jonas A. Barish, "Jonson and the Loathed Stage," *A Celebration of Ben Jonson*, ed. William Blisset, Julian Patrick, and R.W. Van Fossen, Toronto: U of Toronto P, 1973, 27–53, 28.

[27] Patricia Parker, *Shakespeare from the Margins: Language, Culture, Context*, Chicago: U of Chicago P, 1996, 107.

for himself, parsing out the labor of the "good man" from that of others, paradoxically making *material* labor into the *abstract* marker of the ideal poet.

Jonson's experience of building in early modern London might well have schooled him in disjoinery. Bricklaying was introduced in the middle ages, after a series of devastating fires made it necessary that chimneys, wall fillings, and foundations be made of more durable material. Citizens began to build stone houses with foundations, covered with thick tiles, to protect their homes against the flames.[28] Yet in terms of building and architecture, London *circa* 1600 was still a medieval city compared to other European capitals.[29] Standards of brickwork were awkward, involving large bricks of uneven texture. The rough craftsmanship is evident particularly in the uneven joints, which showed evidence of spilled cement:

> The thick joints of early brickwork were the natural result of the irregularity of brick sizes and shapes. The nature of the earths used and very thorough burning (we realize how thorough this burning was when we examine much old brickwork, without finding one brick which has succumbed to the weather) which resulted in hatching or warping. The consequent variations of dimensions often were not absorbed by the thick joint, so that perpends were ill-kept and sometimes cross-joints came immediately over one another.[30]

Although brick was not yet the primary building material in the metropolis, this rough standard must have contributed to the backward appearance that Inigo Jones attempted to correct by introducing Italian architecture into the capital.[31] The awkwardness of London's walls recall the comic ineptitude of "Wall" in *Midsummer Night's Dream* – as Theseus jests, "Would you desire lime and hair to speak better?" [32]

Bricklayers, although sometimes "citizens," sat relatively low among the guilds of early modern London. As will also be the case with John Taylor's Watermen's Company, the fact that the Bricklayers' Company did not engage in trade or commerce means that the Company had little money compared to the wealthy and powerful mercantile companies who played an important role in city governance. In 1600, Elizabeth I's judges determined that bricklayers did not fall within the Statute of Apprentices, which strictly regulated participation in trades, because bricklaying was one of the "arts which require rather ability of body than of skill."[33] This lowly station was reinforced by the very nature of building trades, which caused building to

---

[28] Bell, 4.

[29] See Derek Keene, "Material London in Time and Space" and John Schofield, "The Topography and Buildings of London, ca. 1600, both in *Material London, ca. 1600*, ed. Lena Cowen Orlin, Philadelphia: U of Pennsylvania P, 2000, 55–74, 296–321.

[30] Nathaniel Lloyd, *A History of English Brickwork*, London: H. Greville Montgomery, 1928, 66.

[31] However, to one observer, Jones's London innovations caused even more deformity because they did not fit London's overall look: According to the Museum of London's display on Jones, "The contrast between his new Italianate buildings and their Jacobean neighbours in London was 'like Bug-bears or Gorgon heads' to the average citizen."

[32] *The Riverside Shakespeare*, 2nd edn, ed. G. Blakemore Evans, Boston and New York: Houghton Mifflin, 1997, 5.3.l. 165.

[33] Qtd. in Bell, 17, who calls it "a poor compliment, indeed."

look like wage labor even if the workers were being paid another way.[34] It is difficult to say for certain how Jonson perceived his own craft, but clearly he was exposed to two things: disjoined, awkward craftsmanship and a body-mind hierarchy that resulted in the designation of his non-literary labor as inferior to the work of other guilds. Jonson's interest in Vulcan brings these experiences to bear on authorship.[35]

Bulfinch's Mythology describes Vulcan (the Roman counterpart of the Greek god Hephaestus) as "architect, smith, armourer, chariot builder, and artist of all work in Olympus."[36] The term "artist" invests smithing and metalworking with divine power. Vulcan's creation requires superhuman intelligence:

> He built of brass the houses of the gods; he made for them the golden shoes with which they trod the air or the water, and moved from place to place with the speed of the wind, or even of thought. He also shod with brass the celestial steeds, which whirled the chariots of the gods through the air, or along the surface of the sea. He was able to bestow on his workmanship self-motion, so that the tripods (chairs and tables) could move of themselves in and out of the celestial hall. He even endowed with intelligence the golden handmaidens whom he made to wait on himself.[37]

Wherever an early modern blacksmith's trade might have placed him in the Elizabethan social order, mythological blacksmithing captures the process by which

---

[34] Donald Woodward explains pay scales in a way that makes an important distinction between members of the building trades and actual laborers who worked for a wage:

A shoemaker, tailor, or candle-maker could incorporate the value of his labour – and that of his assistants – in the selling price of an easily recognised and easily valued final product. Such artisans, working with their own tools in their own workshops and marketing their own products, have long been recognised as small-scale, independent producers . . . For building craftsmen things were not so simple. Sometimes they worked by the piece – paving at so much a square yard or casting lead at so much a stone – and sometimes they contracted to build a structure for a set price, but often this was neither possible nor desirable. More frequently, building craftsmen were paid according to the value of the inputs they made, their labour being paid for at a set rate by the day. But the receipt of such a 'wage' did not convert the early-modern building craftsman into a wage-earner in the modern sense. According to the accounts of the larger institutions of northern England, some building craftsmen were employed for weeks or months on end on the same project, and they take on the appearance of wage-earners: but when the same men worked for a day or two repairing broken pews or damaged flagstones in their parish churches they appear in their true colours as independent businessmen, providing raw materials and any extra labour needed.

See *Labourers and Building Craftsmen in the Towns of Northern England, 1450–1750*, Cambridge: Cambridge UP, 1995, 2.

[35] In the ensuing discussion, I borrow the concept of disjoinery from Patricia Parker's treatment of *Midsummer Night's Dream* in the third chapter of her *Shakespeare on the Margins*. Parker argues that theatrical representation is a matter of *mechanical* reproduction – this is what representation with visible seams makes clear. It provides a disruption to aesthetic approaches that insist upon seamless unity (87). As I will argue in the next section, Jonson brings images of "difformity" into the antimasque as a challenge that ultimately validates his own poetic labor, which he calls the true "soul" of the masque.

[36] *Bulfinch's Complete Mythology*, London: Spring Books, 1989, 9.

[37] Ibid.

something is forged divinely into perfect form. Macrobius's commentary on Cicero's *Dream of Scipio* relates that Pythagoras first discovered the relationship between harmony and proportion by observing blacksmiths: "He happened to pass the open shop of some blacksmiths who were beating a hot iron with hammers. The sound of the hammers striking in alternate and regular succession fell upon his ears with the higher note so attuned to the lower that each time the same musical interval returned, and always striking a concord." [38] Physical labor and artistic perfection go together in these accounts. Unlike so many early modern social descriptions that posit material labor as ignoble, Homer's massive, solid Vulcan sweats at his anvil to make objects useful to the gods – his labor at once is bodily and divine.[39] Vulcan is also associated with fire, the element that Prometheus unlawfully seizes and for which he incurs divine punishment. Fire is an emblem of divine prerogative to create and to know.

Early moderns retained some association of labor with godly creation. Sometimes they imagined God as an artificer who crafts the world into perfect form. Examples include Thomas Smith's *De Republica Anglorum* (1583), which designates "lowe and base" laborers as "the fourth sort of men who do not rule"; these include ""day labourers, poore husbandmen, yea marchantes or retailers which have no free lande, copyholders, and all artificers, as Taylers, Shoomakers, Carpenters, Brickemakers, Bricklayers, Masons, and c."[40] Nonetheless, Smith not only describes God as "the Artificer and the Architect,"[41] but he also calls himself an "expert workemaister" whose book is "forged of pure and excellent metal."[42] In a different context, Thomas Dekker's cony-catching pamphlet *The Belman of London* (1608) shows the bellman, as he takes a break from seeking out displaced laborers *cum* criminals, "in Speculation of the admiral workemanshippe of Heaven and of the orders which the Celestiall bodies are governed by."[43] As with Jonson, there is a distinct Platonic logic at work in these texts: although labor in the world is rough and base, there is a divine form of labor that is abstract, perfect, and something that an author can hope to approximate.

Despite Vulcan's role in creating important objects, he also has some distinct social liabilities. In *The Iliad*, Zeus hurls Hephaestus from Olympus, from which Hephaestus falls for nine days before his landing on the island of Lemnos leaves him permanently disfigured.[44] Homer's epic also records that he was born lame and that Hera threw him from Olympus in disgust at her misshapen son.[45] Athenian mythology recounts that Hephaestus wanted to marry (and even tried to rape) Athena (also a

---

[38] Macrobius, *Commentary on the Dream of Scipio*, trans. William Harris Stahl, New York: Columbia UP, 1952, 186–7.

[39] Homer, *The Iliad*, trans. Robert Fagles, New York: Viking, 1990, 18.480–88.

[40] Thomas Smith, *De Republica Anglorum*, London, 1583, F.

[41] Smith, B1.

[42] Smith, A4v.

[43] Thomas Dekker, *The Belman of London*, London, 1608, B4.

[44] Homer, *The Iliad*,1.710–6.

[45] Homer, *The Iliad*, 18.461–73.

patron of smiths) but was rejected on account of his ugliness.[46] Vulcan's disability testifies to his rejection and expulsion from Olympus. In a world of idealized classical beauty, Vulcan is a god with an imperfect and very human physical form; he is ugly and, at times, laughable because of it. His marginality finds further expression in early modern painting. Jan Brueghel's *Venus at the Forge of Vulcan* depicts a luminous Venus standing, with a bemused expression, next to a craggy, dark Vulcan as he bends over to labor at his forge. The ground is scattered with pieces of armor and other misplaced parts from Vulcan's workshop, which is also filled with common, earthly-looking human assistants. Diego Velazquez's *The Forge of Vulcan* (1630) employs similar dark and light contrasts: a radiant, dark Apollo visits Vulcan's workshop, where the dark, fleshly blacksmith and his assistants look up from their work to stare in awe and surprise. These representations support Vulcan's status as an imperfect outsider, a suggestion further bolstered by the fact that, due to danger of fire, his temples were normally located outside the cities – as were the Elizabethan public playhouses as well as the shops of many Elizabethan blacksmiths.

Vulcan also exhibits a level of devotion to his wife, Venus, that leads to his cuckoldry. Embodying a type familiar in Renaissance comic drama, Vulcan becomes the jealous husband outwitted by a shrewd wife and her lover, Mars. Andrea Mantegna's painting *Parnassus* depicts Mars and Venus standing, triumphant, over a dance of muses while, in a cave off to the left, the ugly cuckold Vulcan stands angrily in the shadows. He has sprung out of his forge and gestures in a futile rage at the new couple. Some mythological accounts hold that, upon learning of Venus's affair, Vulcan builds an elaborate net of metalwork so that he can catch the lovers in their embrace.[47] Even a successful plot to catch the lovers does not completely rescue Vulcan from ridicule. Yet Vulcan's ingenuity also testifies to his craftiness, which Jonson highlights in the poem "Why I Write Not Of Love." Love asks, "Can Poets hope to fetter mee? / It is enough, they once did get / *Mars*, and my *Mother* in their net." [48] Vulcan may not be a successful lover (and neither is the poet, as Jonson suggests here and elsewhere), but he has the skill to outmaneuver deceit.

Vulcan exhibits these characteristics in Jonson's masques. He first appears in *The Haddington Masque* as a classical figure "attired in a cassock girt to him, with bare arms, his hair and beard rough, his hat of blue and ending in a cone, in his hand a hammer and tongs, as coming from the forge."[49] He presides over marriages and, during this nuptial masque, an uxorious Vulcan reveals a proportionate sphere: "Which I have done, the best of all my life; / And have my end, if it but please my wife, / And she commend it, to the labored worth. / Cleave, solid rock, and bring the wonder forth!"[50] Vulcan's artistry is refined, potent, and balanced. His sphere is "in due proportion to the sphere of heaven, / With all his lines and circles, that compose

---

[46] Oxford Classical Dictionary, rev. 3rd edn, ed. Simon Hornblower and Anthony Spawforth, New York: Oxford UP, 2003, 682.

[47] Homer, *The Odyssey*, trans. Robert Fagles, London: Penguin, 1996, 8: 300–410.

[48] 8: ll. 4–6.

[49] Orgel, *Complete Masques*, ll. 220–2.

[50] Orgel, *Complete Masques*, ll. 223–6.

/ The perfect'st form."[51] As a maker of perfectly crafted things, completely in accord with nature, he is hailed as "Our great artificer, the god of fire,"[52] one with whom Jonson identifies when he calls himself an "artificer" in the preface.[53]

While Vulcan's creation clearly is a positive, even essential, force in *Haddington*, the later masque *Mercury Vindicated* depicts Vulcan as an enemy and a deceiver. As Lesley Mickel writes, "the emphasis [in *Mercury Vindicated*] seems to be on imposture and the problem of distinguishing true from false creative power," [54] pitting Mercury (representing Nature) against Vulcan and the Cyclops who assist him at the forge (representing Artifice), which results in the defeat of alchemy, an illegitimate and unnatural kind of creation. *Mercury* can thus be read as a meditation on honest versus dishonest types of artistry. In Beaumont's *Masque of the Inner Temple*, Mercury brings forth statues that come alive, "new and strange varieties both in the Musick and paces."[55] However, in Jonson's masque, Vulcan the blacksmith becomes the threateningly powerful figure with the ability to thwart nature through his art. Furthermore, Vulcan is compared negatively to Prometheus, who successfully resists the allure of women, most especially Vulcan's own creation, Pandora: "can you [Chorus] from such beauty part? / You'll do a wonder more than I. / I woman with her ills did fly, / But you their good and them deny" (ll. 252–5).[56] By the time Jonson stages his last entertainment, *Love's Welcome at Bolsover*, Vulcan is a rude comic figure among other mechanicals: Chesil the Carver, Maul the Free-Mason, Squire Sumer the Carpenter, Twybil his Man, Dresser the Plomber, Quarel the Glasier, Fret the Plaisterer, and Beater the Morter-man. No longer the holder of creative power for good *or* for bad, "Captaine Smith", like the mythological Vulcan, stands out for his deformity: "O Captaine *Smith*! or Hammer-armed *Vulcan*! with your three Sledges, you are our Musique, you come a little too tardie; but wee remit that, to your polt-foot, we know you are lame."[57] Vulcan has descended from a maker of royal marriages and a creator of perfect forms, to a perpetrator of false art, to a fool – at last scarcely more potent in the eyes of the court than the rude mechanicals in *Midsummer Night's Dream*.

The late poem "An Execration upon Vulcan" both acknowledges Vulcan's power and tries to contain that power by associating him with the kind of base, material production that opposes Jonson's own poetic production. The poem has received little sustained scholarly attention, which is surprising given its clear thematic footing in Jonson's well-documented authorial ego. Here Jonson casts the god of the forge as the enemy of his own artistic output and, indeed, the enemy of culture itself. The poem relies on conventional antitheses between high and low culture

---

[51] Orgel, *Complete Masques*, ll. 237–9.

[52] Orgel, *Complete Masques*, l. 289.

[53] Orgel, *Complete Masques*, l. 15.

[54] Lesley Mickel, *Ben Jonson's Antimasques: A History of Growth and Decline*, Aldershot: Ashgate, 1999.

[55] Francis Beaumont, *The Masque of the Inner Temple and Gray's Inn* in *A Book of Masques in Honour of Allardyce Nicoll*, ed. T.J.B. Spencer and S. Wells, Cambridge: Cambridge UP, 1967, ll. 60–61.

[56] Orgel, *Complete Masques*, ll. 252–5.

[57] Ben Jonson, *The Workes of Benjamin Jonson, the Second Volume*, London, 1640, 282.

and intellectual and manual work, with Jonson embodying the former and Vulcan the latter. Despite his reliance elsewhere on the image of the forge, in "Execration," Jonson attributes the fire to the forge's Roman god. Jonson nominates his study as the latest important site to be consumed by fire, after the Globe, the Temple of Diana at Ephesus, and the library at Alexandria, among others. Fire and study are pitted against one another as opposites that, due to Vulcan's resentment, cannot coexist – fire continually threatens to erase cultural sites and to usurp their rightful place in history. Vulcan is the enemy of the learned, but at the same time, he is necessary to help define Jonson's claim to permanence. Jonson portrays Vulcan as an envious usurper who deserves banishment back to the sites of vulgar mechanical production, as when he asks a court of equity to "confine him [Vulcan] to the Brew-houses, / the Glasse-house, Dye-fats, and their Fornaces [. . .] Condemne him to the Brick-kills, or some Hill- / foot (out in Sussex) to an iron Mill."[58] Here we find bodily labor again subordinated to mental labor, and both endowed clearly with class terms. "For none but Smiths would have made thee a God," sneers Jonson, musing that Vulcan's deformity and envy make him a natural candidate for becoming a rude mechanical enemy of the higher arts.[59] While it is certainly true that, in the words of David Riggs, the poem "masks a keen sense of victimage,"[60] this victimage is essential to Jonson's definition of his own art.

This poem's version of Vulcan deserves special attention because Jonson posits Vulcan as a *competitor* whose labor does not advance honest art and knowledge, but destroys it. Jonson links him to warfare, as Thomas Wyatt does in "Description of a Gun":

> Vulcan begat me: Minerva me taught:
> Nature, my mother: Craft nourish'd me year by year:
> Three bodies are my food: my strength is in naught:
> Anger, wrath, waste, and noise are my children dear.
> Guess, friend, what I am: and how I am wraught:
> Monster of sea, or of land, or of elsewhere.
> Know me, and use me: and I may thee defend:
> And if I be thine enemy, I may thy life end.[61]

At worst, Jonson's Vulcan is like Wyatt's – a figure of destruction distinguished by "craft." At best, he is like Vulcan in *Mercury Vindicated* – he can produce rough, imperfect hybrids of things that show only art, with no obedience paid to nature. Jonson's aesthetic model, Horace,[62] is concerned also with badly built works, as the first lines of Jonson's translation of Horace's *Ars Poetica* demonstrate:

---

[58] 8: ll. 179–80, 183–4.

[59] 8: l. 117.

[60] David Riggs, *Ben Jonson: A Life*, Cambridge: Harvard UP, 1989, 288.

[61] Rollins, Hyder Edward, ed. Tottel's Miscellany. 2 vols. Cambridge: Harvard UP, 1928.

[62] In *Ben Jonson and Possessive Authorship*, Loewenstein remarks that Jonsonian authorship is, in many ways, distinctly *un*-Horatian and argues for Martial's influence instead. See in particular his fourth and fifth chapters.

> If to a woman's head, a painter would
> Set a Horse-neck, and divers feathers fold
> On every limbe, ta'en from a severall creature,
> Presenting upwards, a faire female feature,
> Which in some swarthie fish uncomely ends:
> Admitted to the sight, although his friends,
> Could you containe your laughter? [. . .]
> Yet, not as therefore wild, and tame should cleave
> Together: not that we should Serpents see
> With Doves; or Lambes, with Tygres coupled be.[63]

The sense of a malformed object is mirrored in Vulcan's own deformed body. In Greek and Roman sculpture, Vulcan/Hephaestus is usually depicted as a merry cripple standing at his anvil. Sometimes he walks with a crutch, he usually has a beard, and he is ugly. Homer depicts him as lame and walking with a stick – a spectacle that amuses the other gods.[64] In archaic iconography, he can even be pictured with his feet turned backwards.

Horace's Roman contemporaries, who held such powerful sway over Jonson, were prone to view anything misshapen or badly put together with disgust or derision. Lloyd A. Thompson explains this prejudice as "a deeply rooted Roman tendency to ridicule 'inappropriate' personal characteristics of all kinds, physical and non-physical."[65] Valuing a somatic Roman "norm" for the body – known as *aspectus, habitus, morphe, idea* – Romans imagined that Vulcan suffered regular mockery from his fellow deities.[66] Jonson's own corpulent body and pockmarked face made him vulnerable to similar ridicule, which twists his anti-materialism into a curious form of self-hatred. Inigo Jones turns the language of deformity back onto Jonson in his poem where he famously dubs Jonson "the best of Poettes but the worst of men" – he calls Jonson an abortive birth and extends the metaphor of deformity to Jonson's language: "Soe longe I have travailed for with thee / But thy neglect hath chaung'd the happier fate / and made thy birth abortive turne to hate / Whose language like thy nature now must prove."[67] Revulsion and amusement at badly assembled bodies accords with Horace's aesthetic preferences when, in *Ars Poetica*, he decries kinds of poetic making that result in distorted, disjointed figures.

Deformity, in Jonson's Horatian outlook, is what art looks like when it is unfinished. When too much art shows, the reader or spectator perceives an unpleasant diversity among the work's components. The *OED* records common slippage between "deformity" and "difformity," a word that means "difference or diversity

---

[63] 8.ll. 1–7, 13–15. Hereford and Simpson use the translation from Jonson's second folio. There was another translation printed in duodecimo titled *Q. Horatius Flaccus: His Art of Poetry, Englished by Ben Jonson*, printed by John Benson in 1640. The folio version of *Ars* was printed in a final section of the volume, along with *The English Grammar* and *Discoveries*.

[64] Homer, *The Iliad*, 1.721–3.

[65] Lloyd A. Thompson, *Romans and Blacks*, Norman, OK: U of Oklahoma P, 1989, 136.

[66] Ibid.

[67] Reprinted in D.H. Craig, ed., *Ben Jonson: The Critical Heritage, 1599–1798*, London and New York: Routledge, 1990, 130–32, 131.

of form; want of uniformity or conformity." Further, the way elements are mixed and forged together is a *moral* matter, as we also see in Jonson's translation of *Ars*: "So mixeth cunningly / Falshood with truth, as no man can espie / Where the midst differs from the first: or where / The last doth from the midst dis-joyn'd appeare."[68] Disjoined creations show their "false" elements and thus announce themselves as "art" divorced from nature – they are visible acts of dishonesty. Like the piebald writings of "Poet-Ape" in *Epigrams* LVI, poorly assembled (and pilfered) materials show only "shreds" and not "the whole peece."[69] "A Fit of Rime Against Rime" attacks rhyme in the same terms, as "Joynting [disjoining] Syllables, drowning Letters, / Fastning Vowells, as with fetters / They were bound!"[70] Rhymes, which the classical poets scorned, require breaking up language in an unnatural fashion. Fittingly, Jonson wishes that "He that first invented thee [rhymes], / May his joynts tormented bee, / Cramp'd for ever."[71] Conversely, a well constructed whole cannot be so easily broken down to its component parts. "On the New Motion" (*Epigrams* XCVII), a poem that Hereford and Simpson believe was aimed at Inigo Jones, describes a fool as a vulgar assemblage of pieces:

> See you yond' Motion? Not the old *Fa-ding*,
> Nor Captayne *Pod*, nor yet the *Eltham*-thing;
> But one more rare, and in the case so new:
> His cloke with orient velvet quite lin'd through,
> His rosie tyes and garters so ore-blowne,
> But his each glorious parcell to be knowne![72]

This figure encapsulates several characteristics repugnant to Jonson: novelty (the "new motion" or new puppet), outward shows (the velvet cloak, the garters), and lack of unity in his aesthetic effects ("by his each glorious parcel"). Disgust at disjoinery extends itself beyond literature and theater into fashion which, in a sense, is another kind of bad theater.

In Jonson's multiple handlings of Vulcan, different discursive contradictions emerge: between the nobility and ignominy of physical labor, between beauty and ugliness, between selfless devotion and foolish gullibility. Jonson vacillates between these themes before he settles on a representation of Vulcan as a comical laborer who nonetheless threatens with the capacity to destroy what is "good" in culture and art. These complexities are thematized in the fact that while fire destroys, it also renews – the seal of the Blacksmiths' Company prominently features a phoenix emerging from flames, evoking the mythological notion that something newer and better can emerge (Figure 3.1). Derek Keene notes that it was, in fact, the Great Fire of 1666 that enabled the rebuilding of the city to a level of splendor rivaling the rest

---

68 8:ll. 215–18.

69 8: l. 14.

70 8: ll. 10–12.

71 8: ll. 49–51.

72 8: ll. 1–6.

Figure 3.1 Seal of the Worshipful Company of Blacksmiths, London

of Europe; this "new appearance of modernity," constructed with brick, paralleled Britain's new prominence in worldwide markets.[73]

At the same time, the *non*-mercantile craftsmen who most evoked fire – the blacksmiths – were everywhere. While most trades tended to collect in certain areas of the city to the point that they actually became identified with those areas, the blacksmiths worked in the suburbs, as well as in different locations inside the city walls. They were highly visible, but at the same time, diffuse.[74] These characteristics feed into Jonson's association of Vulcan with displaced yet transgressive labor – a portrayal that he marshals into masque aesthetics and the quarrel with Inigo Jones. While I do not suggest that "An Execration upon Vulcan" is an allegory of Jones, it has prominent images in common with a poem Jonson wrote during the time that the two artists ended their collaboration. "An Expostulation with Inigo Jones" decries the new fashion for spectacle: "Pack with your pedling Poetry to the Stage, / This is the money-gett, Mechanick Age!"[75] As in "Execration," that which Jonson calls

[73] Keene, 69.

[74] Such was the case with both the blacksmiths and those in Bottom's occupation – the weavers. See Joseph P. Ward, *Metropolitan Communities: Trade Guilds, Identity, and Change in Early Modern London*, Stanford, CA: Stanford UP, 1997, 34–5.

[75] 8: ll. 51–2.

"mechanick" in "Expostulation" is aligned with base material desires, as well as base material itself. As a fantasy resolution, Jonson imagines Jones himself devoured by fire:

> What Posey ere was painted on a wall,
> That might compare with thee? what story shall
> Of all the Worthyes hope t'outlast thy one,
> Soe the Materialls be of Purbeck stone!
> Lyve long the Feasting Roome. And ere thou burne
> Againe, thy Architect to ashes turne!
> Whom not ten fyres, nor a Parlyament can,
> With all Remonstrance make an honest man.[76]

This passage illustrates what is at stake in the symbol of fire: professional anxieties about posterity and the threat of extinction. While Jonson posits fire as a destroyer, he also recognizes it as a symbol of authorial power when he declares in "Praeludium" (*The Forest* X) that "I bring / My own true fire" (VIII, 108). The masques, with their collaborative component and their complex mixture of theater and anti-theater, throw these anxieties into high relief.

"The Bodily Part": Labor and Theatrical Machinery

Jonson's use of Vulcan displays many of the traits attributed to Vulcan by Greek and Roman mythology: his creative potency, his imperfect physical stature, his craftiness, and his vulnerability to ridicule – a picture not unlike Jonson himself. I see in these representations Jonson's wariness of the material realm as it is figured in his varying attitudes toward labor. Katherine Eisaman Maus describes Jonson's anti-materialist bias as an imposition of value onto theatrical work and its participants:

> Jonson repeatedly makes a distinction between the "sensual" people who evaluate everything in terms of the limited, allocatable goods of the material world, and the elite – philosophers, artists, scholars – who seem able to transcend and despise that order. He contrasts the "carcase" or "body" of the masque with its "spirit" or "soul" or "inward parts," reminding us that the former is traditionally torn apart by members of the audience as soon as the revels have ended. Like all "bodies" it can be dismantled, appropriated, redistributed, destroyed. But the latter is exempt by nature from depredation and change.[77]

---

[76] 8: ll. 97–104. In a recent essay, Bernard Capp details early modern arson, showing that fire was commonly employed as a means of revenge not only for subordinates, but between equals and even by superiors. See "Arson, Threats of Arson, and Incivility in Early Modern England," *Civil Histories: Essays Presented to Sir Keith Thomas*, ed. Peter Burke, Brian Harrison, and Paul Slack, Oxford: Oxford UP, 2000, 197–213.

[77] Katherine Eisaman Maus, "Facts of the Matter: Satiric and Ideal Economies in the Jonsonian Imagination," *English Literary Renaissance* 19 (1989): 42–64, reprinted in *Ben Jonson's 1616 Folio*, Jennifer Brady and W.H. Herendeen, eds, London: Associated University Presses, 1991, 64–89, 77. For the criticism that Maus specifically addresses, see her p. 86–7, n. 6.

The notion of "bodies" and "souls" replicates divisions between physical and mental labor, which is what the description of "philosophers, artists, scholars" as members of "elite" vocations suggests. Those who deal in the "bodies" of the masque – costumes, sets, and so forth – merely create empty artifice.

Yet Jonson, active as he was in publishing his works, knew that his poetry had materiality in its own right. Despite his very real dependence on public audiences, technologies of print, the vagaries of the market, and theatrical machinery, he strains to preserve poetry from material trappings as much as possible. As Maus writes, "The consequence of this rhetorical strategy is that relations based upon material considerations must invariably figure as inferior to, or at best secondary to, at worst incompatible with, the cultivation of virtue."[78] Within this framework, Jonson's ascription of "the bodily part" to Inigo Jones in the *Masque of Blackness* is not just a proprietary claim, but a claim that elevates poetry over the material business of theater.[79] The preface to *Hymenai* states:

> This it is hath made the most royal princes and greatest persons, who are commonly the personaters of these actions, not only studious of riches, and magnificence in the outward celebration or show, which rightly becomes them, but curious after the most high and hearty inventions to furnish the inward parts, and those grounded upon antiquity and solid learnings; which, though their voice be taught to sound to present occasions, their sense or doth or should always lay hold on more removed mysteries.[80]

Particularly notable is Jonson's use of the word "mysteries," a term endowed with both religious and vocational significance. Medieval theological uses of the term suggest a revelation beyond the normal human capacity to understand, one that is revealed to a select one or few. The term also applied to anything, religious or not, that presented an enigma to the ordinary person. By the late sixteenth century, "mystery" signified a body of technical knowledge that required special initiation and training. The sixteenth century witnessed an amplification of the medieval associations of "mystery" with the work of craft guilds, as various kinds of work became professionalized areas of expertise to be practiced only by an initiated few.

For Jonson to set his art aside as a "mystery," then, privileges his knowledge. It is essentially a professional claim borrowed from the language of craft guilds, many of whose members held great social responsibility, wealth, and esteem. It provides an early example of the terms that Siskin uses to characterize literary professionalism: "indetermination," or the mystification of a particular kind of work for the purpose of monopolizing it. Combined with "technicality," or the assertion that the exercise of a particular skill stems from a special brand of competence, indetermination renders the poet's work incomprehensible to outsiders. In these terms, poetry is a skill that Jonson "possesses" and thus one that he has the right to explain, distribute,

[78] Maus, 77–8.

[79] Orgel, *Complete Masques*, ll. 71–2.

[80] Orgel, *Complete Masques*, ll. 9–17.

or withhold from others.[81] "To My Old Faithfull Servant" decries the proliferation of writers who eschew the crafts they *ought* to practice:

Now each Court-Hobby-horse will wince in rime;
Both learned, and unlearned, all write *Playes*.
It was not so of old: Men tooke up trades
That knew the Crafts they had bin bred in, right:
An honest *Bilbo*-Smith would make good blades,
And the *Physician* teach men spue, or shite;
The *Cobler* kep him to his nall; but, now
Hee'll be a *Pilot*, scarce can guide a Plough.[82]

Jonson deploys the language of vocation to justify fixed social hierarchies by preserving specific knowledges for specific practicioners. He writes in *Discoveries*, "*In the difference of wits*, I have observ'd; there are many notes: And it is a little *Maistry* to know them [. . .] Some are fit to make *Divines*, some *Poets*, some *Lawyers*, some *Physicians*; some to be sent to the plough, and trades."[83] As if to punctuate the special status of poetic labor, he emphasizes that the removed mysteries, while shadowed by theater, are "removed" from the material plane and from the immediate view of most individuals. When one rests only in the sensuous experience of spectacle, one denies the Platonic/Christian dictum to seek that which is higher. While this model does not deny the power of spectacle, it does contain it. Yet Jonson's efforts to contain Jones's work – and even at times distort it, as I will show – are a struggle against the reality that his theater depends on Jones in order to become manifest.

What we know of Jonson's personality – his ambition, his defensiveness, his delicate ego – suggests that he was jealous of Jones's connections at court. But a less discussed subtext for the rivalry is Jones's alleged predilection for working independently. Jonson satirizes this propensity in *The Tale of a Tub*'s In-and-In Medlay, a joiner who professes himself "*Architectonicus professor*, rather: /That is (as one would zay) and Architect."[84] Medlay is ridiculed by the other characters for his unwillingness to collaborate on a court masque, as if he were the only master:

Hee'll do it alone Sir, He will joyne with no man,
Though he be a Joyner: in designe he cals it,
He must be sole Inventer: In-and-In
Drawes with no other in's project, hee'll tell you,
It cannot else be feazeable . . . [85]

---

[81] Clifford Siskin, *The Work of Writing: Literature and Social Change in Britain, 1700–1830*, Baltimore and London: Johns Hopkins UP, 1998, 116.

[82] 8: ll. 11–18.

[83] 8: 584.

[84] 3:V.ii.1–11. The character of In-and-In Medlay replaces the earlier Vitruvius Hoop, which Jonson was commanded to change.

[85] 3: V.2.35–9

Jonson's play with the word "joyne" both ridicules Jones's origins – Jones was the son of a poor clothworker and had been apprenticed briefly as a joiner in his youth – and trivializes his work.

Jonson's view of Jones as imperious and controlling has some basis in truth. From the period in which Jones was commissioned to restore St. Paul's, a set of reprinted instructions for the pre-fire restoration contains some revealing criticisms and corrections by Jones's nephew and assistant, John Webb. The list of "Officers of the Worke" includes the surveyor, two comptrollers, and a paymaster. Webb adds in the margins, "There were no such officers in the worke but all was managed by ye surveyor: Mr. Inigo Jones."[86] Nonetheless, Webb is anxious to assert his own role: "Mr. Webbe copied all the designes from the Surveyors invention, made all the traceryes in great for the worke, & all the mouldings by the Surveyors direction so that what the Surveyor invented & Mr. Webbe made, the substitute saw putt in worke & nothing else."[87] Meanwhile, craftsmen working for Jones raised formal protests about inadequate pay. The parishioners of nearby St. Gregory's also complained about Jones's predilection for making and executing decisions singlehandedly. Claiming that Jones wished to be "sole monarch" of the restoration, they protested his order to have part of St. Gregory's destroyed without their consent. Reportedly, Jones then "threatened that if the parishioners did not take down the rest of it, then the galleries should be sawed down, and with screws the materials of the said church should be thrown into the street" and warned them that they would be put in the stocks for not complying.[88]

If these difficulties say anything about Jones as a collaborator, it is a small wonder that most of the masque writers with whom he worked chose to defer to him. Samuel Daniel writes in the preface to *Tethys Festival*: "in these things wherein the only life consists in show, the art and invention of the architect gives the greatest grace, and is of most importance: ours, the least part and of least note in the time of the performance thereof; and therefore I have interserted the description of the artificial part, which only speaks M. Inigo Jones."[89] Daniel's rhetoric here is as "proprietary" as Jonson's, in the sense that he gives credit where it is due. However, it is clear that Daniel places himself in a servile position to Jones, prioritizing Jones's work above his own. While Shirley, George Chapman, Aurelian Townshend, and William Davenant do not bow to Jones quite so deeply, they do flatter him in ways that give him the final credit for the masque. Jones and Davenant's *Salmacida Spoila* (1640) ends by crediting Davenant only with words and song, making no claims for Davenant with respect to the production's ultimate success: "'What was spoken or sung, by William Davenant, her Majesty's Servant."[90] The text lists Jones's name

---

[86] Walter H. Godfrey, ed., "Inigo Jones and St. Paul's Cathedral," *London Topographical Record* 18, Cambridge: Cambridge UP, 1942, 41–6, 41.

[87] Godfrey, 42.

[88] Michael Leapman, *Inigo: The Troubled Life of Inigo Jones, Architect of the English Renaissance*, London: Review, 2003, 274.

[89] Samuel Daniel, *Tethys Festival* in *Court Masques: Jacobean and Caroline Entertainments, 1605–1640*, ed. David Lindley, Oxford: Oxford UP, 1995, 54–65, ll. 54–8.

[90] Inigo Jones and William Davenant, *Salmacida Spolia* in *A Book of Masques*, ll. 476–7.

first. After Chapman's *The Memorable Masque* was performed in 1613, Chapman (who, like Jonson, was anxious about protecting his identity as "poet") complained that he wasn't sufficiently paid and thus ranked among "tailors, shoemakers and such snipperados!"[91] Yet nowhere do we see him quarreling with, satirizing, resisting, or denigrating the work of his collaborator. The titlepage also lists Jones first.

In contrast, Jonson satirizes Jones's work as merely mechanical, and thus, inferior. The reconstruction of Paul's began around the same time that *Love's Welcome at Bolsover* was staged (1633), and the instructions annotated by Webb include a list of "Articens of the worke" that looks similar to the dance of mechanics in Jonson's entertainment: mason, carpenter, plumber, smith, and glazier. Accordingly, Jonson constantly uses figures of mechanical labor to put Jones in his place. In-and-In Medlay, Iniquo Vitruvius from *Love's Welcome*, the Cook in *Neptune's Triumph*, and Vangoose in *The Masque at Augurs* all portray Jones as a fool whose pretensions outweigh his true capacities. In "Expostulation with Inigo Jones," Jonson calls him "tire-man, Mountebank,"[92] relegating Jones to the component parts of the masque – costumes, acting, and theater devoid of poetry. Jones subjects poetry, history, and architecture to "Shows! Mighty shows! [. . .]What need of prose, / Or verse, or sense, to express immortal you? / You are the spectacles of state!"[93] "The Town's Honest Man" excoriates Jones's reputation for honesty by portraying Jones as "Iniquity," "Vice," and an Italian mime[94] – all figures which align Jones with empty performativity, playacting without soul. In these portrayals, Jonson draws a paradoxical connection: Jones, as a mere joiner, only works mechanically on earthly material. On the other hand, his labor is empty and lacks real substance. Jonson seems to reserving "true" labor for himself, yet the only thing he seems to be able to define clearly is where – or among whom – the best kind of labor does *not* exist.

With respect to the quarrel's dynamics, the masques become, among other things, meditations on kinds of artistic labor. *The Masque of Queens* represents an important moment in the development of the Jonsonian masque because it is the first to introduce a full antimasque. Earlier masques clearly distribute ownership and authority among collaborators: *Blackness* grants "the bodily part" to Jones, while *Haddington* carefully apportions the work of the production, saving the best (in Jonson's view) for last:

> The two latter [dances] were made by Master Thomas Giles, the two first by Master Hierome Herne, who in the persons of the two Cyclops beat a time to them with their hammers. The tunes were Master Alfonso Ferrabosco's. The device and act of the scene, Master Inigo Jones his, with addition of the trophies. For the invention of the whole and the verses, *Assertor qui dicat esse meos, Imponet plagiario pudorem* [The man who testifies that they are mine will bring shame on the plagiarizer].[95]

---

91 John Gardiner, *The Life and Times of George Chapman, 1559–1634*, Hitchin, UK: The Dogs of Tilehouse Street, 37.

92 8: l. 16.

93 8: ll. 40–42.

94 8: ll. 5, 26–8.

95 Orgel, *Complete Masques*, ll. 298–303.

As is the case in much of Jonson's work, paranoia about plagiarism validates the ultimate authenticity of his verse.[96] Moreover, unlike Jones's other collaborators, Jonson attributes "invention of the whole" to himself.

The Masque of Queens, with the help of similarly value-laden "proprietary" claims, effects a separation of poetry and spectacle. Spectacle retains its power, but the portion of the masque that most highlights Jones's work, the antimasque – or "false masque," as Jonson calls it[97] – draws a picture of malevolence. As A.W. Johnson observes, "The problem of evil passes almost unnoticed in Jonson's earliest masques. Blackness is not malignant, Vulcan is not malign, the Humors and Affections are subsumed into the tempered benevolence of *Hymenaei*, and Hecate frees the masquers from envious night in *The Masque of Beauty*."[98] The antimasque of *Queens*, however, rehearses dangerous, marginal elements that trouble the masque's overall objective of unity, even as the masque finally contains them. Among an "ugly hell . . . flaming beneath,"[99] the witches use magic, sorcery, and illusion as menacing forces. Jonson and Jones offer "twelve women in the habit of hags or witches, sustaining the persons of Ignorance, Suspicion, Credulity, etc., the opposites to good Fame, should fill that part, not as a masque but a spectacle of strangeness, producing multiplicity of gesture, and not unaptly sorting with the current and whole fall of the device."[100] The images of fire and smoke recall Vulcan's workshop and anticipate the malevolent potency in *Mercury Vindicated* and "Execration." Unnatural creators themselves, the witches produce inversions, malformations, misjoinings, and strange and malignant disorder. Deformity and "difformity" appear in their costumes: they come out "all differently attired: some with rats on their head, some on their shoulders; others with ointment pots at their girdles; all with spindles, timbrels, rattles or other venefical instruments, making a confused noise, with strange gestures."[101] Jonson pointedly remarks that the "device of their attire was Master Jones his, with the invention and architecture of the whole scene and machine" while, far from taking credit for the whole, Jonson states that "Only I prescribed them their properties of vipers, snakes, bones, herbs, roots and other ensigns of their magic, out of the authority of ancient and late writers, wherein the faults are mine, if there be any found, and for that cause I confess them."[102] Jonson's appeal to "ancient and learned writers" assures the audience that his small part in the malevolent show is grounded in classical authority, not in whimsy or in any "evil" imaginings of his own. He does not even own the songs, charms, and verses that the witches speak.[103] While claiming his role in the antimasque, he disassociates his poetic labor from it as much as possible.

---

[96] Loewenstein sees Jonson's obsession with plagiarism as another important development in the move toward "possessive" models of authorship. See *Ben Jonson and Possessive Authorship*, chapter four.

[97] Orgel, *Complete Masques*, l. 12.

[98] A. W. Johnson, *Ben Jonson: Poetry and Architecture*, Oxford: Clarendon, 1994, 176.

[99] Orgel, *Complete Masques*, ll. 21–2.

[100] Orgel, *Complete Masques*, ll. 14–19.

[101] ll. 27–30.

[102] ll. 30–35.

[103] In a recent article, Lynn Sermin Meskill plots Jonson's relationship to the witches' antimasque as one that guards his posterity as a poet. Envy is a beguiling, witchcraft-like

When Hecate enters, the witches descend into a confused babble. The lack of verse on the printed page is deliberate, for the witches' talk is "a most piteous hearing, and utterly unworthy any quality of a poem."[104] At the same time, Jonson "trusts" his aristocratic spectators to understand his decision to refrain, commenting that only the lowest individuals would insist on words to accompany the witches: "a writer should always trust somewhat to the capacity of the spectator, especially at these spectacles, where men, beside inquiring eyes, are understood to bring quick ears, and not those sluggish ones of porters and mechanics that must be bored through at every act with narrations."[105] Given Jonson's insistence that spectacle depends on poetry in order for the masque to achieve its highest purpose, his withdrawal from the witches' babble indulges the audience in raw, terrifying spectacle while not allowing the show to have the last word. Furthermore, he draws the elite spectators into a community with himself, much as he does readers elsewhere. Audiences of noble mindset – those to whom Jonson refers elsewhere as the "understanders" – can comprehend spectacle as simply spectacle, something that beguiles in its own right, but is not inherently worthy of poetry. Only "mechanics" cannot grasp the separation between the two; unlike their aristocratic counterparts, they retain no critical judgment. They are like Juniper the Cobbler and the servants in the *The Case is Altered*, who listen with rapt attention to Valentine's stories about foreign theater. Audience members' expectations depend a great deal on their social stations, be they noble "understanders" or "sinfull sixe-penny Mechanicks." With laborers held out as the ultimate foolish spectators, nobles are encouraged to seek the "soul" instead.

By using labor to examine spectatorship, poetry, and creation, Jonson shows himself to be intimately familiar with numerous social contexts and what they might suggest to his audiences. The plays, poems, and masques that represent laborers do so as comic relief, but also as a foil for Jonson and his ideal spectator. The figure of the laborer is a complex one, though, involving a variety of discourses about social privilege and marginality. In the case of the king's favorite masque, *The Gypsies*

---

power that Jonson has to continually stave off in order to vindicate the worth of his text and his reputation. Authorial labor involves resurrecting and continually cutting off those threatening forces: "There is always the danger of the vessel holding reputation leaking and emptying if the poet is not vigilant" (184). This way of reading *Queens* offers a helpful analogue to my own, because both concern the uses of the antimasque for crafting the poet's persona. See "Exorcising the Gorgon of Terror: Jonson's *Masque of Queens*," *ELH* 72:1 (2005), 181–207.

Later, Jonson also credits Jones for the magnificent House of Fame, "The structure and ornament of which (as if professed before) was entirely Master Jones his invention and design. . . . Nor are these alone his due, but divers other accessions to the strangeness and beauty of the spectacle, as the hell, the going about of the chariots, the binding of the witches, the turning machine with the presentation of Fame" (Orgel, *Complete Masques*, ll. 450–2, 465–8). It may be objected fairly that Jonson does not attribute *only* visions of evil to Jones. However, not only is Jonson still disassociating himself from spectacle, but his acknowledgment of Jones is laden with undercurrents of expectation and self-flattery: "All which I willingly acknowledge for him, since it is a virtue planted in good natures that what respects they wish to obtain fruitfully from others they will give ingenuously themselves" (ll. 468–70).

[104] ll. 94–5.

[105] ll. 95–9.

Metamorphos'd, the *displaced* laborer – or "vagrant" or "masterless man" – becomes a dangerous other who is an expert performer.

The Gypsies Metamorphos'd was so popular that it was performed three times; no other masque was ever performed more than twice. Seventeenth century readers would transcribe "The Ballad of Cock Lorel" more than any other poem by Jonson. Jonson was also almost offered a knighthood, was almost made Master of the Revels, and reportedly had his pension increased from 100 to 200 pounds per annum.[106] At nearly 1500 lines of text, it is the longest of his masques. When *Gypsies* was published by John Benson in 1640, it appeared in a duodecimo volume with other texts that expound on the value of true poetic labor over the multitudinous forms of "false" labor in literary and social life: "Execration against Vulcan," "Epigrams," and another translation of *Ars Poetica*, which features on the titlepage as the main text. The volume, which presents a dedicatory poem by Sir Edward Herbert hailing Jonson as the "the *Horace* of our times," showcases the late Jonson's practice of poetic labor. Benson's dedication to "To the Right Honourable Thomas, Lord Windsore" stresses Jonson's "strenuous lines" and "sinewy labours"[107] as a trademark of the author. Barton Holyday's dedication imagines the lines themselves as fit bodies, "Well-bodied works were fram'd, whilst here we see / Their fine Anatomee."[108] Zouch Townley's ode describes the works as having the "strength" to outlast death, when Jonson returns his creative fire to his heavenly muse: "I prophesie more strength to after time, / Whose joy shall call this Isle the Poets Clime, / Because 'twas thine, and unto thee returne / The borrowed flames, with which thy Muse shal burn."[109] As examples of the "learned sweat that makes a language cleane," Jonson's "strong" lines, forged by the muse's fire, mark his text as a product of diligence and true craftsmanship.

Within this volume, *Gypsies* shows the prevailing power of poetry to both create and dissolve theater according to its own determinations. The Patrico, who presides over much of the masque, evokes issues of labor that are close to Jonson in another sense – *scholarly* labor and the blur between legitimate and illegitimate scholarly work. A "patrico" is as a type of hedge-priest – illiterate and inferior to other kinds of clergy. The cony-catching pamphleteers John Awdeley and Thomas Harman mention the patrico; he also appears in the second act of Jonson's *Bartholmew Fair*. Usually accompanied by a "jackman," a rogue who creates counterfeit seals for documents, the patrico's main business was presiding over false marriages. The jackman and the patrico go together because their crimes are of a similar kind: they ape learned labor and the learned professions. The writers of the Elizabethan statute *An Acte for the Punishement of Vacabondes, and for Releif of the Poore and Impotent* (1572) show their awareness of such abuses. Vagabonds subject to discipline include:

> all Comon Labourers being persons able in Bodye using loytering, and refusinge to worke for suche reasonable Wages as ys taxed and comonly gyven in suche partes where such persones do or shall happen to dwell; and all counterfeytures of Lycenses

[106] Riggs, 271.

[107] *Q. Horatius Flaccus: His Art of Poetry, Englished by Ben Jonson*, London, 1640, A5v.

[108] A9.

[109] A10.

> Passeportes and all users of the same, knowing the same to be counterfeyte; and all Scollers of the Universityes of Oxford or Cambridge that goe about begginge, not beinge aucthorysed under the Seale of the said Universities, by the Comyssarye Chauncelour or Vicechauncelour of the same.[110]

It particularly would have alarmed Jonson that learning, that province of strenuous activity, could be counterfeited, for it raises the question of what status learning, ungrounded in other marks of status, can truly have when it can be merely performed. As the alleged proliferation of false "Schollers of the Universityes" challenges the meaning of acquired intellectual prestige, intellectual labor presents one possible area for successful criminal activity, as Jonson (although himself not a university graduate either) is aware in his anxieties about plagiarism.

The Patrico, like other rogues, is an actor. A figure to excite the wrath of any antitheatricalist, he is a vagabond who mimics learning and its privileged offices well enough to blur the line between the performer and the "real" thing. Moreover, the Patrico mocks the rhetoric of professionalism itself by claiming that gypsy life, like any other station, requires special initiation:

> Ye aim at a mystery
> Worthy a history.
> There's much to be done
> Ere you can be a son
> Or a brother o'the moon;
> Tis not so soon
> Acquired as desired.
> You must be bene-bowsy
> And sleepy and drowsy
> And lazy and lousy
> Before ye can rouse ye
> In shape that avows ye [...][111]

The humor in this speech derives from the assertion that a "mystery" – a vocation in which one supposedly exercises diligence – can actually be founded upon idleness, being "sleepy and drowsy / And lazy and lousy." Yet this paradox captures conventional discourse about vagabonds – that they are poor because they are naturally shifty and indolent, not because they are out of work or involuntarily displaced for some other reason.

There is a further cultural link to be made between labor and the gypsy. As Mark Netzloff notes, James I actively persecuted nomadic cultures within the realm, attempting to stabilize what was perceived as slippery cultural difference among certain groups on the island.[112] Along with burgeoning colonial projects abroad and their attendant racialization of labor (in the form of enslavement of African and

---

[110] *Tudor Economic Documents*, 3 vols, ed. R.H. Tawney and Eileen Power, London: Longmans, 1951, 2: 329.

[111] Orgel, *Complete Masques*, ll. 1080–92.

[112] Mark Netzloff, "'Counterfeit Egyptians' and Imagined Borders: Jonson's *The Gypsies Metamorphosed*," *ELH* 68:4 (2001), 763–93, 765.

Atlantic peoples), European governments also turned a regulatory eye on Europeans who did not measure up to the new standard of "Europeanness" as the embodiment of "reason" – all of which was figured in recognizably "white" bodies and customs.[113] In England, domestic groups who failed at Englishness included "rogues" of the supposed criminal underworld, including the "counterfeit Egyptians" – or "gypsies" – who inhabited the borderlands between England and Scotland.

The gypsy and the rogue are linked by the category of labor, for the "counterfeit Egyptians" were thought to be displaced laborers who assumed "Egyptian" identity in order to evade antivagrant statutes.[114] "Counterfeit Egyptians" appear multiple times in rogue literature of the period. Dekker equates the counterfeit Egyptians with "moon-men" (i.e. madmen) and characterizes them as repulsive to putatively normal, morally upright Englishmen:

> They are a people more scattered than Jews, and more hated. Beggarly in apparel, barbarous in condition, beastly in behavior, and bloody if they meet advantage. A man that sees them would swear they had all the yellow Jaundice, or that they were the Tawny Moors' bastards, for no Red-ochre-man carries a face of a more filthy complexion.

But rather than ascribe the behavior of the rogues to any inherent difference, Dekker makes their difference a matter of performance: "they are painted so . . . yet they are not good painters neither, for they do not make faces but mar faces. By a byname they are called Gypsies; they call themselves Egyptians."[115] Dekker's criminals practice illicit performance, as he describes the counterfeit Egyptians in explicitly theatrical terms. They appear almost like a group of traveling players, wearing patchwork costume that reveals their "difformity," inherent lack of unity, and "scattered" existence:

> Their apparel is odd, and fantastic, though it be never so full of rents. The men wear scarves of Calico, or any other base stuff, having their bodies like Morris dancers with bells, and other toys, to entice the country people to flock about them, and to wonder at their fooleries, or, rather, rank knaveries. The women as ridiculously attire themselves, and, like one that plays the Rogue on a Stage, wear rags and patched filthy mantles uppermost, when the undergarments are handsome and in fashion.[116]

Like the rude mechanicals' play, this is bad theater – theater that exposes its own fissures, is rudely comical, and yet at the same time powerfully disruptive.

Labor, vagrancy, and non-British identity converge in the spectacle of the gypsies. The blackened faces of the masque's "Egyptians" are ultimately handled in a similar fashion to those in *The Masque of Blackness* – by restoring them to a reassuring white Europeanness. In each case, the disappearance of the black makeup from the players' "real" faces testifies both to the artificiality of theatrical machinery and its power.

---

[113] Kelvin Santiago-Valles, "'Race,' Labor, 'Women's Proper Place,' and the Birth of Nations," *CR: The New Centennial Review* 3:3 (2003), 47–69, 51.

[114] Netzloff, 773.

[115] *Rogues, Vagabonds & Sturdy Beggars: A New Gallery of Tudor and Early Stuart Rogue Literature*, ed. Arthur F. Kinney, Amherst: U of Massachusetts P, 1990, 243.

[116] Kinney, 244.

The epilogue to *The Gypsies Metamophosed* makes the power of theater explicit, while still assigning the ultimate authority to "the poet." That is to say, theatrical illusion (the province of Jones) may achieve a base rudimentary kind of illusion, but it is the poet (Jonson) who gives the illusion its smooth finish, dissolving the sutures that would betray the artificiality of illusion into, paradoxically, *true* illusion. The epilogue makes this division clear in terms of a distinction between the work of a "barber and tailor" and the "power of poetry":

> [. . .] lest it prove like wonder to the sight
> To see a gypsy, as an Ethiop, white,
> Know that what dyed our faces was an ointment
> Made and laid on by Master Wolf's appointment,
> The court *lycanthropos*, yet without spells,
> By a mere barber, and no magic else.
> It was fetched off with water and a ball,
> And to our transformation this is all,
> Save what the master fashioner calls his;
> For to a gypsy's metamorphosis
> Who doth disguise his habit and his face,
> And takes on a false person by his place,
> The power of poetry can never fail her,
> Assisted by a barber and a tailor.[117]

In the context of delivery to a sophisticated courtly audience, the epilogue comes across as coy, as if the poet's power had really fooled spectators into believing the players to be real Egyptians. More importantly, poetry's "power," guided by its supposed higher purpose, exposes the marginality of the displaced, idle laborer *cum* beggar as an empty pose. When the masque concludes by dispelling the gypsy's power, it also dispels the power of theater in favor of poetry. Given the wanderer's association with idleness in the period, the end of the masque again sets up poetry as a "more removed mystery" and a moral ideal.

Thirteen years later, *Love's Welcome at Bolsover*, with its foolish Vulcan and the character of Coronell Vitruvius, appears as Jonson's final theatrical response to Jones – one that is meant to defeat Jones, but is actually predicated on Jonson's own defeat. The status of Jones's art as theater thus puts Jonson in a bind – as Orgel remarks, Jonson needs spectacle, and yet spectacle constantly threatens to eclipse poetry: "Inigo Jones's masque settings were making the most far-reaching statements about the nature of theatrical illusion, for a realistic scene implies that seeing – not hearing, or understanding – is believing."[118] Jonson's response to the increasing importance of spectacle rests on a paradox – he seeks to expose the illusory, transitory nature of theatrical illusion by insisting on its base, mechanical, bodily qualities, while reserving the essential "soul" of the masque for poetry, the foundation on which theater rests. Jonson's epigram to the Lord Treasurer (printed both in *Underwood* and in the duodecimo volume of *Ars*) perhaps best sums up

---

[117] Orgel, *Complete Masques*, 1385–98.

[118] Orgel, *Complete Masques*, 24.

Jonson's anxiety and the complex discursive web of contradictions on which it is built. Jonson fashions himself as too "humble" to give lavish gifts, unlike "an architect" who erects pyramids and "glorious piles" unto the Lord Treasurer's honor. What Jonson *does* have, however, is a "song" which, done aloud, "may last as long" as those pyramids.[119] In fact, by implication, it will last longer. This is Jonson's aspiration for his own work – that it evade associations with material labor, and yet is solid enough to give his writing some claim to permanence. Much of this validation depends on containing kinds of labor that Jonson deems "mechanical," expunging them through the poet's prerogative, and melting them into a cohesive whole – in short, putting them in their place.

Conclusion: "laborious, yet not base"

If one reads certain masques in isolation from Jonson's whole *oeuvre*, it is easy to think that Jonson merely tries to place himself with royal privilege and that his laboring background is inconsequential. But Jonson imagines the honest practice of poetry, founded upon true diligence, as a special distinction that separates him from men of other professions and estates. The poet decries popular culture and the masses, but he also detaches from the morals of the court and posits himself as their corrector, even as an advisor to the prince who, with the laborious poet as a model, must study to improve his affairs. It is here that the double signification of labor comes into play: on the ground, it is something to leave behind in scorn as one struggles to fulfill one's ambition, yet it is also the realm that informs Jonson's experience as an author who goes from the laboring classes, to education, to an appointment at court. This brings us to "labor" in the second sense – as a store of metaphors that inspires one to reach beyond what is possible in the merely representational fields of theater and print.

The position of the Jonsonian poet is a social one in which the poet holds status in the commonwealth and among great men. Like the "laureates," he is neither aristocratic dilettante nor vulgar upstart. But unlike the rest of the laureates and more like the laboring poets I identify here, labor is a major part of his self-presentation. To borrow from a line from another masque writer of humble origins, Jonson presents himself as "laborious, yet not base."[120] Like Nashe, but more explicitly, he makes laborious writing into a professional platform by rendering his art a special privilege for the initiated few. Orgel writes that Jones's view of the stage as a "unified machine" is "the first step toward the poet's becoming superfluous."[121] Jonson's strategy to combat superfluity is to embrace obscurity as a position of professional superiority.

Yet paradoxically, his intense attention to the idea renders "real" labor mystified and immaterial. The further Jonson divorces his labor from material literary and artistic systems, the more difficult his standard is to grasp. Jonson would have it that "true" labor marks him as honest in a world of mere pretenders. But where, in the end, does "true" labor reside? How can one imitate what is obscure and elusive?

---

[119] 8: ll. 25–9.

[120] George Chapman, *The Memorable Masque* in *Court Masques: Jacobean and Caroline Entertainments*, ed. David Lindley, Oxford: Oxford UP, 1995, 74–91, l. 380.

[121] Ibid.

Is it simply another Platonic "more removed mystery," a goal to be striven for but never seen? Labor is not with the actual laborer, as Jonson's continual disdain for the lower orders suggests. Nor is it with other non-aristocratic writers like Dekker, whose non-gentle status earns him Jonson's ridicule during the War of the Theatres. Nor is it with the "painting and carpentry" of Inigo Jones, whom Jonson sarcastically calls "The Town's Honest Man."[122] So when Jonson is the only figure still standing with a quality he struggles to define, one wonders if his "honest," authentic labor finally is just an abstraction – one that, in the market *and* at court, is as elusive as honesty itself.

I by no means wish to suggest a resolution to this paradox – to do so would take for granted the complexity of the social discourses that Jonson works within, not to mention the fact that all literary careers have a right to their inconsistencies and contradictions. Rather, the paradox marks an important moment in literary history for two reasons. First, Jonson's struggle to both detach from and embrace labor represents an authorial attempt to carve out a place for his profession through the assertion of privilege based on knowledge and skill. As an author who writes for pay, Jonson faces a class-based discourse that manages print participation by encoding it with vulgar economic necessity.[123] Its most extreme implications class writing for pay as wage labor and its authors as wage-earning grunts – mere mechanics who, as Shakespeare writes, "never labor in their minds."[124] Jonson's rhetoric about himself exhibits consistent denial of this status through his persistent denigration of the lower orders as workers, readers, and spectators. Yet the language of labor allows him to claim poetry as legitimate work, as opposed to the amateur, court-centered writing that he *cannot* claim. The author becomes self-consciously unique, exercising a vocation based upon special competence. He is not a writer of poetry, but a "poet," an abstract label that for Jonson is a matter of character as well as of skill.[125] Second, Jonson's insistence on the labor that goes into his writing represents an attempt to call attention to the *process* of writing in addition to its final product. This strategy introduces matters of character – or the "good man" formulation – into writing, making the author's individual disposition, which is ideally oriented toward honest diligence, into a means by which to evaluate the worth of literary texts.

While I am certainly not the first to notice the connection between text and character in Jonson, I wish to emphasize that Jonsonian labor articulates a newly emergent standard of composition, one in which work is embraced over casual

---

[122] "An Expostulation," 8: l. 50; *Epigram* 115.

[123] This term was originally coined by J. W. Saunders in "The Stigma of Print: A Note on the Social Bases of Tudor Poetry," *Essays in Criticism* 1: 2 (1951), 139–64.

[124] William Shakespeare, *A Midsummer Night's Dream*, Act V, Sc. 1.

[125] As Boehrer writes, "The individual constituents of [Jonson's theory of authorship] – the emphasis upon labor, the problematical claims to originality, the concomitant tendency to charge others with plagiarism and incompetence, and the insistence that writing reflects one's inmost self – are not necessarily unique to Jonson; however, Jonson integrates them into a cohesive whole through the sheer energy of assertion and repetition. To this extent, he becomes one of early modern England's first self-conscious representatives of literature as vocation" ("The Poet of Labor," 302–3). I agree with this assessment and hope that this chapter has usefully uncovered some material bases for Jonson's professional claims.

sprezzatura. Any vulgar upstart can produce a poem, but the best poems are informed by something felt but not seen – the habits of diligent composition and the care for learning that informs these habits. The emphasis on the author's character fits with Jonson's faith that the "understanders" will be drawn to his texts, because "character" is a means by which to navigate the multiplicity of authors and readers generated by the market for print and public theater. The experience of purchasing and reading texts is in part indebted to knowing something about authors themselves and the conditions of their writing. For Jonson, the infusion of process into the finished text reintroduces hierarchy into the leveling effects of literary market systems, allowing for new standards of distinction that counter his evident anxiety about participating in these markets. Given his proximity to labor in all its forms, the language of labor becomes the best way of capturing process and developing an incipient sense of authorship as a vocation – a "mystery" of a new kind, one that makes a mere writer of poetry into a "poet" of his own creation.

Chapter 4

The New Bourgeois Hero: The Self-Presentation of John Taylor "The Water Poet"

John Taylor "The Water Poet" (1578–1653)[1] was an admirer of Thomas Nashe. His true inspiration, however, was Ben Jonson. Jonson is a complex enough figure to allow readers of a variety of subject positions to see themselves in him; what Taylor seems to have seen is a model for non-elite authorship. Fourteen years after the appearance of Jonson's first collected works in folio, Taylor issued an edition of his own collected works in an effort to establish himself as a poet of similar stature. Shortly after Jonson made a famous walking tour to Scotland, Taylor undertook a journey of his own, with no money, and made it into the subject of popular travel writing. Jonson was well aware of Taylor's affinity for self-publicizing activities and responded with disdain. This is due in part to the fact that Taylor embraced his lowly roots in ways that Jonson did not, by putting his non-literary identity as a lowly sculler at the forefront of a highly successful literary persona.

The few modern scholars who touch on Taylor's career attribute his uniqueness to exactly these traits.[2] "His 'project' was himself," writes Bernard Capp, who dubs Taylor "the first modern 'personality'."[3] Taylor's novel combination of two kinds of work – rowing and writing – made him a celebrity throughout Britain, and

---

[1] The *DNB* supplies 24 August 1580 as the year for Taylor's birth, while Capp definitively cites the year 1578. Because Capp's biography is the more recent of the two sources, I use his date here.

[2] Earlier critical opinion mixes awe at Taylor's celebrity with disparagement of his literary merit. In his *Brief Lives*, John Aubrey remembers Taylor as "very facetious and diverting company; and for stories and lively telling them, few could outdo him", ed. Richard Barber, Totowa, NJ: Barnes and Noble, 1983, 298. Wallace Notestein remarks upon "how unrhythmical was his verse, how diluted and commonplace his thought," yet numbers him among four "thoroughly English" individuals who "have much to tell of the times in which they lived," *Four Worthies: John Chamberlain, Anne Clifford, John Taylor, Oliver Heywood*, London: Jonathan Cape, 1956, 207. Robert Southey includes him in his *Lives and Works of the Uneducated Poets* as one whose poetry had "no intrinsic merit alone" but is useful "to illustrate the manners of his age"; yet Southey sees Taylor's social status as paradoxically enabling for his career: "if the Water-Poet had been in a higher trade of society, and bred to some regular profession, he would probably have been a much less distinguished person in his generation," ed. J.S. Childers, London: Humphrey Milford, 1925, 86.

[3] Bernard Capp, *The World of John Taylor the Water-Poet*, Oxford: Clarendon, 1994, 196.

he consciously cultivated his fame as he gained the amused notice of audiences from a range of regions and degrees, including servants, urban trades-people, and aristocracy. Alexandra Halasz, remarking on Taylor's publishing activities, calls him a "capitalist" who harnessed print market relations for his own gain. Halasz views his novel decisions as an attempt to imagine unmediated exchange between producers and consumers. As Taylor engages his readers in a contractual exchange relationship, "Discourse itself becomes a form of labor, a matter of time and energy endlessly repeating itself, a continual process of loss and surplus."[4] In other words, Taylor conceived of his authorship as a form of marketplace labor and expected payment from those who benefited from his efforts. What I will add here is that which is suggested, but not elaborated, by Halasz – that Taylor's self-presentation partakes of an emerging democratic discourse, assisted by changes in print market relations, that mirrors larger democratic pressures within the commonwealth itself.

Thus Taylor's approach, while inspired by Jonson's, is more explicitly political. As Capp's biography shows, the revolutionary context for Taylor's career is crucial to his story. Taking Capp's work as a starting point, I will offer detailed readings of Taylor's texts to show how, on the level of textual self-presentation, the affirmation of the common self partakes of the fantasy of democratization as well as its problems. The revolutionary context of Taylor's writings leads him to a place that Jonson never went – to participation in the explosion of print that attended the intense political debates surrounding monarchy, religion, and governance in the mid-seventeenth century. This more overtly politicized setting, along with Taylor's personal experience of the upheaval within his own non-literary occupation, lends further complications to the rhetorical pose of the laborer. Specifically, authorial self-presentation becomes bound up in pressing questions concerning the fate of the commonwealth itself.

Yet in many respects, Taylor's place in early seventeenth-century England's literary culture was singular. Even as he published approximately 150 books and pamphlets over a forty-year span, he spent most of his career either working as a Thames waterman or as an officer in the Watermen's Company. His publications encompass a wide array of popular genres – travel writing, verse essays, miscellanies, political prose, and jest books, to name a few – on an equally vast variety of contemporary topics. Throughout, he makes his identity as a waterman a central feature of his self-presentation, even as he often feels the need to vindicate his association with one of London's rowdiest trades. His works include numerous apologies for watermen, who contemporaries regarded as a shifty and unruly lot, and argues for the importance of watermen's services to the realm. But it is not simply the promotion of his trade that sets him apart, for in doing so, he follows the tradition of the "Elizabethan bourgeois hero-tale" exemplified by the earlier stories and plays of Deloney, Heywood, and Dekker. Taylor departs from these predecessors in that he weaves his menial occupation into an authorial persona that is distinctly self-promoting, individualist, and entrepreneurial. In addition to such attention-grabbing stunts as walking from London to Scotland with no money and cruising down the river in a brown paper boat, he printed many of his works at his own cost and sold

4 Halasz, *Marketplace*, 194.

them through public subscription – an unusual strategy in the early seventeenth century. Even when he did not publish by subscription, Taylor actively courted customers' pocketbooks by elaborate rhetorical strategy.

Another characteristic of Taylor's self-presentation, which is not found among previous writers of popular works about merchants and craftsmen, is his propensity for presenting a portrait of his own inner life as an example to readers. As is often the case with authors who promote their own labor, like Whitney and Jonson, labor and character are linked together to emphasize the process of writing over and above its status as a commodity. The effect is one of literary autobiography. Taylor writes about himself as often as he does the myriad contemporary topics he treats. In particular, his discussions of the watermen's trade nearly always connect the labor of scullery to his own habits of being. For example, the "Apologie for Water-men" in his early book of verse, *The Nipping and Snipping of Abuses* (1614), declares "So well I like it, and such love I owe / Unto it, that I'll fall againe to Rowe: / 'Twill keepe my health from falling to decay, / Get money, and chase Idleness away" (*Workes* 267).[5] In contradistinction to the aristocratic qualities of magnificence, benevolence, liberality, justice, and care for servants that Laura Caroline Stevenson attributes to such tradesmen heroes as Simon Eyre of Dekker's *The Shoemaker's Holiday* and John Winchcombe of Deloney's *Jack of Newberry*,[6] Taylor presents honest labor as conducive to physical health, industry for its own sake, and modest earning. Moreover, these virtues represent the fulfillment of the market laborer as his best self, and they become most pronounced in his encounters with customers. Stevenson notes that the heroes of the Elizabethan tales were never lauded for their mercantile activities, but only for "gentle" characteristics like martial valor, generosity, and poise. As we shall see, Taylor's attitudes toward labor bespeak an entirely different set of standards. In a move that exemplifies Agnew's observation that the market eventually saturates all social and economic relations, Taylor posits behavior in the marketplace as the essential test of virtue for subjects of all classes and occupations.

Perhaps more than any other case in this book, Taylor's career shows that rooting one's authorship in labor is necessarily fraught with contradiction, because early modern labor itself shifted between traditional and wage-earning models, even within the same profession. My analysis of Taylor's attitudes toward textual labor will include several interrelated developments. First is his involvement with the Watermen's Company, reputed to be a particularly turbulent company comprised of coarse, obstreperous men in dire need of surveillance and discipline. Although

---

[5] Unless otherwise noted, all quotations from modern rerprints of Taylor's works have been drawn from the following two collections: *Works of John Taylor, The Water-Poet, Comprised in the Folio Edition of 1630*, 5 vols (Manchester: Spenser Society, 1869), whose volumes were published by the Spenser Society as issue numbers 2, 3, and 4; and *Works of John Taylor, The Water Poet, Not Included in the Folio Volume of 1630*, 5 vols (Manchester: Spenser Society, 1870–78), whose volumes were published as issue numbers 7, 14, 19, 21, and 25. Material taken from the original texts (i.e. not from the Spenser Society reprints) will be cited parenthetically by signature number.

[6] Laura Caroline Stevenson, *Praise and Paradox: Merchants and Craftsmen in Elizabethan Popular Literature*, Cambridge: Cambridge UP, 1984, 6.

many companies faced internal divisions as the nation moved toward civil war, as a ruler Taylor witnessed firsthand a member-led revolution against the oligarchic power of the company officers in the 1640s. I read the dissention in the company, and Taylor's responses to it, as an interruption of equilibrium between the old ideal of guild fellowship and the new realities of economic competition during the early seventeenth century.[7]

Taylor's role in the Watermen's Company was that of governor, so not surprisingly, he looked with dismay upon the members' protests and viewed them as part of a larger trend of rebellion against authority. Yet at the same time, Taylor was imagining a more horizontal form of social organization in his publishing activities. I will read Taylor's early pamphlets to explore how he conceived of his role as a literary producer in a total social field of potential customers. Here, despite the conservative politics we see in Taylor elsewhere, he actively questions pre-capitalist notions of social privilege by subordinating all classes to the marketplace as a test of honesty. Furthermore, he promotes free will, honest labor, thrift, industry, and the affirmation of ordinary subjects and their experiences.

Then I will return to a discussion of Taylor's social conservatism and the confrontations that his embrace of the market pose to his concomitant belief in a natural order of hierarchy and obedience. While it is unsafe to view Taylor's fantasy of social leveling in the marketplace as a conscious political program, he nonetheless raises the question of political self-determination in doing so. The radical religious reformers and anti-Royalists who surfaced in England during the last years of Taylor's career saw this possibility as well, but Taylor reacted to their activities with horror and derision in pamphlets against sectarian tradesmen and mechanics who took up preaching. Also, he linked the success of these reformers to their ability to manipulate an "unlearned," gullible reading public – the very field of purchasers to which he could attribute his own success as an author. Like all of the cases in this study, Taylor's has compelling paradoxes. If, as Frederick Jameson suggests, contradiction can be read as a response to the losses incurred by social change,[8] then the contradictions so conspicuous in Taylor should point the way to what exactly was changing, and why.

"The Honest Vocation": Taylor and the Watermen's Company

If it occurred to anyone before Taylor to write a tale in praise of the civic virtues of a waterman, that author would have had little on which to draw. The primary question at the heart of the Elizabethan bourgeois hero-tale concerns the role of wealth in social status. For this reason, merchants and tradesmen – producers and sellers of

[7] I borrow this language from George Unwin, who views early modern guild identity as having a dynamic of "free fellowship" where "the upward thrust of the new life and the downward pressure of the old formula" inadvertently promote the liberty of the individual to the degree that free fellowship "may be an aimless and even anarchic social force," *The Gilds and Companies of London*, New York: Barnes and Noble, 1964, 12.

[8] Frederic Jameson, *The Political Unconscious: Narrative as a Socially Symbolic Act*, Ithaca: Cornell UP, 1981, 166–7, 253–4, 296.

commodities at home and abroad, and generators of great wealth – provide the writers of these tales with their heroes. The typical Elizabethan narrative charts the rise of its hero from humble means to the possession of great capital, and perhaps later, high office in City government or a seat in Parliament. In reality, the riches of these tradesmen were an immense source of civic pride for Londoners. Thus it is through the virtuous acquisition and use of wealth that the merchants and craftsmen of these tales provide extravagant feasts for apprentices and monarchs alike, intermarry with landed aristocracy, or obtain a costly, influential office like that of Lord Mayor or alderman.[9]

By contrast, like all of the professions I have examined here, the waterman's work afforded no opportunity for the accumulation of capital – thus the process of the work, rather than the end result, becomes an important measure of the work's worth. While the skillful sale and trade of commodities promised substantial monetary gain, the performance of a mere service, such as transportation, could not. Using no raw material but a boat, an oar, and his own physical strength, the waterman ferried passengers between the north and south banks of the Thames for a modest fare agreed upon in advance. Even after their incorporation as a company, watermen shared the status of porters and lightermen as laborers with no need of merchants of middlemen; for this reason, George Unwin describes the Watermen's Company as "more of a federation than a single gild."[10] Taylor complains of the status difference between watermen and merchants in a mock-heroic pamphlet entitled *The Shilling or, the Travailles of Twelve-pence* (1621). The emblem on the title page depicts a coin with wings flying away from an oar, shovel, and flail to a "Furre-gowned" alderman. The ensuing lines explain, "Money to the Mizers Coffers flies. / Whilst unto those that paines and labor take, / It doth a creeping, sleeping dull pace make" (A1^{v}). Had they experienced similar poverty in their trades, John Winchcombe and Simon Eyre could never have exercised the virtues that they exhibit in their respective tales.[11]

Another characteristic of watermen that rendered them unfit for the lavish display of pseudo-aristocratic "gentility" is the fact that members of the Watermen's Company never enjoyed the same citizen status, or "freedom of the city," as members of the more prestigious guilds. During times of war, all watermen except the company rulers were eligible for conscription into the navy. Freedom of the city would have exempted them from impressments. During the reign of Elizabeth, the press gangs worked constantly; Taylor himself was pressed seven times. So while apprentices, but not freemen, in other companies could be pressed into service, watermen enjoyed no similar protection. Furthermore, unlike other company members with

[9] Stevenson, *Praise and Paradox*, 1–27.

[10] Unwin, *The Gilds and Companies of London*, 365.

[11] I describe the waterman's *typical* situation here, but on rare occasion, opportunities for corruption presented themselves to those who enjoyed positions with the monarch or gentry. Shortly after his apprenticeship, Taylor served as "bottleman" to the Tower, a job that involved bringing cargoes of wine into the river and asserting the Lieutenant of the Tower's right to two large leather bottles. Given the bottleman's proximity to stores of saleable goods, it was possible to buy small wares from mariners and resell them for a profit by evading Customs. *Taylors Farewell to the Tower-Bottles* (1622) relates the story of his service and asserts that he never engaged in such practices while in office, although he could have.

the "freedom," they typically did not engage in any other incorporated trade. These factors further constrained the possibility of a waterman amassing wealth.

Just as Whitney and Nashe both adopt marginal identities, Taylor's waterman status is marginal as well. The conditions of the watermen's incorporation marks a clear difference between their company and the more celebrated trades: it was the only company formed by Act of Parliament for the express purpose of controlling its members' behavior. While commodity producers were assets for society, the watermen were more like a liability in their legendary fondness for drinking brawling, swearing, lying, and wagering. Moreover, they were known to quarrel with customers and with one another over fares, pitch for new fares once they got passengers into the middle of the river, and rob, assault, push overboard, or even murder those who refused to pay a higher fare. The reactions of contemporaries who wrote about this behavior range from disgust to outright alarm. For example, Wye Saltonstall writes, "When you come within ken of them, you shall hear a noise worse than the confusion of Bedlam," and concludes, "the oars think you no gentleman."[12] Playwright William Davenant corroborates this opinion by remarking that watermen treat passengers with disturbing familiarity and characterizes the passenger as a virtual prisoner to the waterman's greed.[13] Thomas Overbury, in his *Characters* (1615), relates that the waterman is "evermore telling strange news, most commonly lies" and, like the players he transports to and from the south bank theaters, his "daily labour teaches him the art of dissembling."[14] In the cony-catching pamphlet *Greenes Ghost* (1626), Samuel Rowlands remarks that watermen "will be readie & very diligent for anie man, until they can get them to their boates, but when they come to land to paie their fare, if you paie them not to their owne contentments, you shall be sure of some gird or other."[15] Thus, for most observers, to attribute "gentle" civic virtue to a waterman would have stretched the limits even of fantasy.

The 1555 "Act touching Watermen and Bargemen upon the River Thames" similarly describes them as dangerous, immoral, and even vagrant. The Act proclaims that watermen, "for lack of good government and due order," routinely take advantage of nobles and commoners alike, who are "robbed and spoiled of their goods, and also drowned" and "daily put in fear and peril of their lives."[16] A description of the "rude, ignorant, and unskilful" watermen estimates that they have "for the most part been masterless men, and single men."[17] Being both "masterless" and "single," they operate outside of the systems of family and service. Further, their lack of commitment to a stable, predictable, and easily identifiable course of life is evidenced by a makeshift economic existence in which they survive by

[12] Qtd. in Capp, 10.

[13] Capp, 10.

[14] Sir Thomas Overbury, *The Miscellaneous Works in Prose and Verse of Sir Thomas Overbury, Knt.*, ed. Edward F. Rimbault, London: John Russell Smith, 1856, 135.

[15] Samuel Rowlands, *The Complete Works of Samuel Rowlands, 1598–1628*, Glasgow: Hunterian Club, 1880, 38.

[16] Qtd. in Henry Humpherus, *History of the Origin and Progress of the Company of Watermen and Lightermen of the River Thames, with numerous historical notes*, 3 vols, Sudbury, UK: Lavenham, 1999, 1: 101.

[17] Qtd. in Humpherus, 1: 100.

"all kinds of occupations and faculties" and "do work at their own hands" while performing none of this work with skill.[18] The habit of working in many trades at once, all "out of the rule and obedience of any honest master and governor"[19] makes watermen a "great and evil example for others; yet they are also guilty of idleness, as they waste "the most part of their time . . . [in] dicing and carding, and other unlawful games."[20] The Act presents the additional complaint that when watermen are faced with impressment into naval service, they "absent and convey themselves into the country, and other secret places, practising their robberies and felonies, and other evil, detestable facts."[21] In short, watermen exhibit a combination of criminal attributes: idleness, a propensity to wander, an affinity for telling tales, and disrespect for passengers and their property.

By creating a Watermen's Company, then, the Act imposed oligarchic rule on a group of apparently shiftless individuals and gave them a chance at civic respectability. The authors mandated a period of apprenticeship for all who rowed on the river and further decreed that all watermen would henceforth be ruled by eight "householders . . . the most wise, discreet, and best sort of watermen" to be appointed annually by the Lord Mayor and Court of Aldermen.[22] As with other companies, the rulers were invested with the authority to discipline all members who took their individual earning capacities into their own hands. The rulers would hold the power to limit and assess all fares, as they did with a published fare table they implemented in 1559.[23] Any freeman who touted for fares above the set price was liable to a forty-shilling fine and half a year in prison.[24]

Taylor served as an overseer once in 1630 and for two more terms in 1638–40, once again that decade as a company assistant, and once as the company's clerk in 1642. Like most older watermen, he no longer rowed during his tenure in office. But because of his celebrity, he was well positioned to advocate for his company. Two major developments threatened the trade in the early seventeenth century: the building of theaters on the north side of the river and the spread of hackney coaches throughout the metropolis. On these issues, Taylor often directly petitioned the king or Parliament. But his activism also included writing pamphlets – some serious, some humorous – for general distribution to the public. The prose pamphlet *The World runnes on Wheeles* (1631) employs humor and hyperbole to win widespread sympathy for the company's campaign against hackney coaches. Punning on his own name, Taylor employs a self-promoting gesture by likening the piece to a trusty, well-made garment: "I have embroidered it with mirth, Quilted it with materiall Stuffe, Lac'd it with similitudes; Sowed it with comparisons, and in a word, so playd the Taylor with it, that I thinke it will fitte the wearing of any honest mans Reading,

---

18 Ibid.

19 Ibid.

20 Ibid.

21 Humpherus, 1: 101.

22 Humpherus, 1: 102. In 1603, "An Act concerning wherrymen and watermen" would increase the apprenticeship to seven years. See Humpherus 1: 159.

23 Humpherus, 1: 110.

24 Humpherus, 1: 106.

Attention, and Liking" (A4). His appeal classes coaches with other signs of wasteful, destructive consumership; for example, the coach signifies "sloath and effeminacie" (B4) and is compared to a whore. Coaches are also "toyes and trifles . . . whose beginning is Folly, continuance Pride and whose end is ruine" (A8^{v}). The pamphlet implicates the entire world in the noise, destruction, and conspicuous consumption wrought by hackney coaches; this point is made in the titlepage, where a sideways illustration shows the devil and a whore pulling a globe in a coach to portray "The World turn'd upside downe, as all men know" (A1^{v}) (Figure 4.1).

Taylor also pressed the watermen's causes in a more sober tone, as in one earlier piece, *The Cause of the Watermen's Suit Concerning Players* (1613). Here he casts the threatened northward migration of the theaters as an economic competition between actors and watermen. Players, he argues, deal in mere entertainment and pleasure; watermen, however, provide a necessary service, and therefore, the realm should put their concerns first. While conceding that "there are many rude, uncivil fellows in our Company," he asserts that watermen comprise "the greatest Company" and challenges readers to "consider other trades and faculties of higher account, and I am sure they will come short in honesty, perhaps not of watermen, but of the honest vocation of a waterman."[25] Reversing characterizations of rowing as conducive to deceit, Taylor argues that scullery is in fact more conducive to honesty than any other trade. As he champions "so useful and necessary" a trade and the worthiness of its members, he asserts that "many of the meanest scullers that rows on the Thames, was, is, or shall be if occasion serve, at command to do their prince and country more service, than any of the players."[26] These very arguments, made in prose, would be versified a year later in the "Apologie for Water-men."

Taylor's writing and petitioning achieved notable short-term results. However, these small successes ultimately failed to contain the building of new theaters and the spread of coaches. The trade also faced another problem: the long years of peace under the early Stuart monarchs meant that fewer watermen served abroad in the navy, and thus, there was an oversupply of them on the river. In the reign of James I, the City already had proven itself increasingly reluctant to extend financial help to the company. When the river froze in 1608, the Lord Mayor turned down the Company's request for frost relief, reasoning that if the City helps one trade, it "must do the like for all." Although the City eventually authorized the delivery of a small sum to the Company, the Lord Mayor prayed that "the watermen might be left to help themselves by their own industry, in the same manner as other manual trades."[27] As a result of these mounting economic pressures, business slackened and competition among individual watermen intensified.

Some watermen viewed these problems as the rulers' failure to protect their interests. Their resentment culminated in a "democratic revolution" in the 1640s that

---

25 Humpherus, 1: 184–5.

26 Humpherus, 1: 184.

27 Qtd. in W. Culling Gaze, *On and Along the Thames: James I, 1603–1625*, London: Jarrold and Sons, 1900, 374–5.

The World runnes on VVheeles: Or

Oddes, betwixt *Carts* and *Coaches*.

LONDON
Printed by E. A. for *Henry Gosson*. 1623.

The meaning of the *Embleme*.

THe *Deuill*, the *Flesh*, the *World* doth Man oppo
And are his mighty and his mortall foes:
The *Deuill* and the whorish *Flesh* drawes still,
The *World* on Wheeles runs after with good wi
For that which wee the World may iustly call
(I meane the lower Globe Terrestriall)
Is (as the *Deuill*, and a *Whore* doth please)
Drawne here and there, and euery where, with
Those that their Liues to vertue *heere* doe frame,
Are in the *World*, but yet not of the same.
Some such there are, whom neither *Flesh* or
Can wilfully drawe on to any euill;
But for the *World*, as 'tis the *World*, you see
It *Runnes on Wheeles*, and who the Palfreys be
Which Embleme, to the Reader doth display.
The *Deuill* and the *Flesh* runnes swift away,
The Chayn'd ensnared *World* doth follow fast,
Till All into Perditions pit be cast.
The Picture topsie-turuie stands kew waw;
The World turn'd vpside downe, as all men

Figure 4.1 John Taylor. *The World runnes on Wheeles: or Oddes, betwixt Carts and Coaches*. (1623)

would permanently change the company's organization.[28] Around 1630, freemen and apprentices of numerous London companies complained against their rulers, perceiving them as out of touch with the whole of the membership. In the Watermen's Company, such complaints already had been brewing for at least a decade. In 1622, a dissident member tried to have all the rulers arrested for corruption. Nine years later, after a number of watermen faced naval conscription, one Joshua Church led a group of them in accusing the rulers of forging royal warrants so that they could extort bribes from men facing impressment. The following year, Church accused Taylor himself of accepting a ten-pound bribe. It was not the only time Taylor met such accusations. During the campaign against the players, Taylor faced charges that he had taken bribes from players whom he had befriended while on the river. Also, when a 1636 royal proclamation banned hackney coaches from carrying passengers on any journey less than three miles, many members were disappointed that the ban was not more thorough and reacted by accusing Taylor of fraud over his expenses.[29]

The 1640 calling of Parliament led to protests in many companies against their rulers, while among the watermen, Church and his fellow dissidents protested the rule of oligarchs whom they had never elected. Although the rulers attempted to reassert their control through their own petitions to Parliament, the reformers publicly accused the current rulers of fraud and oppression and pressed the Commons to permit company elections in which all watermen could vote. The rulers answered these allegations by declaring that the agenda of Joshua Church and his ilk had reduced an otherwise respectable trade to anarchy. Indeed, many of the reformers talked of lynching the rulers, whose authority had, by then, all but collapsed.[30]

Taylor felt that no officers in any company were obliged to account for their actions to the membership. He scoffed at the reformers and particularly at his old enemy, Church. In his writings, he portrayed them as threatening to all order. In a 1642 petition to the Commons, he describes them as men who had "boasted, that now during this parliament-time, they were free from all Government" and "would cut some of your petitioners in pieces" (A2). In another pamphlet, *John Taylors Manifestation and Just Vindication Against Joshua Church* (1642), Taylor accuses Church of foul-mouthed malice – a legacy handed down from Church's mother, whose "Baboon Monkeyfied visage" he inherited as well (*Works* 19: 2). Taylor imagines that Church was bound apprentice to her and, to obtain his freedom, spent everything he earned at the alehouse, forcing her to enter one of the company's almshouses as he slept in a pile of dung and earned the nickname "Vermin" (19: 3). "In these kinde of courses you came to be a Waterman" proclaims Taylor, as he purports to expose Church as unworthy of the "honest" trade (19: 4). He includes Church's cohort in this accusation, mentioning one dissenter who served "but 4 years Apprentiship in all, for before 7 years were expired he had two wives" and then "turned Recusant . . . and said lately, that there would be Roman Catholickes

[28] The term "democratic revolution" is suggested by C. O'Riordan in "The Democratic Revolution in the Company of Thames Watermen, 1641–2," *East London Record* 6 (1983), 17–27.

[29] Humpherus 229–37, Gaze 381–2, Capp 31–3.

[30] Humpherus 233–7, Capp 146–7.

enough left as might drink a health to all our confusions" (19: 3). By lumping low breeding, railing, adultery, and dishonesty together with the Catholic threat, Taylor presents the most alarming possible picture of the reformers to his audience. He suggests that the disorder that lurks behind the "cloake of Reformation" has begun on the river, which has become "a Wildernesse: for there is neither command nor obedience" there (19: 5). The disorder that Church has wrought upon the company, Taylor further implies, will inevitably corrupt the entire realm. But his arguments ultimately failed to persuade. In February of 1642, the City ordered changes to the Company's electoral rules: each year, fifty-five watermen would choose twenty candidates for office, and from this group, the aldermen would choose eight new rulers. Taylor's association with the company ended.

The extent to which the reforms truly were democratic in the end is debatable, particularly since several of the reformers once had been rulers themselves and neither Church, nor any of his close associates, was elected to office. The latter fact indicates that Taylor's portrayal of Church as violent and disreputable may have had some basis in truth. "The protest movement," writes Capp, "was most probably a powerful but unstable alliance between genuine reformers and the disorderly elements for which the trade had long been notorious."[31] To this "unstable alliance," I would add several more. First, because many of the inter-company protest movements of the 1640s were influenced by radical Protestantism and its democratic implications, the reform movement can be read in part as a conflict between the drive for political self-determination and a belief in absolute order, authority, and governance – that is, "rulers" and "ruled." It seems that both the dissidents and the rulers perceived democracy and oligarchy as finally irreconcilable: oligarchy precluded democracy, while democracy threatened structures of governance, and thus became "anarchy." Second, despite Unwin's description of the company as a "federation" of men who retained a certain equality,[32] hierarchies clearly existed in the company's organization. Although the officers ruled over a relatively poor trade, they were nonetheless elected by the City and, in that sense, connected to the civic elite. Hence, the rulers also viewed themselves as having a certain prerogative. Finally, we can discern an old ideal of fellowship cracking under the new reality of economic competition that watermen felt both from other trades and amongst themselves. Taylor, like other laboring writers, will find himself reconsidering community in light of a new set of socioeconomic relations that pressures its participants into increased self-interest.

Taylor, like many company rulers, was a staunch Royalist and Anglican; thus it is not surprising that, after leaving the company, he began a successful career as a Royalist pamphleteer. He no doubt viewed the dissention in his company as part of the larger "rebellion" he witnessed taking place against the authority of the monarch and the English church. Yet prior to the 1640s, he frequently writes in an anti-hierarchical and democratic vein, particularly when he imagines his place in society as both a waterman and a producer of literature. As I have detailed here, one of the challenges that the laboring author faces is the pressure to re-organize the terms of literary professionalism in a way that designates him or her as virtuous, diligent,

[31] 150.
[32] 354.

and honest. In this instance, Taylor works toward a notion of individual virtue that relies upon self-knowledge and proving oneself in an economic and social landscape saturated with deceit. Because this suggests values like self-determination and horizontal forms of dependency, it is initially difficult to reconcile with Taylor's faith in a vertical social order. To understand the dynamics of this apparent contradiction, we shall now turn to the first side of the equation.

"Plain Dealing": The Self-Marketing Self

From the beginning of his literary career, Taylor used his occupation as a waterman to cultivate the novelty that would later gain him celebrity status. A few outstanding examples include the title page of his first book of verse, *The Sculler, Rowing from Tiber to Thames* (1612),[33] which shows a simple woodcut of the author rowing his boat through calm waters to deliver a "hotch-potch" of sonnets, satires, and epigrams. The emblem of a later book, *Taylor's Motto* (1621), depicts the author steadfastly standing on a rock in a storm-tossed sea, with an oar in one hand, an empty purse in the other, and a book balanced on a globe between his legs. The title page from the folio edition of his collected works, *All the Workes of John Taylor The Water Poet* (1630), presents a portrait of the author flanked by oars and fish, with another picture of two rowers ferrying a man across the waters. The regular use of the name "Water Poet" alone demonstrates the marketing potential that Taylor saw in the novel pairing of his manual and intellectual occupations.

The self-conscious visibility of Taylor's waterman status suggests how Taylor, unlike Deloney, promoted his own authorial ambitions by creating a self-image for public consumption. If he was, as Capp suggests, a "modern" personality, then Taylor's self-conscious image-making testifies to the inherently public quality of this personality. The implications of the plebian self-image for Taylor's handling of print market relations are several. First, it allows him to defend his experience as a waterman and reflect on his role as a manual laborer. In other words, by announcing himself as an "author" while refusing to abandon his humble occupation, he constructs a situation in which it is necessary, as well as informative and entertaining, to write the life of the plebian self for a wide range of audiences. In a mode akin to the spiritual autobiographies that proliferated during these decades, the "inner life" of the ordinary subject becomes a topic worth exploring. As with Whitney, the affirmation of everyday experience lends itself to a reflection on the role of laborers and producers in social life – not as contributors to the glory of the city and the realm, but as providers of everyday goods and services in a market context. Because Taylor thinks of himself as a laborer – whether it be as a provider of transport or a producer of texts – he positions his customers as consumers who engage him in horizontal, not vertical, relationships of dependency, as Whitney does when she posits George Mainwaring as a "friend" rather than as a patron. Furthermore, the exchange of money for goods and services requires "honesty" on both sides in order to work, and all kinds of customers are subject to the same expectations. Similar to

[33] The 1614 edition of *The Sculler* is renamed *Taylor's Water-worke*.

Jonson's fantasy of "understanders" among the rabble of illiterates, Taylor's own fantasy places himself and his readers on equal terms, striking a bargain that is putatively pure, compared to the deceit and dissembling so prominent in the literary marketplace.

Michael Mascuch offers a helpful model for connecting non-aristocratic self-fashioning with marketplace exchange. He calls autobiography "a peculiarly modern institution" and proposes that a concept of individualist self-identity is necessary to write in an autobiographical vein; the individualist subject must have the capacity to think of himself as his own maker, or *telos*.[34] For the "self-maker" and his audience, the question "who am I?" holds value and meaning, and the self is fundamentally *capable*, even if damaged in practice. Thus, self-professed marginality, so often invoked by the laboring authors I treat here, is turned toward crafting a virtuous self-image. But the expression of the individualist self in discourse also relies upon audience response, "and so will be a unique product of the public situation of its bearer."[35] Moreover, the public promotion of the individual requires a set of material and social conditions to make this kind of representation possible. Taylor's propensity for writing autobiographically is unique among members of his lowly station. The witnesses of his public self-image come not from a coterie, but from the field of consumers who engage him in marketplace transactions. As in the case of Whitney, Taylor utilizes the market to create a new kind of textual community – not a manuscript-based coterie, but one in which producers and consumers are sharply defined in a relationship of exchange. In the epilogue to *The Pennyles Pilgrimage* (1618), Taylor connects his own subjective experience to the audience's judgment: "what mine eyes did see, I doe beleeve; / And what I doe beleeve, I know is true: / And what is true, unto your hands I give, / That what I give, may be beleev'd of you" (G3). "Belief" binds the writer and his audience in a contract of horizontal exchange: "Thus Gentlemen, amongst you take my ware, / You share my thankes, and I your moneyes share" (G3). If the individualist self needs mutuality and reciprocity to register itself, then in Taylor's case, it is the network of purchasers that validates the public self-image and gives it its chance for expression.

These are fundamentally different values than those of the quasi-feudal Elizabethan order, with its emphasis on hierarchies of dependency. It seems that Taylor found the witnesses to his self-presentation on the riverbanks as well as in the bookstalls, for he uses the same standards – honesty, transparency, choice, mutuality, and trust – to describe his encounters in each venue. These values become the test by which to judge a person's character, regardless of occupation or degree. Although Taylor sometimes pitched for aristocratic patronage, particularly early in his career, he more frequently aims his work at "everybody": for example, "To Every Body" in *Taylor's Motto*, to "Most Mightie, Catholicke (or Universall Mounsier Multitude" in *Taylors Water-worke* (1614), to "no matter who" in *A Common Whore* (1622), to "any Reader He or Shee, / It makes no matter what they be" in *An Errant Thiefe* (1625), and "To the World" in his collected works. Also, he often pokes fun at

[34] Michael Mascuch, *Origins of the Individualist Self: Autobiography and Self Identity in England, 1591–1791*, Stanford: Stanford UP, 1996, 7.

[35] Mascuch, 18.

traditional patronage relationships, as in *Sir Gregory Nonsense His Newes from no place* (1622). The pamphlet's address "To Nobody" accompanies another dedication to "(Sir Reverence) Rich Worshipped, Master Trim Tram Senceles, great Image of Authority" and addresses the fake nobleman as "Most Honorificicabilitudinatatibus" (A3). Here, the deference inherent in patronage relationships is held up to ridicule; the fake dedication comically demonstrates how exaggeration becomes tired convention in a hierarchical literary system – a convention that, Taylor imagines, the market promises to reinvent.

The language of inclusiveness that we find in these addresses also defines Taylor's approach to the trade of scullery. In a defense of watermen from *Taylor's Motto*, he remarks, "Some say we carry whores and theeves. 'Tis true, / I'l carry those that said so, for my due: / Our boats like hackney horses, every day, / Will carry honest men and knaves, for pay." Noting that the sun shines alike on all people, he argues that the market's bounty, like that of nature, should be available to everyone: "All tradesmen sell their ware continually, / To whores, or knaves, or any that will buy. / They ne'r examine people what they are: / No more can we, when we transport a fare" (D6^{v}). In the same terms, Taylor was fond of describing his writings as a "boat" for anyone's use, as in *Taylor's Water-worke*: "my Boat (like a Barbers shop) is readie for all commers be they of what Religion they will, paying their fare" (A2). This egalitarian philosophy of commerce articulates, for Taylor, an ideal marketplace scenario.

However, this standard also calls for trust on both sides, which Taylor realized was not always borne out in practice. In the "Apologie for Watermen," Taylor defines rowing as an honest trade precisely because it deals in *services* and not goods – services are transparent, whereas goods hide the intentions of their producers and thus hold an infinite capacity to deceive: "[Watermen] keepe no shops, nor sell deceitfull wares, / But like to Pilgrims, travell for their fares" (*Workes* 267). In *The Watermen's Suit Concerning Players*, Taylor argues for the worthiness of scullery over the retail trades:

> If a waterman would be false in his trade, I muse what falsehood he could use, he hath no weights or measures to curtail a man's passage, but he will land a man for his money, and not bate him an inch of the place he is appointed: His shop is not dark like a woollen draper's on purpose, because the buyer shall not see the coarseness of the cloth, or the falseness of the color: no, his work and ware is seen and known, and he utters it with the sweat of his brows.[36]

The open river provides the waterman with his shop, and all his labor takes place at the very moment that the customer enjoys the service for which he or she paid. The transaction between a sculler and his passenger is putatively pure because it is transparent and unmediated. It is particularly important to Taylor that the waterman's labor is "seen and known," because if his labor is watched, then the customer may trust his or her own eyes. An actual retail object, by contrast, would obscure the labor that went into its production, putting the buyer in the position of blindly trusting a possibly untrustworthy merchant. The cultural fact of this untrustworthiness in the trade of commodities is what fuels Taylor's fantasy of direct exchange.

[36] The entire text is reproduced in Humpherus, 1: 186.

To Taylor, then, honest labor is that which can be shown to potential buyers; labor speaks for itself through its very visibility, as when the sculler "utters" it "with the sweat of his brows." Without this transparency, exchange is a hazardous business. But as Taylor also is aware, it is more difficult to make *textual* labor transparent, because the final outcome of writing is, of course, a book. Taylor wrestles with this difficulty when promoting his works – hence a tendency to dress them in "plain" shows that bespeak his honesty. In every such case, Taylor assures his readers that the text directly reflects his worthy intentions. But these displays of virtue also depend upon the customer's ability to see things rightly and judge accordingly. In the prefatory material to *Taylors Travels to Prague in Bohemia* (1621), he imagines a buyer examining the book among numerous other wares in the stalls, and remarks, "because I would not have you either guld of your mony, or deceived in expectation, take notice of my plain dealing" (*Works* 4: 574). When he describes *The World runnes on Wheeles* as a garment that will "fitte the wearing of any honest mans Reading, Attention, and Liking," he asks the "honest" man to examine the workmanship for himself and consider it suitable for his own wearing (A4). In short, Taylor's ideal marketplace scenario assumes that the buyer will navigate the world of false commodities by self-selecting: in a very Jonsonian formulation, honest books attract honest people. The *Motto*'s emblem allows the book and the oar to "plainely shew" themselves alongside a book dressed in "plaine dealing Satyrs Equipage" (A2^{v}). Yet as the emblem supplies visual evidence of the book's integrity, Taylor also hopes to preserve his book for those who will understand the signs according to his intentions: he aims "not to every Reader . . . But only unto such as can Read right" (A3). So casting his net wide enough to include "Every Body" involves a leap of faith: that the "right" readers will emerge from the faceless mass of purchasers to validate his true intentions through their own ability to discern truth.

At first, the idea of "right" and "wrong" readers sounds like another status distinction, for "right" discernment presumes a certain level of literacy. Indeed, it is true that Taylor sought the attention of upper-middle class urban merchants (and of course, aristocrats inclined toward patronage) and disdained the illiterate rabble. Further, as the publication of his collected works in folio attests, he wanted to be viewed as a poet, not as a penny scribbler. However, the initial courting of audiences that Taylor undertakes in his prefatory material rests on an egalitarian and inclusive premise, because the capacity to read "right" depends not only on literacy, but on an *inner* quality of good judgment rather than on outward marks of distinction that affiliate one with a certain socioeconomic class. Everyone gets a chance at market participation through the purchase of the pamphlets, and everyone has a choice to act honestly. For an expression of this view, we may again consult *The Watermen's Suit Concerning Players*:

> we know that men are free to buy their cloth at *what drapers they please*, or their stuffs at *which mercers they will*, *what tailor they list* make their garments; and *what cook they like* may dress their meat: and so forth, of all functions *every man is free to make his choice*; and so amongst watermen, *men may take whom they please*, because they are bound to none, he that goes with me shall have my labour, and I am in hope to have his money, he

> that will not go with me goes with another, and I have the more ease the while, he doth me no wrong in not going with me, and I will do him no injury for going from me.[37]

This passage directly responds to the common belief that watermen bully passengers into going with them over the river, aggressively steering them away from other watermen; it replaces a picture of uncivil competition with one that is mutually respectful. The language used to describe the inclinations of customers – "they please," "they will," "they list" – emphasizes "choice" and freewill on the part of potential buyers, with voluntary participation and mutual understanding on both sides. Openness and transparency define this idealized picture of exchange, and when openness is not present, the balance of mutual benefit is interrupted. To demonstrate the potential for imbalance, Taylor recalls a common watermen's experience involving a "roaring boy (or one of the cursed crew)" who, wearing "nothing about him but a satin outside to cover his knavery," orders his waterman to row vigorously, asks the waterman to wait at the other side of the river to collect his fare, and "having neither money nor honesty," never returns.[38] With a sumptuous cloth to "cover his knavery," the roaring boy symbolizes the outer aspect of a customer who does not deal fairly. The satin actually betrays the opposite of what it would suggest – not money, but the lack of it – and the fact that he covers himself in such a cloth betrays his lack of honesty too.

The roaring boy epitomizes the dishonest customer who benefits from the market without fully participating in it, exhibiting a parasitism that Taylor often attributed to upper-class privilege. The pamphlet *A Kicksey-Winsey: or a Lerry Come-Twang* (1619) praises his paying subscribers and excoriates his debtors. Here, he divides subscribers into seven types, or "heads," from "Those that have paid" to "Those Rorers that can pay, and wil not" (A8). The "rorers" of the last category, for which Taylor saves most of his venom, consist almost entirely of aristocratic types. The typical debtor dresses well and carries himself with haughtiness: "His carcasse cased in this borrowed case, / Imagines he doth me exceeding grace; / If when I meete him, he bestowes a nod, / Then must I thinke me highly blest of God" (B6–B6ᵛ). Taylor deems not paying a particularly aristocratic habit when he quips "One part of Gentry he will ne're forget, / And what is, that he ne're will pay his dett" and pines for "good men in meaner Rayment" (B6ᵛ). Whether Taylor attacks actual members of the gentry we cannot be sure, since he deliberately refrains from listing names. What is certain is that he attacks upper-class *habits* of prodigality and dissimulation, which may be just as present (if not more) in commoners with pretensions as in the nobility itself. Perez Zagorin notes that the word "courtier" functioned as a byword for dishonesty and faithlessness, as can be seen in the proliferation of anti-courtier literature alongside courtiers' handbooks.[39] The image of a parasite in "borrowed" raiment looking down upon an honest "plain dealer" serves as effective ridicule.

---

[37] Humpherus, 1: 188–9, emphasis added.

[38] Humpherus, 1: 187.

[39] Perez Zagorin, *Ways of Lying: Dissimulation, Persecution, and Conformity in Early Modern Europe*, Cambridge, MA: Harvard UP, 1990, 7.

Because "no man was inforc'd against his will" to sign on to the subscriptions, then Taylor considers publicly satirizing the debtors a justifiable act (B7^{v}).[40]

The ideals of fairness, plainness, and transparency comprise the self-image that Taylor conveys to the public in *Taylor's Motto*, his most overtly autobiographical piece. As its title suggests, the work is best described as a verse manifesto that displays the author's habits of being. Taylor's self-construction promotes him as a complete, self-sufficient subject and interrogates status hierarchies to allow a new set of distinctions to emerge. The emblem of the title page is accompanied by a set of verses ("The Embleme Explained") to highlight each symbol in the illustration. Small banners around the figure proclaim the subtitle of the piece, "Et Habeo, Et Careo, Et Curo" (I Have, I Want, I Care), and beneath the figure sits another banner that reads, "Happy in miserye" (A2) (Figure 4.2). The book and oar in the pictures signify his dual occupations: "I have a Muse to write, A Boat to rowe, / Which both the booke and Oare doth plainely shew" (A2^{v}). As these objects announce what "I Have," the empty purse signifes what "I Want": "The empty purse proclaimes, that monie's scant, / Want's my fee simple, or my simple fee, / And (as I am a Poet,) dwells with me" (A2^{v}). Each element of the picture serves the exterior manifestation of the author's inner self. Taylor further explains the placement of the figure's feet, which one facing forward and the other turned away: "The one's like steadfast hope, the other then / Presents temptations which encompasse men, / Which he that can resist with Constancy, / Is a most happy man in Miserie" (A2^{v}). Through the centrality of the "I," the emblem makes it clear that this plebian author will focus the book on himself and invites curious readers to look further. "Reader, in the booke, if you inquire for," promises Taylor, "Ther's more of what *I have*, and *want*, and *care* for" (A2^{v}). The poet/sculler offers himself as a subject of interest to a wide range of readers (as evidenced by the opening epistle "To Every Body") and an exemplary guide to cultivating inner integrity in the face of exterior compromises.

The discursive self-identification in *Taylor's Motto* relies upon distinguishing the self as honest and unpolitic – in a word, "plain."[41] This designation interrogates hierarchies of social organization through anti-aristocratic comparisons. From the emblem to the rest of the book's seventy-four pages, Taylor purports to bear his soul to readers as a man who, in a politic and dissembling age, has nothing to hide: "I want a bragging or a boasting vaine; / In words or writing, any wayes to frame, / To make my selfe seeme better then I am . . . I want that undermining policy; / To purchase wealth with foule dishonesty" (C5). Declaring a different value system from "dishonest" purchasers of wealth and status, including wealthy urban tradesmen, Taylor claims to acquire whatever he has through scullery: "I have a trade, much like an Alchymist, / That oft-times by extraction, if I list, / With sweating labour at a woodden Oare, / I'le get the coyn'd refined silver ore. / Which I count better then

[40] Apparently, this public shaming worked: although the 1619 edition names 800 debtors, the number decreases to 750 in the version that appears in the 1630 folio.

[41] Stevenson notes that Elizabethan writers, particularly writers of sermons, sometimes advertised the "plain style" of their works to insure accessibility to readers with only a basic education (52). What is new about Taylor's "plainness" is that it is not only a style, but a characteristic of the self as reflected in writing.

Figure 4.2 John Taylor. *Taylors Motto. Et habeo, Et Careo, Et Curo.* (1621)

the sharking tricks / Of cooz'ning Tradesmen, or rich Politicks, / Or any proud foole, ne'er so proud or wise, / That doth my needfull honest trade despise" (C2). In other words, "honest" labor in an "honest" trade becomes a mode of distinction for the self. Moreover, the inability of this labor to translate into wealth preserves him from moral danger: "if (perhaps) I had their [rich men's] meanes, I thinke / I should (as they doe) dice and drab and drinke" (A8v). Unlike the chronic debtors that he finds among gentility, he insists that he maintains good credit and a modest appetite: "I care for food and lodging, fire and rayment, / And (what I owe) I care to make good payment" (E3v). In a Jonsonian move, Taylor extends his claims to moderation and diligence into his habits of composition. Demonstrating discipline in the use of his time, he asserts (in a kind of commoner's *sprezzatura*) that he put together the entire *Motto* in "houres . . . three dayes at most" and promises to write another book before breakfast (E4). Thrift, industry, honesty, and plainness all define the self that Taylor describes, a self that is fundamentally different in habit and outlook from his upper-class counterparts. Finally, this self is essentially capable and self-determining, as when he declares, "I have had time and pow'r to write all this" (C2v). The presence of the text itself testifies to the expenditure of labor, the judicious use of time, and the persistence of the will in spite of material want. Customers bear witness to this self-construction when they purchase the book and read it, thus fulfilling the desired end of public self-making.

Taylor's idealized relationship with his customers, then, rests on a validation of both consumer power and the labor power of the producer. Moreover, the performative transparency of Taylor's public self-image challenges consumers to look critically at the field of commodities and the intentions of the commodity producers who compete for their money. Each aspect of Taylor's approach to market relations – the advertisement of the inner self and the faith in the critical individual – anticipates the later arrivals of a "bourgeois public sphere." However, the reorganization of existing structures of privilege and autonomy does not necessarily erase hierarchy itself, nor does it automatically eliminate notions of fixed identity, or squelch the desire for an authorizing structure outside the self to hold society together. As I have noted throughout this study, non-aristocratic identity always possesses its complications, straining against the same revisionary formulations it proposes. On the eve of the English Civil War, such competing impulses coexisted long before the outbreak of war demonstrated their ability to continue doing so. A look at the language of Taylor's writings during the early years of revolution will show that, in fact, the ability to imagine personal autonomy and the desire for structural order could exist in the same person.

The Age of "Impudence": Taylor and Revolutionary Politics

After leaving the Watermen's Company, Taylor turned to writing as his sole source of income and continued to publish entertaining pieces that he hoped would sell. He undertook several more journeys that he made into travel accounts, including a visit to the king in *Tailors Travels to the Isle of Wight* (1648) and a tour of Wales in *A Short Relation of a Long Journey . . . encompassing the Principalitie of Wales*

(1652). He also turned to "nonsense" as a motif for jests and humorous verse, as in *Mad Verse, Sad Verse, Glad Verse and Bad Verse* (1644), *Mercurius Nonsensicus* (1648), and *Nonsence upon Sense* (1651). To reawaken reverence for the institution of royalty, he also composed pieces in honor of England's past and present monarchs. Taylor had served as a King's Waterman for part of his career, a post of special honor (the emblem of *Taylor's Motto* depicts him in royal livery). Even after his tenure as royal waterman, he still liked to view himself as a servant of the king. In 1641, during a short-lived revival of popular support for Charles I, he wrote the following occasional verse on Charles's return from Scotland and delivered it to him in person: "through my power (which my poor muse inflames) / A greater wonder is performed by me; I have transformed a boat from off the Thames / Unto a horse, to come to welcome thee. / And now thy gracious sight I do attain, / Ile turn that horse into a boat again." In answer to those who do not exult at Charles's return, he adds, "Let them be hang'd and then they have their right."[42] At this early point in the revolution, Taylor could still count on wide popular agreement for such sentiments.

In the years immediately subsequent, Taylor focused his writing on the rise of religious radicalism in the commonwealth, a development that profoundly challenged his Anglican and Royalist sympathies. After the king fled from London early in 1642, it was difficult to maintain a Royalist position publicly; thus, he penned a number of his pamphlets anonymously. Other pamphlets he wrote in his own name, with the initials "J.T.," or under the anagram "Thorny Alio." Because the authorship of certain pamphlets thought to be Taylor's is difficult to know with certainty, I will refer to these pamphlets only by way of providing context for the pieces that Taylor definitively wrote.

Around the time of the democratic reforms in the Watermen's Company, Taylor turned his critical attention to one consequence of religious radicalism that particularly alarmed him: the proliferation of self-appointed preachers he saw emerging from the ranks of laborers and artisans. In such satirical pieces as *A Swarme of Sectaries, and Schismatiques* (1641), *New Preachers New* (1641), and *An Apology for Private Preaching* (1642), he describes cobblers, weavers, butchers, and brewers who leave their trades to try their hands at preaching and/or printing "seditious" pamphlets. In *The Whole Life and Progress of Henry Walker the Ironmonger* (1642), he homes in on a specific case by relating the life of an ironworker who neglects his trade and occupies himself as an illegal printer and anonymous writer of pamphlets against the king. Taylor describes these artisans and mechanics as impudently seizing a privilege for which they have no "calling," and because they have no calling, they neglect their trades and rebel against their superiors. He presents these mechanic-preachers as shifty, unstable in character and occupation, and opportunistic. Here, Taylor's conception of his own calling runs aground with his conservative uses of the idea. On the one hand, the pull he feels to write his own life and ideas transcends his lowly status. On the other hand, he deploys the "calling" as a means of keeping political

[42] Qtd. in Humpherus, 289.

elements he deems repugnant in check. Thus the mechanic-preachers become the externalized Other that Taylor finds, in part, within himself.[43]

Taylor's perception of the mechanic-preachers as dangerous to the realm has an additional element that more directly implicates him as a participant in the print market: he views the general public as unable to discriminate between "right" and "wrong" doctrine and therefore vulnerable to seditious ideas. Heretical preachers pose a serious threat because they have access to two major institutions of public discourse – preaching and printing – and thus can mislead a gullible public with relative ease. A view of "the people" as both easily misled and potentially menacing held place in both literary representations and the minds of government officials, even Parliamentarians. Citing numerous such examples, Christopher Hill remarks that, in the minds of many observers, "'The people' were fickle, unstable, incapable of rational thought: the headless multitude, the many-headed monster."[44] Taylor's earlier publications, for all their egalitarianism, also betray a sense of bewilderment at the public's diversity. For example, the address to "Most Mightie, Catholicke (or Universall) Mounsier Multitude" in *Taylors Water-worke* describes the audience as anything but catholic: "(whose *many millions of Hydraes heads*, Argos eyes, and Briarcus hands,) are (if you please) to judge of my Water-Muses travels, to looke with *hundreds of aspects* on the prospect of my Sculler, or to lend a few of your *many hands* to helpe to tugge me a shore at the haven of your good-wills" (A2, emphasis added). In light of this diversity, Taylor perhaps ironically wishes that his lines "might please like Cheese to a Welchman, Butter to a Fleming, Usquebaugh to an Irishman, or Honey to a Beare" as he signs the address, "Yours ten thousand wayes, John Taylor" (A2). However he might wish to gain universal positive regard, his choice to address "neyther Monarch, nor Miser, Keafer nor Caitife, Pallatine or Plebian" exposes the text "to be censured as it shall please their wise-domes to screw their Luna-like opinions" (A2). The address "To the World" in the collected works attributes the confusion of the people to the circulation of money. He calls his time a "Golden Age," for "Gold can doe any thing; it can both cleare and bleare the eies of Justice: it can turne Religion into Policie, Pietie into perjurie" (A3). It is also a "Silver Age" for similar reasons, since "without it there is no market kept in Church or Commonwealth: For whosoever is King, Pecunia is Queene" (A3). Additionally, it is a "Brass Age," as is apparent in everyone's "impudence" toward authority and one another (A3). The result is that "we are so credulous, that when the whoremaster is called honest man, the Knave will believe himselfe to be so" (A3^{v}). Thus, as we saw in the subscription scenario, entering the marketplace with the expectation of profit calls for a degree of faith in the judgment of consumers, or as Halasz terms it, a "wager."[45]

As the nation approached civil war, the detrimental effects of religious and political diversity became more clearly drawn, and faith in the discrimination of

---

43 Helgerson also notices the dynamic of authors isolating parts of themselves as "other" in order to achieve their goals in self-presentation. See *Self-Crowned Laureates*, 10.

44 Christopher Hill, *Change and Continuity in Seventeenth-Century England*, Cambridge, MA: Harvard UP, 1975, 181.

45 Halasz, *Marketplace*, 196.

the public wanes. *Heads of all Fashions* (1642), a pamphlet possibly written by Taylor, portrays the public as a plethora of "heads" pulling in different directions according to their multitudinous opinions.[46] The woodcut on the title page depicts these diverse heads "Butting, Jetting, or pointing at vulgar opinion," and the roster of heads includes "light," "empty," "hollow," "plaine," and "round" heads, according to their different religious and political inclinations (A1–A1ᵛ). The introductory epistle to the reader depicts the heads exulting, "Each City and each Towne, yea every village, / Can fill us now with newes, we need not pillage" (A1ᵛ). The heads depend upon a market network of news that has multiplied throughout the realm, and the author presents the hunger for news as a drive toward novelty and a sublimation of independent judgment: "Some brings us newes from Ireland, false or true / How ever all is call'd both true and new" (A2). The successful combination of the "true" and "new" in popular printed material, including cheap ballads and broadsheets, emerges here with respect to a misled, gullible public. The heads represent the opposite of Taylor's ideal, independent "right" reader – they are victims of marketing who devour all kinds of "news" without respect to the likelihood of the fantastical stories proclaimed. By intervening with his own pamphlets, Taylor competes for the attentions of a public he regards as too easily swayed in dangerous times.

Taylor's pieces on heretical preachers combine these concerns – laborers stepping out of their stations and seizing control of public opinion, and a scattered, diverse public with infantilized judgment – to present a picture of impeding rebellion against governance.[47] I focus on these pamphlets because I view them as an attempt to come to terms with the questions of non-aristocratic self-determination, individual judgment, and social reorganization that Taylor raises in his earlier writings. Furthermore, the mechanics' participation in public discourse implicates Taylor's own position as a manual laborer who himself achieves print. The similarity between his case and that of the mechanics calls for a set of distinctions on Taylor's part that defines proper motives and venues for publishing and public speaking, as well as an appropriate view of oneself within social hierarchies. But the distinctions that Taylor attempts to impose are problematic.

The title page of *A Swarme of Sectaries, and Schismatiques* announces an intention to "discover" the "strange preaching (or prating) of such as are by their trades Coblers, Tinkers, Pedlers, Weavers, Sow-gelders, and Chymney-Sweepers" (*Works* 7: 5). The introductory address "To he that will" anticipates that Taylor's own pamphlet might not be initially distinguishable from the false printed ideas that buyers encounter daily; in response, Taylor appeals to the reader to "look thou understand before thou judge" (7: 6). As he describes self-appointed preachers from a variety of trades, he deems them worthy in their given trades, but out of order in any other capacity: "Tis past a Butchers, or a Brewers reach, / To pearch into a Pulpit,

[46] The STC attributes *Heads of all Fashions* to Taylor, although it is signed "J.M.," which might be the initials of the printer, John Morgan.

[47] Mechanic-preachers were a fairly popular topic and were treated in other pamphlets not by Taylor, such as a 1647 broadsheet entitled "These tradesmen are preachers in and about the city of London," the titlepage of which depicts twelve heretical craftsmen. See Unwin, 336–7.

or to preach . . . Yet all these, if they not misplaced be, / Are necessary, each in their degree" (7: 7). The defiant sectaries include a "zealous" cobbler named Samuel Howe who sways ignorant audiences who "hold learning in small estimation" through his own "unlearned" speeches (7:12). The main thrust of Taylor's argument rests on an idea of occupation as a category of natural order – because the mechanics were not "call'd or sent" to preach, they are "impudent" for stepping out of their stations to do so (7: 14). The mechanics, like vagrants, "ne're are well imploy'd, nor never idle" as they incite rebellion against the proper order of church and king (7: 19).

Another pamphlet, *New Preachers New*, depicts laborers and artisans engaging in "this new kinde of talking Trade, which many ignorant Coxcombes call Preaching," and identifies them on the title page as "Greene the Feltmaker, Spencer the Horse-rubber, Quartermaine the Brewers Clarke, with some few others" (A1). Whether these names refer to caricatures or actual people, we cannot be certain, but Taylor sees them as propelled to success by the public's fascination with newness. As in *A Swarme of Sectaries*, Taylor portrays the mechanics as "proud spirits" boldly stepping out of their natural stations "to be Ambassadours of God, to teach your teachers" (A1v). He denies the possibility that any one of them might have a true calling, for such would go against the tradition of "any well setled Church in Europe," to "ordaine such as you" who spend the day "in the forenoone making a hat, or rubbing a horse, in the afternoone preaching a Sermon" (A2). This language represents the mechanic-preachers as unable to commit to a single trade, unstable, and therefore suspicious. He describes "Spencer the Horse-rubber" as "a wavering minded fellow, a stable unstable companion in all his waies" who partakes of "as many trades almost as religions" (A2). Arguing that the preachers also inflict economic damage by neglecting their trades, he commands them to leave their "trickes" and "vizards" and "turne honest men, follow your trades painfully, pay your debts honestly" and of course, "obey your governors readily" (A3–A3v). The preachers, then, display a variety of criminal attributes – they eschew consistent affiliation with a trade, are "dishonest," carry debts, and ignore the authority of their betters. In similar language as that which was used to describe unincorporated watermen, the mechanic-preachers form a class of vagrants. Just as vagrants threaten the realm through their immorality, so do the preachers, as Taylor ends the pamphlet by warning the "good Reader" to "Consider and avoid these disorders" (A4v).

For Taylor, the case of Henry Walker "The Ironmonger" exemplifies the danger of unlearned mechanics who rebel against their stations, yet gain enough control over public forms of discourse to inspire the general public to flout the natural order as well. Unlike the caricatures in *A Swarme of Sectaries* and *New Preachers New*, Walker was a real figure who became notorious for his radical writings and views. *The Whole Life and Progress of Henry Walker the Ironmonger* is a later installation in a public feud, carried out in print, between Taylor and Walker. The *Life and Progress* responds to Walker's arrest at the Old Bailey for seditious printing. Here Taylor offers a narrative of how Walker fell "at odds" with his trade (and thus "at odds" with occupational stability and civic respectability) and finds a "foster occupation" in bookselling, an activity to which Taylor also alleges Walker "fell" (*Works* 7: 2). Taylor depicts Walker composing books that he feels will sell "amongst such people as understood them not, loved contention, or were willing to beleeve any thing that tended to rend or shake the piece of either Church or State" (7: 2). Walker, then, remedies the loss of his former occupation by capitalizing on the ignorance of the people and their inclination to rebellion. At the same time, Taylor reports on "some hundred of thred-bare scriblers," chiefly "Vagrants and Vagabonds" from the shires around London who "would bee called Poets"; recognizing an opportunity to cozen credulous purchasers, they flock to the trade of "scandalous Writing" and "Newes making." These vagabonds transform themselves into "wandring Booke sellers . . . commonly called Mercuries and Hawkers" (7: 3). Bookselling, then, becomes a trade most attractive to wanderers with nothing better to do. Furthermore, they discern the potential to earn money from the sale of cheap, scandalous pamphlets to people predisposed to unrest.

Walker's portrayal as a vagrant gains further support from the fact that, when questioned, he is "not able to give a good account of himselfe" (7: 3), a common characteristic of arraigned vagabonds and a contrast to Taylor's own propensity for openly narrating his life. Although he is released under condition of never returning to the trade, Walker collaborates with a printer to produce the seditious pamphlet *To your Tents, O Israel*, which he hurls over the heads of a crowd into the king's coach. Despite Walker's efforts to cover his tracks by imputing authorship to another source, the printer verifies that Walker indeed penned the pamphlet himself. Walker then escapes from jail several times and cloaks himself under numerous guises: among a gang of rebels, in holes and cellars, as a minister who preaches rebellion against City governors. The last disguise links Walker's shiftless criminality to radical preachers who exhort rebellion against authority. But it is still his activities as a pamphleteer which cause the most damage; when he is finally arrested for good, Taylor concludes that "hee hath done more mischiefe by his Pamphlettizing seditions, scandalous ridiculous Lyes, and rayling Libells, then one thousand of his heads are worth" (7: 6). The jury reprimands him for *To Your Tents, O Israel* and he confesses that "it was his owne worke, & done by night" to cloak his true identity and his libelous intent (7: 8).

The story of Henry Walker demonstrates not only the danger of seditious pamphlets to the state, but explores the causes of rebellion through a discussion of personal character and individual intention. Taylor's explanation for the spread of heretical religious ideas resides not in faults of the king, church, or economic order, but within the sins of shiftless individuals who cannot remain content with their modest stations in life. In short, Taylor attributes the greed and instability he finds in society on the eve of revolution to the success of greedy and unstable individuals who craftily manipulate public discourse for *personal* (never ideological) ends. This conclusion short-circuits the possibility raised by revolutionaries, "heretics," and indeed, discontented tradesmen like Joshua Church, that old orders of hierarchy and obedience can no longer support the growing presence of individualist ideas and economic competition.

In the face of this contradiction, it makes sense that Taylor responds by reasserting hierarchy. The application of rebellious impulses to the greedy self-interest of unstable individuals represents an attempt to come to terms with change. On the rhetorical handling of the anxiety that accompanies social transformation, Stevenson suggests that an appeal to tradition serves as a means for coping with the losses that accompany progress:

> in times of social and economic change, social fact changes more quickly than vocabulary and ideology, and so men frequently find themselves describing observations of the present in the rhetoric of the past. To dismiss this rhetoric as mere lip-service to tradition is to ignore the pain that attends social change and the confusion that attends formulation of new social ideology. In times of social change, tradition has greater psychological appeal than innovation. Before men abandon old paradigms and develop new ones that accurately describe what they observe, they strain their rhetorical concepts to the snapping point in an attempt to deny the possible ramifications of what they see.[48]

These remarks occur within the context of a discussion of Elizabethan bourgeois-hero tales, but they have a similar application here. Taylor's career as both writer and waterman involved living and working within stark contradictions: he was both a manual laborer and an elite ruler, a successful writer and an aspiring poet on the downside of the social scale, and an entrepreneurial figure who viewed accumulation as greed. Although he liked to believe that his "low" social status and modest means posed no limitation to his achievement, he also viewed his station as a non-negotiable fact that determined his fortunes and place in society. In other words, Taylor inhabited a world in which self-determination was imaginable, but not without the loss of security one may find in a natural order outside the self. More specifically, the possibilities that he saw within print culture for the cultivation of a critical public, self-representation, and monetary gain involved acceptance of his own role within an unstable marketing network that threatened pre-capitalist notions of social organization. If the market for print can authorize a waterman to write, present himself, and make money for it, then it also confers the same privilege on men like Henry Walker.

Conclusion: An Unstable Society, A Stable Self

Taylor's case tells us several things about the situation of the non-elite writer in early modern England. First, it shows that, for the common subject to attain "representative publicness," it was necessary to gauge virtue by a new set of terms. While Tudor theories of hierarchy defined virtue in a circular way – with gentility as the embodiment of virtue and virtue the expression of gentility – those who challenged hierarchy erected a politics of inwardness and "character" that interrupted the theoretical coherence between blood and the interior disposition. Second, positive figurations of authorial labor involved representing the marketplace not as something to be shunned, but as a test for character. The market becomes a total social field, replacing the question of whether one participates with *how* one participates – assuming that, in reality, everyone does. The debtors in *A Kicksey Winsey* believe that their privilege supersedes the rules of exchange, but in the pamphlet, their behavior in commercial transactions reveals them to be the inferiors

---

[48] Stevenson, *Praise and Paradox*, 6–7.

of "good men in meaner Rayment." Thus the market becomes a new set of social laws in which the "plain dealer" emerges as the one with true virtue. Third is the related issue of profit. Whereas the stigma of print held profit of any kind to be vulgar, Taylor notes that everyone earns. The real question is *how* one earns, why, and how much: does one greedily accumulate through deceitful means, or does one modestly earn with honesty? In all, Taylor's case shows how the market can be deployed to challenge older forms of ascribed status that denigrate work and profit by posing new options for self-representation and new standards of self-definition.

In a sense, Taylor's case is the most straightforward illustration of an argument I have made throughout these chapters – that the advent of print, in conjunction with the interruption of class-based hierarchies of work, allowed an early manifestation of the professional author to flourish. This development depends upon claiming labor as a positive basis for authorship and, often, this claim extends beyond labor as mere metaphor. Out of the authors I have discussed in depth, Taylor has the least reservation about making such claims and seems to extend them the furthest. However, Taylor also most clearly illustrates the degree to which the new possibilities for non-aristocratic self-representation attended historical changes disturbing even to those whom these changes benefited. Market participation in the late sixteenth and early seventeenth centuries is fraught with moral significations that render it socially problematic for individuals steeped in a society that is still, in many ways, dominated by quasi-feudal systems of organization. For this reason, claiming the labor of authorship as an enabling part of authorial identity involves both a sense of emancipation and a sense of unease.

In Taylor's case, the problem becomes how to participate profitably in the market while distinguishing oneself among market vagaries – and the market's "vagrants." Particularly with the impending collapse of church and state as he had always known them, the authoritative space inhabited by traditional institutions threatens to become vacant. Taylor spent the last years of his life running a tavern called "The Poet's Head," where he hawked his verses to customers in hopes of eking out a living in his old age. Over the door of the tavern, he hung a sign bearing his own portrait, which he explained in *Of Alterations Strange, Of various Signes* (1651): "I oft have seen a saint's head for a sign, / And many a king's head too, then why not mine?".[49] These lines reveal the double aspect of egalitarianism with which Taylor struggled. On the one hand, he saw the opportunity to manipulate traditional iconographies in order to make *himself* into an icon, while on the other hand, the affirmation of himself as "common man" interrupts the authority of traditionally revered institutions. For better or for worse, the result of the new system of signs is that one "head" is as good as another, and that any head may compete for authority in a society that has become "headless." De Certeau describes the development of autonomous selfhood as a process of gain and loss:

> When the speaker's identity was certain ("God speaks in the world"), attention was directed toward the deciphering of his statements, the "mysteries" of the world. But when

[49] Qtd. in Capp, 155. Other commentators give varying accounts of these lines, and some report that it was written on the sign itself. See Capp 155, n. 68.

> this certitude is disturbed along with the political and religious institutions that guaranteed it, the questioning is directed toward the possibility of finding substitutes for the unique speaker: who is going to speak? and to whom? The disappearance of the First Speaker creates the problem of communication, that is, of a language that has to be *made* and not just *heard and understood*. . . . In other words, it is because he loses his position that the individual comes into being as a *subject*.[50]

As de Certeau argues and the authors in this study illustrate in varying ways, the development of a sense of autonomous selfhood requires the loss of older authorizing structures outside the self. Furthermore, as some radical religious sects realized, the space of authority may be assumed by anyone, regardless of ascribed status. As a conservative thinker, Taylor perceived the very indeterminacy of this proposition as threatening. Hence, within his appeal to an old order of "rulers" and "ruled," we can detect an attempt to articulate a new system of social classification before the language is available. The terms that Taylor adopts to describe what he sees evoke not only traditional governing structures, but a standard of *self*-government and right intention, expressed as ideals of occupational stability, non-aristocratic authenticity, "honesty" in business, good credit, and transparency of character.

Thus, while Taylor's appeals to order indicate the rhetorical management of anxiety, I wish to suggest that his contradictions – which bring to a head the contradictions that belie all the constructions of authorship I describe here – point toward something larger: a construction of the self as locus of stable meaning. When Taylor decries the occupational instability of the heretic preachers, he positions this itinerancy as reflective of a generally unstable character and implicitly erects an ideal of loyalty to one's trade as a measure of individual virtue. For this reason, it is rhetorically useful for him to claim consistent affiliation with the waterman's trade in spite of its detriment to readers' perceptions of him as a serious author. As he tells us in the "Apologie for Water-men," he continues in the trade not because he must, but because he "likes" it and finds it morally and physically salutary. Once again, what appears as base necessity is transformed into a mark of character. For Taylor, loyalty to the trade signifies a refusal to give in to social ambition and thus promotes the image of a constant self who "knows [him]self to be" (D). Consistent affiliation with a trade is an ideal that had little basis in fact for many of Taylor's degree, for as Patricia Fumerton points out, the realities of a market economy required many lower- to middle-class people to hold multiple jobs, thus engaging in a kind of "continuing and displaced labor" anathema to occupational stability.[51] In this sense, Taylor's performative constancy can be read as an attempt to stabilize the conditions of a "vagrant market" within the self – that is to say, the self assumes the stability that seems lacking everywhere else. Furthermore, the turn to individual character as a mode of evaluation is a means by which to create new social distinctions that replace those which the market threatened, leveled, or even erased altogether.

---

[50] *Practice of Everyday Life*, 138.

[51] Patricia Fumerton, "London's Vagrant Economy: Making Space for 'Low' Subjectivity," *Material London, ca. 1600*, ed. Lena Cowen Orlin, Philadelphia: U of Pennsylvania P, 2000, 206–25, 215, 211.

In his own individualist project, Taylor found himself unwittingly participating in the revolutionary pressures that he feared. As some historians argue, the English Revolution was not made by or consciously willed by the bourgeoisie, but represents the dominance of a new order of capitalist relations that older social structures could no longer support. Hill attributes the revolution to "not only the individualism of those who wished to make money by doing what they would with their own but also the individualism of those who wished to follow their own consciences in worshipping God, and whose consciences led them to challenge the institutions of a stratified hierarchical society."[52] The "inward turn" of individualism, then, is conditioned by a social and economic structure that promotes individual self-interest, creating a fiction of personal autonomy that can be expressed in a variety of ways: speculative economic ventures, a direct and unmediated relationship with God, or a desire to challenge one's subordinate position in a hierarchy.

Taylor, while neither a radical revolutionary nor a wealthy merchant, seized the opportunity to cultivate an individualist self in both his publishing activity and in his self-presentation. If, in doing so, he inadvertently promoted an ideology whose implications he did not consciously support, then his experiment with self-making is profoundly ironic, for it anticipates and hastened changes that he loathed to see. The tavern sign where he substituted a king's head with his own thematizes the ambiguity of the situation, as the transfer of authority from outside government to individual conscience is met with vision, playfulness, disillusionment, and resignation. The sign, like Taylor's own celebrity and the struggles of other non-aristocratic early modern writers, testifies not only to the beginnings of the "modern personality," but also to its costs.

[52] Christopher Hill, "A Bourgeois Revolution?", *The Collected Essays of Christopher Hill*, Vol. 3, Sussex, UK: Harvester, 1986, 94–124, 96–7.

Chapter 5

"One Line a Day": George Wither's Process

> Before Wither no one ever celebrated its power at home, the wealth and strength which this divine gift confers on its possessor. Fame, and that too after death, was all which hitherto the poets had promised themselves and their art. It seems to have been left to Wither to discover that poetry was a present possession as well as a rich reversion; and that the Muse had promise of both lives, of this, and of that which was to come.
>
> Charles Lamb

Lamb's remarks on "the power of poetry" show why George Wither is frequently classed with John Milton as a self-proclaimed visionary poet of prophetic power. While it may be inaccurate to say that Wither was "the first" poet to concern himself with matters besides fame, the suggestion that he viewed poetic possession as involving "both lives" – the present and the one to come – reminds us of how deeply Protestant spirituality influenced the writings of certain figures in mid-seventeenth century England. Like his contemporary Milton, Wither saw in writing the potential for spiritual justification, Christian immortality, and even political change. Most especially, both figures demonstrate the sense of poetry as a calling grounded in deep, often iconoclastic spiritual conviction. In these instances, the embrace of writing as a "calling" is intrepid, for writing becomes a means of exercising the critical intelligence of the independent Christian spirit, or as David Gay puts it, "the representation of poetic voice as a source of power and truth in conflict with authority and error."[1] For Wither, as well as for Milton, the sources of "authority and error" could frequently be found in publishing practices themselves.

It may fairly be asked why I conclude this study with Wither rather than Milton, a poet of proven consequence for the history of authorship. After all, Milton's career can certainly be described as one in which writing-as-work is evident, as he regarded authorial diligence as a manifestation of spiritual fitness. However, Wither is of current interest due to his alleged role in the history of intellectual property. During Wither's struggle with the Stationer's Company over the royal patent granted to his *Hymnes and Songs of the Church*, Wither had numerous opportunities to assert his writing as not only property, but as *labor*. A contemporary of Taylor, Wither is becoming increasingly well known as a major figure in the history of intellectual

[1] David Gay, "'Lawfull Charms' and 'Wars of Truth': Voice and Power in Writings by John Milton and George Wither," *Papers on Language and Literature* 36: 2 (Spring 2000), 177–97, 177.

property due to his battle with the Stationers Company over the royal patent for his book *Hymnes and Songes of the Church* (1622–1623). While Wither was not the first to challenge the stationers' privileges, he was, according to Joseph Loewenstein, their "boldest authorial adversary."[2] Wither's claim for the product of his labor is legible in several of his texts, but most especially *The Schollers Purgatory* (c. 1625), which he dedicated to "honest stationers." His elaborate arguments amount to the defense that "I am an author, and that is to say I am a worker"; Loewenstein characterizes Wither as a self-styled "poet-prophet" for whom "poetry is a vocation and a *job*."[3] Ultimately, Loewenstein assesses *The Schollers Purgatory* as a major historical development for authorship: "This assertion of legal property constitutes a breakthrough in the history of authorship," because it generates a notion of natural property.[4]

Certainly, the seriousness by which Wither approaches his labor is the major component of his sense of property. To develop this notion further, I ask from where his sense of labor itself comes. Wither's idea of labor itself merits closer scrutiny, for the conviction that he is entitled to his labor as property is undergirded by confidence that writing is something to which he has been called. The legal moment brings to fruition a sense of author-as-laborer that is informed by religious and cultural discourses that encouraged such thinking; Wither represents a major development in these stories as well.

Wither has much in common with the laboring authors I treat here, a fact that places his legal struggles in a broader cultural context to include the struggles of authors in other social positions. For example, just as Ben Jonson often liked to represent himself in contrast to the amateurism of courtly dilettantes, a writer's willingness to labor and to live in penury is configured as a testament to his professionalism and his commitment. Wither himself liked to proclaim his own poverty, extending his personal misfortune toward the embrace of a "humble" writing style and choice of subject matter. Despite his status as an Oxford graduate and onetime member of the Inns of Court, Wither strives to present himself as lowly. In *The Scholler's Purgatory* he likens himself to a laborer, much as the female and putatively poorer Whitney does:

> And as some cheerefull laborer, by carrying stones & morter (by encouraging his fellows, and giving now and then a word of direction) may further the building of a house more then many others, and winn great commendation in that imployment; who would be rather a let (if not the ruin of it) if he should take upon him to lay the stones; So, I that have as a common labourer seriously and some way profitably endevoured; presuming into the place of a master workman, may become lesse serviceable, and peradventure a trouble to the business which I thought to further. (12: 43)

---

[2] Joseph Loewenstein, *The Author's Due: Printing and the Prehistory of Copyright*, Chicago: U of Chicago P, 2002, 142.

[3] Loewenstein, *Author's Due*, 147.

[4] Loewenstein, *Author's Due*, 149.

Here, as elsewhere, the laborer pose suggests the sense of one's own marginalization; the attempt to erect this marginal status as not only deeply moral, but as a platform for the diligent exercise of poetic skill.

But the author with whom Wither has the most in common is John Taylor, despite their very different political orientations. Wither's self-portrait, *Withers Motto*, had inspired Taylor to write a motto of his own, *Taylors Motto*; Wither's self-defense in *The Scholler's Purgatory* follows in the same vein by describing his development as a writer in terms akin to spiritual autobiography. In revolutionary context, both authors take what Lamb calls "present possession" of their poetic faculties. The sense of the *present* moment as one that is highly fertile for change becomes the context for narrating the self's experiences; it also becomes the context for an unfolding narrative of the process by which the text came into being, a process that highlights the daily work of the diligent self. Thus, regardless of the author's conscious political sympathies, this appeal to present experience and daily authorial labor helps forge a kind of non-aristocratic poetics that is registered in a tendency for authors to represent themselves in traditional seats of authority that are now left vacant. Thus laboring authors demonstrate a highly ambiguous relationship toward authority.

On the one hand, they maintain an anxious awareness of authority at all times, be it ecclesiastical, scriptural, political, cultural, class or gender-based. At the same time, they operate within transitional moments where traditional seats of authority appear highly vulnerable to disruption as, for example, the growing prominence of market models unseats feudal economic relationships in favor of wage labor. Manuscript-based models of publication confront the new possibility of print publication, wide dissemination, and a buying public of literate commoners. And in the case of Wither and his contemporaries, we witness an impending revolution in which new forms of government, including *self*-government, become possible. Taylor imagines his own head on an alehouse sign as a substitute for the king's detached one. Likewise, Wither envisions himself as a direct recipient of guidance from God and even God's minister. This affirmation of the self's own perceptions happens in a historical context where Wither, like Taylor, notices that the traditional seats of authority are open or, as they both express it, "headless." Wither writes in *Vox Pacifica* (1645):

> A *King*, is but a *substituted-head*,
> Made for *conveniencie:* And, if thereby
> The *bodie* seem to be indangered,
> (If *Power* it hath) it hath *Authoritie*
> To take one off, and set another on;
> Aswell, as, at the first, to make it one.
> And when that *Body* shall be represented,
> As this hath been, according to the *Law*,
> Or, shall be by *necessity* conventented;
> Therein resides, that *Soveraignty*, that Awe. ($K5^v$)[5]

[5] George Wither, *Vox Pacifica*, London, 1645.

The empty seat of external authority opens up a space for the self to enter. As we shall see, it is the combination of professed independence with the embrace of process that makes Wither's sense of himself as a professional possible.

Here I will examine Wither primarily as a conclusion to this study. By noting his use of labor in several representative texts, I seek to elaborate Wither's own conception of the calling by linking it to his sense of authorial labor. Wither provides a culminating instance of how the embrace of writing as labor represents a key moment in the establishment of "modern" authorship as a vocation, a profession, and a matter of personal commitment.

Time and Process

Wither's discursive self-presentation reveals him to be a Christian of the self-interested kind, one that would suit Max Weber's classic definition of the "Protestant ethic." This is not to accuse Wither of greed or disingenuousness so much as to identify him as one who took full advantage of the present revolutionary moment by using it to create a rudimentary sense of literature as a vocation. His career does much to anticipate modern "professional" modes of authorship, not only because he sought to define his writerly labor as a kind of property over which he had certain rights, but because he claimed to be destined for, and thus wholly dedicated to, writing as a course of life.

In fact, it could even be argued that Wither's drive for literary success conditioned his revolutionary commitments, especially if, as David Norbrook has argued, Wither's attitude toward change was more reluctant than is commonly believed.[6] Even among some of the more overtly "political" writings, Wither's authorial ego becomes apparent in his insistence on a style and persona that is unique among authors. As he writes in *The Shepheards Hunting*, "Though I'me young, I scorn to flit / On the wings of borrowed wit." (4.209–10).[7] These lines represent one of the simplest gestures by which authors can distinguish themselves – by maintaining a fantasy that their verses are completely non-derivative, an imaginative break with tired precedent. It would seem that this resistance to convention might inform Wither's attraction to radical thought, but it can temper his radicalism just as much. As he notes in *Major Wither's Disclaimer* (1647), where he tells of a royalist pamphlet inaccurately ascribed to him:

> This *Bastard* is not like me in the *pace*,
> Nor in the *language*: neither in the *face*,
> Nor in *condition*, so resembling me,
> As that, it mine, it may appeare to be.
> For, when two Parties I do guilty know,
> I strike not one, and let the other go,

[6] David Norbrook, "Levelling Poetry: George Wither and the English Revolution, 1642–1649," *English Literary Renaissance* 21: 2 (Spring 1991), 217–56.

[7] Quotes from *The Shepheards Hunting* are taken from Hunter's edition.

> But give them all their due, without regard,
> Or feare, of what may follow afterward . . . (7)

Although he clearly repudiates the idea of having penned a royalist text, he does not side with any other political position. Rather, he objects to the idea that any pamphlet might resemble him in style without actually being authored by him – essentially, he resists the idea that he is prone to duplication. The "bastard" text "is not like" him on any level: the style (that is, "the language" and "the pace"), the presentation (that is, "the face"), or in its status as cheap, circulating commodity (that is "in condition"). The political statement – that "two Parties I do guilty know" – elevates his authorial persona above the workings of politics, crafting a self with superior wisdom as well as skill. The poem not only testifies to an inimitable poetic style, but helps modify any partisan reputation that Wither might have incurred.

This constructed uniqueness, however, was limited. Special as Wither claimed to be, he was as likely as any of his contemporaries to participate in literary trends. When he tried his hand at these genres, though, they became opportunities to expound on one of his favorite topics: writing itself. One example is his *A Collection of Emblemes, Ancient and Moderne* (1635). Emblem books enjoyed great popularity in the early to mid-seventeenth century. Following the trend, the publisher Henry Taunton convinced Wither to write verses for engravings by Crispin de Passe. Wither's democratic – albeit condescending – wish for the volume is that it will attract the illiterate to learning, moreover, he strongly urges diligence, modesty, piety, and the use of one's abilities for service to the public (A).[8] As this goal suggests, emblem poetry was primarily a type of religious verse. Within this generic context, Wither's emblem verses can be read as an inkblot test of sorts, for the lines that accompany each engraving tell us much about the spiritual signification that certain symbols and associations held for him.

The majority of Wither's interpretations are grounded in Christian stoicism; in these instances he takes the emblems as an opportunity to preach such themes as patience in adversity and the choosing of virtuous labor and spiritual zeal over worldly pleasures. Occasionally he encounters a particularly obscure engraving and freely admits that he has no clue what it means, yet manages to eke out some verses for it anyway. But the emblem of special interest for the labor of authorship is one where Wither meditates on writerly diligence and professional commitment. Emblem 24 of Book 3 (Y4[v]) begins, "Each Day a Line, small tasks appeares: / Yet, much it makes in threescore Yeares." The emblem pictures a hand coming out of clouds to write down a single line, while the sun shines onto the scene (Figure 5.1). Wither takes this occasion to examine the laborious process of composition in lines persuasive enough to inspire writers struggling with their own processes:

> Here's but *one Line*; and, but *one Line a Day*,
> Is all the *taske* our *Motto*, seemes to say:
> And, that is thought, perhaps, a thing so small,

[8] George Wither, *A Collection of Emblemes, Ancient and Moderne*, London, 1635.

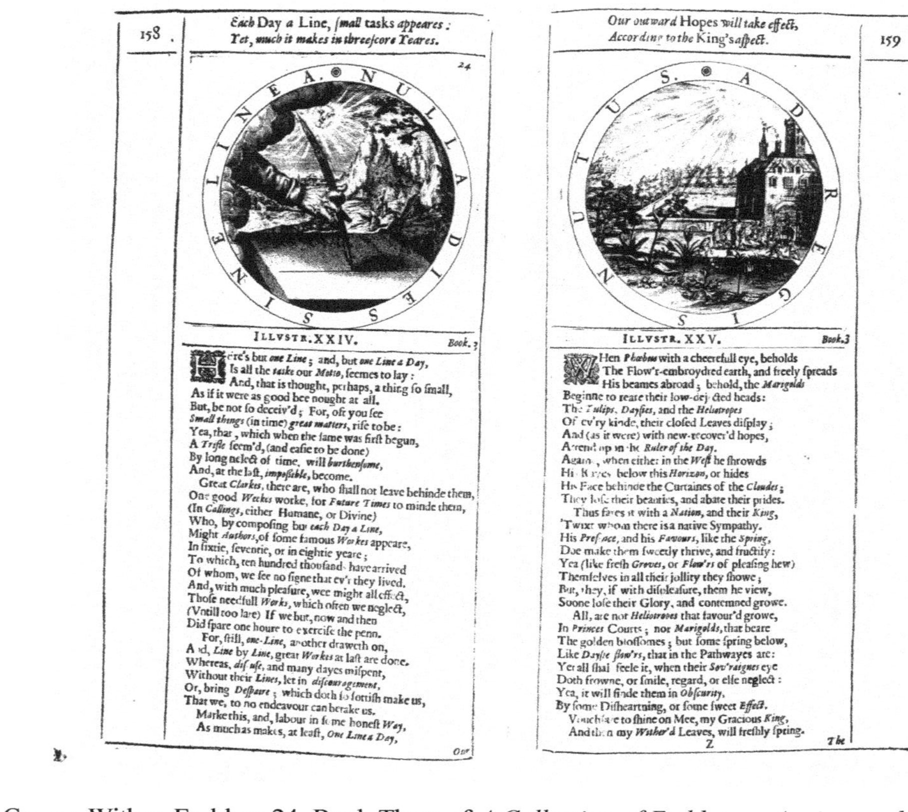

158 .

Each Day a Line, ſmall tasks appeares:
Yet, much it makes in threeſcore Yeares.

24

NULLA DIES SINE LINEA.

ILLVSTR. XXIV. *Book. 3*

Here's but *one Line*; and, but *one Line a Day*,
Is all the *taske* our *Motto*, ſeemes to lay:
And, that is thought, perhaps, a thing ſo ſmall,
As if it were as good bee nought at all.
But, be not ſo deceiv'd; For, oft you ſee
Small things (in time) *great matters*, riſe to be:
Yea, that, which when the ſame was firſt begun,
A *Trifle* ſeem'd, (and eaſie to be done)
By long neleƈt of time, will *burthenſome*,
And, at the laſt, *impoſsible*, become.
Great *Clarkes*, there are, who ſhall not leave behinde them,
One good *Weekes* worke, for *Future Times* to minde them,
(In *Callings*, either Humane, or Divine)
Who, by compoſing but *each Day a Line*,
Might *Authors*, of ſome famous *Workes* appeare,
In ſixtie, ſeventie, or in eightie yeare;
To which, ten hundred thouſands have arrived
Of whom, we ſee no ſigne that ev'r they lived.
And, with much pleaſure, wee might all effeƈt,
Thoſe needfull *Works*, which often we negleƈt,
(Vntill too late) If we but, now and then
Did ſpare one houre to exerciſe the penn.
For, ſtill, *one-Line*, another draweth on,
And, *Line* by *Line*, great *Workes* at laſt are done.
Whereas, *diſ-uſe*, and many dayes miſpent,
Without their *Lines*, let in *diſcouragement*,
Or, bring *Deſpaire*; which doth ſo ſottiſh make us,
That we, to no endeavour can betake us.
Marke this, and, labour in ſome honeſt *Way*,
As much as makes, at leaſt, *One Line a Day*,

Our

Our outward Hopes will take effeƈt,
According to the King's aſpeƈt.

159

AD REGIS NUTUS.

ILLVSTR. XXV. *Book. 3*

When *Phœbus* with a cheerefull eye, beholds
The Flow'r-embroydred earth, and freely ſpreads
His beames abroad; behold, the *Marigolds*
Beginne to reare their low-dejeƈted heads:
The *Tulips*, *Dayſies*, and the *Heliotropes*
Of ev'ry kinde, their cloſed Leaves diſplay;
And (as it were) with new-recover'd hopes,
Attend upon the *Ruler of the Day*.
Againe, when either in the *Weſt* he ſhrowds
His Rayes below this *Horizon*, or hides
His Face behinde the Curtaines of the *Cloudes*;
They loſe their beauties, and abate their prides.
Thus fares it with a *Nation*, and their *King*,
'Twixt whom there is a native Sympathy.
His *Preſence*, and his *Favours*, like the *Spring*,
Doe make them ſweetly thrive, and fruƈtify:
Yea (like freſh *Groves*, or *Flow'rs* of pleaſing hew)
Themſelves in all their jollity they ſhowe;
But, they, if with diſpleaſure, them he view,
Soone loſe their Glory, and contemned growe.
All, are not *Heliotropes* that favour'd growe,
In *Princes* Courts; nor *Marigolds*, that beare
The golden bloſſomes; but ſome ſpring below,
Like *Dayſie flow'rs*, that in the Pathwayes are:
Yet all ſhall feele it, when their *Sov'raignes* eye
Doth frowne, or ſmile, regard, or elſe negleƈt:
Yea, it will finde them in *Obſcurity*,
By ſome Diſheartning, or ſome ſweet *Effeƈt*.
Vouchſafe to ſhine on Mee, my Gracious *King*,
And then my *Wither'd* Leaves, will freſhly ſpring.

Z *The*

Figure 5.1 George Wither. Emblem 24, Book Three of *A Collection of Emblemes, Ancient and Modern: quickened with metrical Illustrations, both morall and divine, and Disposed into lotteries [..]..* (1635)

As if it were as good bee nought at all.
But, be not so deceiv'd; For, oft you see
Small things (in time) *great matters*, rise to be:
Yea, that, which when the same was first begun,
A Trifle seem'd, (and easie to be done)
By long neglect of time, will *burthensome*,
And, at the last, *impossible*, become. (Emblem 24 of Book 3 Y4v)

The lines exhibit a remarkable awareness of the minute elements that comprise large things, reminding those who write that every project consists of small, incremental steps. Moreover, the idea that "small things" may eventually become "great matters" supports the inherent importance of everyday experience. There is nothing specific in the emblem itself to suggest such an idea. Rather, Wither's verses offer a clear indication of his own personal approach to composition, one that is thoroughly infused the sense of writing as a "calling":

Great *Clarkes*, there are, who shall not leave behinde them,
One good *Weeke*s worke, for *Future Times* to minde them,
(In *Callings*, either Humane, or Divine)
Who, by composing but *each Day a Line*,
Might *Authors*, of some famous *Workes* appeare,
In sixtie, seventie, or in eightie yeare;
To which, ten hundred thousands have arrived
Of whom, we see no signe that ev'r they lived.
And, with much pleasure, wee might all effect,
Those needful *Works*, which often we neglect,
(Untill too late) If we but, now and then
Did spare one houre to exercise the penn. (Emblem 24 of Book 3 Y4v)

In expressions that seem to anticipate Benjamin Franklin's counting up of time and tasks in his *Autobiography*, Wither betrays a distinct sense of time as a finite set of blocks, easily wasted, to be used for fulfilling divine purpose. While the end – a completed work – definitely is important, the means is equally so if not more, because it is in the constant exercise of the calling that one fulfills it. Acknowledging the secular world, he also notes that callings can be not only "divine" but "humane," as in the case of clerks, whose daily output authors would do well to emulate a little at a time. This routine discipline has everything to do with character because, for Wither, the steady application of self to one's tasks constitutes "honest" labor:

For, still, *one-Line*, another draweth on,
And, *Line* by *Line*, great *Workes* at last are done.
Whereas, *dis-use*, and many days misspent,
Without their *Lines*, let in *discouragement*,
Or, bring *Despaire*; which doth so sottish make us,
That we, to no endeavour can betake us.

Marke this, and, labour in some honest *Way*,
As much as makes, at least, *One Line a Day*. (Emblem 24 of Book 3 Y4v)

To commit to writing, then, is to commit to the regular exercise of one's faculties. To neglect one's work admits guilt and despair, resulting in a downward spiral toward becoming "sottish" and therefore useless. On the other hand, daily labor keeps one not only busy, but "honest" and spiritually fit. In short, labor represents the fulfillment of the true writer's ideal spiritual path. Echoing Jonson's and Taylor's insistence on good character as informing good writing, Wither makes "honest" process paramount in his definition of what writing ought to be – a fusion of strong individual ethics and solid product.

For Wither, writing is not simply play, as the typical courtly amateur might regard it. All his life, Wither admired the ethical function of the poet. He calls poetry "the first root and ground / Of every Art" and the oldest "Science."[9] This vocational language becomes a foundation for literary professionalism and gestures toward the eventual development of vocational authorship. Wither represents an extension of Nashe's and Jonson's conceptions of poetry as a "mystery," except without Nashe's and Jonson's explicit class antagonism. Wither retains the sense of poetry as a mystery because he regards it as a spiritual matter, but also because it is a serious matter, one at which he works rather than plays: simply put, the writer is a writer because he *writes*.

Wit and Money

Wither's interpretation of the emblem as illustrative of the writer's discipline appears in the same book as a characteristic defense of his writing as property. Process is paramount, but it is also an example of the means justifying the end – labor entitles him to profit. The emblem book concludes with a scurrilous verse letter "to all them, whose custome it is, without any deserving, to importune Authors to give unto them their Bookes" (Oo2^v). The letter to the stationers informs us that his god-given capacity for invention is indeed worth money:

These many years, it hath your Custom bin,
That, when in my possession, you have seene
A Volume, of mine owne, you did no more,
But, Aske and Take; As if you thought my store
Encreast, without my Cost; And, that, by Giving,
(Both Paines and Charges too) I got my living;
Or, that, I find the Paper and the Printing,
As easie to me, as the Bookes Inventing. (Oo2^v)

Here Wither corrects the assumption that a writer loses nothing concrete when he hands over the rights to his manuscript. On the contrary, he compares his loss to the stationer's, claiming that his own is far greater: "What hee Gives, doth onely Mony Cost, / In mine, both Mony, Time, and Wit is lost." (Oo2^v). Wit is seen as both

[9] Qtd. in Charles S. Hensley, *The Later Career of George Wither*, The Hague and Paris: Mouton, 1969, 21.

expendable and commodifiable, as Wither makes it clear that his wit is his livelihood and therefore must be carefully guarded. The emblem book reinforces this point both in its content – verses that expound both the moral and economic value of writing – and in its form: a large, attractive volume that apparently was so costly that it never sold well enough to be reissued in Wither's lifetime.

Despite the New Testament's injunctions against wealth, Wither demonstrates Weber's notion of the "Protestant ethic" by conflating Christian duty with the impetus to earn. This is a paradox to be sure, but a familiar one in the United States, where books that employ Protestant Christian spirituality to justify personal prosperity often become instant bestsellers. (Recent examples include Joel Osteen's *Your Best Life Now: 7 Steps to Living at Your Full Potential* and Bruce Wilkinson's *The Prayer of Jabez: Breaking Through to the Blessed Life*.) However, as David Hawkes recently has argued, early modern print authors operate in a transitional period with respect to the morality of the market; that is to say, they are caught between market participation as an *option* (laden with moral and spiritual significance) and market participation as a *given*, which opens up an array of choices as to how one might participate, but assumes that one necessarily does. Hawkes situates post-Reformation repugnance toward idolatry within a larger market context in which, initially, participation "involves a fatal materialism – an unhealthy, irrational orientation toward the things of this world and the pleasures of the flesh – and it fosters the twin addictions of covetousness and sensuality."[10] Later, after the new economics increasingly takes hold, "virtually everyone in a capitalist society exchanges a portion of their lives for an objectified representation of life,"[11] as the world of money presents an abstraction of social and economic relations. If "everyone" lives there, then moral conflicts become internal struggles – not merely social struggles between classes or groups – that are internally, and then externally, justified. The so-called Protestant ethic, with its emphasis on diligence in a calling, represents one manifestation of the spiritualization of earning that the early modern period makes possible.

In keeping with the doctrine of the calling, Wither's arguments against the stationers link his claim for profit with divine will. His use of God as the authorizing force of his ambition comes across in bold and startling ways in *The Schollers Purgatory*. In addition to Loewenstein's incisive analysis, more can be said on Wither's idea of labor and with respect to religious discourse – i.e. his deployment of the "calling" to argue for his writing's intrinsic worth in the marketplace. This is not to say, however, that Wither's justifications are clear and straightforward, even to himself. In *The Schollers Purgatory*, we see that the social meaning of the calling is highly subject to scrutiny and debate.

It is the insistence on a calling that allows Wither to justify his own self-interest, while at the same time damning that of the stationers, by permitting him to assert that his interests are the same as God's interests; thus, to interfere with him is to interfere with the will of God. This supposed alliance with God is registered in a variety of ways. First, he relates his struggles with the stationers in a manner akin to

---

[10] David Hawkes, *Idols of the Marketplace: Idolatry and Commodity Fetishism in English Literature, 1580–1680*, New York: Palgrave, 2001, 6.

[11] Hawkes, *Idols*, 14.

spiritual autobiography. Identifying with Christ, he cites poverty as evidence of his sacrifice for a certain "integrity" of authorship, a lofty ideal: "Nay, even those who are grapes of the mysticall vine Jesus Christ, must bee crushed in the winepresse, or brused on the tongue, at the least, before they yeald any profitable nourishment. If it be so with me . . . " (12: 2). In keeping with the virtue that Wither claims to share with Christ, the Palm Sunday hymn in *Hymnes and Songes of the Church* emphasizes Jesus's exemplary poverty: "His glorie, and his royall right / (Ev'n by a power divine) / As if in worldly pomps despight, / Through poverty did shine" (D^v).[12] Wither's identification with Christ even goes so far as to imagine himself as Christ's own substitute teacher. Like Milton, Wither opposed the Archibishop Laud's campaign against lecturers, ministers appointed by parishes without approval from higher church authorities. Understanding the lecturer to be an independent preacher of the Gospel, Wither sees not only Jesus as a lecturer, but himself as one too, when in *Britains Remembrancer* he portrays Jesus casting merchants out of the church and then himself lecturing there instead. Given Wither's propensity to see himself in this way, his struggle with the stationers thus becomes a means of taking up the cross, rendering his struggle a holy mission. Wither's proclaimed poverty makes him both godly and, as he was wont to argue, somewhat of an original, as he writes in *Emblemes*:

> But, O my God! though groveling I appear
> Upon the ground (and have a rooting here
> Which hales me downward) yet in my desire
> To that which is above me I aspire;
> And all my best affections I profess
> To Him that is the sun of righteousness.
> Oh, keep the morning of His incarnation,
> The burning noontide of His bitter passion,
> The night of His descending, and the height
> Of His ascension ever in my sight,
> That imitating Him in what I may,
> I never follow an inferior way. (Ff)

This construction of "happiness in misery" allows Wither not only to claim independence from all other authority but God's, but to craft an authorial voice supposedly untainted by the traffic in money. Wither's embrace of poverty and identification with Christ thus further infuse his defense with voluntary martyrdom:

> My weake fortunes, my troubles, and the chargablenesse of a studie, that bringes with it no outward supplie, put me unto a kinde of necessity to cast my thoughts a side unto worldly respects: but I have since been sory for it upon better consideration. And as a just reward for my too earnest looking after vaine hopes, I doe now accept of my present trouble, that outwardly is like to impoverish me. (12: 30)

Wither likens stationers to preachers who profit from leading ignorant people astray – and these people seem to come from the "mechanical" class: "Yea; Brockers,

[12] George Wither, *The hymnes and songes of the church*, London, 1623.

and Costermongers, and Tapsters, and Pedlers, and Semptsters, and Fydlers, and Feltmakers, and all the Brotherhoods of Amsterdam, have scoffingly passed sentence upon me in their conventicles, at taphouses and Tavernes. So that . . . some of the stationers have by traducing it, given ignorant people occasion to speake the more in contempt of those Ordinances which they ought reverently to obey" (12: 64–65). The stationers, like the preachers, are guilty of deceiving ignorant people. This assumes a gullible, misled public, and the presence of the "brotherhood of Amsterdam" clearly links this to insubordination and radical religion. When one speaks against Wither, one thus speaks not only against the public's well-being, but against the true, untainted religion that his direct knowledge of his calling supposedly represents.

The story of Wither's election to writing is presented as a unique private experience that he now makes public. He relates how he first undertook his serious writing in jail, isolated, "shutt up from the society of mankind." Thus begins a narrative about his time in jail and, then, coming into his vocation. He tells of how he was not only denied human companionship but was not allowed to write, either, and this deprivation gave him strength: "So that if God, had not by resolutions of the minde which he infused into mee, extraordinarily inabled me to wrestle with those, & such other aflictions as I was then exercised withall, I had beene dangerously and everlastingly overcome" (12: 3). The successful weathering of this trial is deployed as evidence that Wither is a writer of both holy and personal election. His jail narrative becomes a defense against stepping out of his proper calling into that of the stationers: he posits that his writing *is* his calling and that it is his duty to defend it against infringement. He also asserts that his calling became evident early on, with a childhood love for the study of divinity. Eschewing the pursuit of a good reputation as fruitless, he spends three years preparing himself for the vocation of authorship.

While Wither seems particularly concerned to defend himself, his alleged persecution is rhetorically useful because it allows him to cast himself as a martyr: "For the Stationers have not onely labored to deprive me of the benefit due to my labours, but also to make me appeare without Christianity in my intentions: by affirming that I sought myne owne benyfit onely, in composing my booke of Hymns, & in publishing it according to the kinges commaund" (12: 24). He justifies his self-interest as a matter of intrinsic right to his own labors, which he undertakes strictly at God's command: "why should I be the man more accused, then all others, for seekeing after the just hyre of my labours? am I the only One guilty of studyinge myne owne profit, in the course of my paynefull endeavours for religious ende?" (12: 25). Yet at the same time, Wither's ownership of his own self-interest becomes confused by statements that seem to *deny* it. He claims that he resolves to publish at this time only to "stirre up in them that obedience and reverence, which they ought to expresse towards the pious ordinances of the Church" (12: 14). Later, he again denies any interest in "private benifit" (12: 17). Self-interest, he argues, is a sin of which only the stationers are guilty.

These contradictions are understandably frustrating to readers. Assuming that Wither recognizes them as such, he resolves the question by trying to impose the morality of the calling onto the question of self-interest in order to draw the difference between the stationers and himself. Firstly, Wither shares Taylor's fantasy that "true" labor *ought* to be self-evident in the way the laborer practices it. Both take visible "sweate" as a sign that one labors honestly, independent of the market's obfuscations of character and quality, as Wither declares, "Insomuch that there can be no publike grievance truly named or probably pretended which that priviledge is cause of: except it bee a griefe to some fewe Idle drones, to behould the laborious lyving upon the sweate of their owne browes" (12: 30–31). Again, labor becomes a moral designation – not merely labor itself, but the *kind* of labor undertaken and the premises for performing it. In presenting his case, Wither particularly is concerned with defining "honest" versus "dishonest" uses of the calling. Here his notion of occupation is conservative in the sense that it does posit exclusivity. Thus it proceeds that, because writing is a calling for him, he cannot possibly be intruding on an undeserved privilege; it is not "a taske fitter for a Divine then for me" (12: 40). In laboring, he is carrying out these gifts and making them manifest in the world: "God hath appointed me . . . There are divers guyftes, and diversitys of callings; and by the guift of God hath given him, every man may guesse at his calling, as the souldier may know in what part of the battell to range himselfe, by those Arms his Captayne appointed him unto: and that place he ought to make good, untyll he finde himselfe furnished and authorized for another Station" (12: 42). Labor is evidence of this special appointment – otherwise, no one would spend time at it: "I did not leape on a suddaine, or irreverently into this employment; but, having consumed almost [?] yeares of an Apprenticeshipp, in studies of this kinde, I entred therinto conscionably & in the feare of God: nor have I proceeded without his assistance, as the difficulties and discouragements which I have passed thorugh, do witness unto me" (12: 36). As with Jonson, "difficulties and discouragements" become evidence of a higher aim – in Wither's case, a distinctly spiritual aim.

However Wither, like Taylor, knows that the book, because it circulates as a commodity among commodities, cannot not exhibit the "sweat" he claims he exerts in creating it. This problem informs the division he seeks to make between honest and dishonest market participants. Like his contemporaries Jonson and Dekker, Wither imposes distinctions onto the print market by excoriating the flooding of the market with ballads and cheaply printed books: "how many dung-botes full of fruitless Volumnes doe they yearely foyst upon his Majesties subjectes, by lying Titles, insinuations, and disparaging of more profitable Books! how many hundred reames of foolish prophane and sensles Ballads do they quarterly disperse abroade?" (12: 29). The way to negotiate this minefield, as Jonson shows us, is to connect "honest" texts to honest readers, opening up the rest of the market for the proliferation of dishonest texts, readers, and producers. Wither insists that his text is "imprinted for the honest stationers," and Wither takes great pains at the end of the text to describe the "honest stationer" (12: 116–18) versus the "mere stationer" (12: 119–27). Charles Hensley notes, "In the poet's eyes, a 'meere stationer' prints anything for profit; he pirates material, even blots the author's name. Worst of all, he presumes to criticize all books yet has no respect for learning. He sets the interests of his 'Mystery above God, the State, and all good causes.'" (12: 37). The honest stationer works with an eye toward the glory of God rather than toward his own advantage, while the mere stationer works toward the latter. Undergirding the mere stationer's greed and ambition is the fact that he illicitly desires another walk of life; as Wither answers those who accuse him of intruding on the stationer's calling – which the stationers have characterized as not merely impertinence, but "blasphemy"[13] – he counters that it is the stationers who try to step out of their station, having "wished themselves of some other calling." Because of the typical mere stationer's resentment, he has enslaved authors and debased learning: he "hath brought Authors, yea the whole Common-wealth, and the liberall Sciences into bondage. For he makes all professors of Art, labour for his profit, at his owne price, and utters it to the Common-wealth in such fashion, and at those rates, which please himselfe" (12: 10). Wither's dramatic claim is that reaching outside of one's calling not only is detrimental to authors, but to the commonwealth itself. Also, discrediting the stationer's profession divorces the author from the actual material book and the agents of its production, even as he over-determines his responsibility for his creation, and thus advances a claim for authorship – that in its true, elemental form, it is about *writing*, not about packaging and selling.

The profession of honesty is paramount here, because it allows the writer to assert that he is different – and virtuously so – from an economic landscape that is defined by corrupt, dishonest practices. Like Taylor, Wither's definition of honest labor depends not only on a professed sense of election, but on a prejudice against mercantile activity as a breeding ground for deceit. Wither reminds his readers that it was the merchants who Jesus cast out of the temple; thus he likens the booksellers to "the Silver Smithes of Ephesus" (12: 6). Elsewhere, in language similar to that which Taylor uses to describe the roaring boy, Wither describes the stationers as those who "craftily cullor their ayme with the cloak of sanctity, and zeale of true religion. Yea they are growen so malepert, and arrogant, that being but the peddlers of Books, and for the most part ignorant fellows (acquainted with nothing concerning them, but their names, and pryses) they neverthelesse dare take upon them the miscensuring of any mans labours though allowed by authority" (12: 8). Wither's response to the idea of books as petty commodities emerges from a paradox: on the one hand, he wishes to cast books as things merely bought and sold, while needing to present his own book as superior, the product of true labor in a calling. Thus he draws the distinction between labor and selling or peddling, labor clearly being represented as more noble and honest because it is (supposedly) divorced from profit. It is of course highly ironic that this putative purity of motive becomes the basis for seeking profit. Wither even employs the metaphor of a merchant to dramatize his own losses: "All which expence, together with my paynefull endeavours, are now in danger to be lost, to the overthrow of my hopes; and (which is my greater griefe) to the hinderance of those my friends, who have adventured their goods in my sinking vessel" (12: 6). The "friends" who have risked their investments might be subscribers, or patrons, or they might simply be friends who have lent Wither money. The ship metaphor borrows mercantile language while still insisting on honesty (and not wishing harm to others)

[13] Gay reads the accusations of blasphemy as meaning "that the Stationers were attacking the very nature of his voice and not simply his economic practices and privileges" (184). Gay does not state the obvious here – that "blasphemy" also entails the deliberate flouting of God's authority. In such a case it makes sense that Wither would counter by arguing that, in fact, God's authority is on his side and that anyone who stands in his way is effectively the blasphemer.

as Wither strains to draw the distinction between "labor" (as in making something that one later owns) and trafficking.

As Wither's slippery, often self-contradictory arguments demonstrate, the rhetorical deployment of "labor" as a means of self-presentation rests upon anxiety about what it means to participate in the market for print. Like the other authors I have treated here, Wither wishes to both disassociate himself from the market and to adopt it as a means by which to argue for his own superior virtue and diligence. In the context of the radical Protestant Wither's career, the discourse of vocation is one way to enhance labor, making it moral and noble, rather than a means to achieve money.

The Shepheard's Calling

Although his increasing religious radicalism is certainly crucial to understanding Wither's sense of his profession, Wither also articulates vocational consciousness in secular genres and contexts. The pastoral poem *The Shepheards Hunting* (1614), which he wrote while in Marshalsea prison, proclaims his honesty and states that all of his pains are "to avoid idlenesse" rather than to go for praise (137). (In *The Schollers Purgatory*, he also claims that this is the period in which he learned to practice "content of mind" – another version of the Taylor-esque "happiness in misery.") His address "To the Reader" also makes a promise in the style of the young, ambitious Milton: he will in the future move on from the "slight matter" of pastorals to the "greater matter" of epic. This is not a new rhetorical pose for Wither or for the period in general, but Wither's pastoral exploration of idleness and industry specifically applies to the craft of poetry, particularly in Eclogue 5, where Wither "raises the still difficult issue of how a poet can write and at the same time support himself."[14] Wither's answer is that, society being what it is and poets having the standing in it that they have, one must try to do both, although this certainly is not the ideal condition for one whose calling is poetry alone. In *The Shepheards Hunting*, the shepherd Philarete assures his friend Alexis need not forsake shepherding, nor need he abandon poetry. Alexis frets that the two cannot possibly coexist:

> Yea, but if I appli'd mee to those straines,
> Who should drive forth my flocks unto the plaines,
> Which, whil'st the *Muses* rest, and leasure crave,
> Must watering, folding, and attendance have?
> For if I leave with wonted care to cherish
> Those tender *heards*, both I and they should perish. (5.143–8)

In answer, Philaster advises that he not:

> Neglect thy calling for thy *Muse*.
> But, let these two, so each of other borrow,
> That they may season mirth, and lesson sorrow.

[14] William B. Hunter, ed., *The English Spenserians: The Poetry of Giles Fletcher, George Wither, Michael Drayton, Phineas Fletcher and Henry More*, Salt Lake City: U of Utah Press, 1977.

> Thy Flocke will helpe thy charges to defray,
> Thy *Muse* to passé the long and teadious day. (5.152–6)

In a way that recalls Taylor's equation of rowing and writing, Philarete links shepherding to writing in a way that enables both kinds of labor. Thus, in a departure from early modern social descriptions that erected class-based differences between intellectual and manual work, Philarete suggests that one might succeed at both. Whereas the self-interested and defensive Wither of *The Schollers Purgatory* maintained that poetry required full commitment, here Wither adopts the position that a poet can (and often must) take on two occupations at once. While *The Schollers Purgatory* uses the discourse of callings in a conservative way, to manage the stationers and keep them from impeding on Wither's writing, Philarete's notion of occupation suggests its more liberal nuances, by positing that even the humble shepherd can attain the gift of poetry. Indeed, any early modern pastoral can be safely taken as an allegory for something else, be it the individual poet's social frustrations, a larger political problem, or both. But I believe it is no accident that notions of occupation, poetic and otherwise, are taking place in a pastoral by an author who spent much of his career defending his right to an authorial vocation and the earnings from its products.

The Shepheards Hunting, like many of Wither's writings, is not only concerned with the practice of poetry; Wither also seeks to delineate the identity of "the poet" in general. As in Jonson's case, the "poet" gets abstracted from a mere writer of verse to a social identity with its own gifts and responsibilities. "The poet" is self-possessed, if a bit antisocial:

> What is't to us, if they (o'reseene) contemne
> The praises due to sacred Poesie,
> Let them disdaine, and fret till they are weary,
> Wee in our selves have that shall make us merry:
> Which, he that wants, and had the power to know it,
> Would give his life that he might die a Poet. (5.175–82)

In yet another formulation of poetry-as-mystery, "Poesie" is deemed sacred and thus a realm to be understood and practiced only by the initiate. That Wither conceives of poets as a special group – "Wee in our selves" – is notable, given that laboring poets so often present themselves in isolation. But it also reveals the extent to which Wither considers poets the practioners of an occupation, as with clerks, shepherds, brewers, and so forth. The "poet" emerges as part of a special class.

Even if he is part of a group though, the poet still is misunderstood and defiantly marginal. Philarete, whose name means "love of virtue," proclaims himself highly independent in judgment:

> Nor care I greatly; for it skils not much,
> What the unsteady common-people deemes,
> His *Conscience* doth not always feele least touch,
> That blamelesse in the sight of others seemes:
> My cause is honest, and because 'tis such,

> I hold it so, and not for mens esteemes:
> If they speake justly well of mee, I'me glad;
> If falsely evill, it ne're makes me sad. (2. 33–40)

This pronouncement asserts that the speaking subject is both the author and the assessor of his own worth. The scorn of others merely presents further evidence of his virtue. Moreover, the primacy of "conscience" demonstrates the spiritual underpinnings of this fundamental "honesty." Philarete expresses the fundamental peace of mind that Wither claims to have had while in prison:

> I have *Mirth* here thou would'st not beleeve,
> From deepest *cares* the highest *joyes* I borrow.
> If ought chance out this day, may make me grieve
> I'le learne to men, or scorne it by to morrow.
> This barren place yeelds somewhat to relieve:
> For, I have found sufficient to content me,
> And more true blisse then ever freedome lent me. (1. 65–72)

Marginality becomes evidence of his superior virtue. In a formulation that appears continually in the works of laboring authors, Philarete's sense of security in his occupational identity stems precisely from his suffering:

> So, when I will be merry, I aswell
> Something for mirth from every thing can draw,
> From *Miserie*, from *Prisons*, nay from *Hell:*
> And as when to my *minde*, *griefe* gives a flaw,
> Best comforts doe but make my woes more fell:
> So when I'me bent to *Mirth*, from mischiefes paw,
> (Though ceas'd upon me) I would something cull,
> That spight of *care*, should make my *joyes* more full. (3.206–13)

Philarete brings this Christianized form of contentment into pastoral, a genre with classical pagan roots. While I do not go so far as to suggest that Philarete is an autobiographical figure for Wither, he echoes much of what Wither has to say about his struggles to own his labor. Moreover, as we have seen with Taylor, the claim to have invulnerable peace of mind and autonomy becomes a strategy for navigating the marketplace: the author attracts readers by claiming not to care what they think, at least not if they are "common-people." Readers are thus invited to self-select – if they too are "honest" and virtuous, they will participate in the author's self-construction by buying and valuing his books.

Although Philarete's scorn for "common-people" certainly marks him as elitist, the total profile of Philarete is really one of independence from both elite and popular culture. His stance is one that mirrors those all the laboring authors I treat, who eschew both "amateur" and "professional" tastes and modes of composition. Philarete draws a clear distinction between himself as a hardworking shepherd and from courtly pastimes and courtly poetry:

Here my neighbouring Sheepe
Upon the border of these Downes I keepe:
Where often thou at Pastorals and Playes,
Hast grac'd our Wakes on Summer Holy-dayes:
And many a time with thee at this cold spring
Met I, to heare your learned shepheards sing,
Saw them disporting in the shady Groves,
And in chaste Sonnets wooe their chaster Loves:
When I, endued with the meanest skill,
Mongst others have been urg'd to tune my quill.
But, (cause but little cunning I had got)
Perhaps thou saw'st me, though thou knew'st me not. (5.21–32)

Casting himself as an anonymous, but not invisible, figure to the viewer who "knew'st me not," Philarete injects his voice into a kind of pastoral distinctly concerned with the work of writing. Whereas previous shepherds engaged in love poetry and sonnets, Philarete applies "meanest skill" to his endeavors, resisting advice to "tune my quill" to something perhaps more conventional or less rough. The practice of a rough style resembles Taylor's insistence on "plainness," as though lack of decoration implies lack of deceit. In *The Schollers Purgatory*, Wither offers an apology for the kinds of poetry normally deemed "bad": "we make use of the most excelent expressions of the holy ghost in rude, and barbarous Numbers, whilst our own wanton fancies were paynted, & trymed out in the most moving language" (12: 12). Thus the Christian dictum of humility is extended into an approach to literary style; the more decorated the style, the more suited to "wanton" subject matter far from the spirit of the "holy ghost." Similarly, *The Schollers Purgatory* betrays a preference for "plainness" over "circumlocution," while treading lightly on the criticism of other styles. Wither even goes so far as to claim that the Bible is written in the same rough, jerky style in which his detractors accuse him of writing. Moreover, in a statement that challenges easy elisions between print and "popular" (i.e. non-elite) literature, Wither links the stationers to the proliferation of forms he regards as profane (despite occasionally having written in such forms himself); he ties "Flesh and the Devill" to "vaine Songes, and prophane ballads stored up in Stationers warhouses" (12: 19), making the stationers complicit in the spread of sin.

While it is certainly in keeping with *sprezzatura* to claim that one has "mean" skill when one does not, Philarete explicitly defines his own skill *against* acknowledged modes. Instead, he embraces the putatively rough standard that accounts for his difference from other poets who create within the confines of established forms. Thus, something new and "original" is discursively formed. Philarete's rejection of literary precedent (even as Wither embraces it in his imitation of conventional forms) mirrors Wither's own theological outlook, one in which reason and conscience are elevated over the Fathers of the Church, and experience takes precedent over authority. Thus Wither's approach may be properly understood as spiritual, cultural, and political all at once as, in the 1612 poem "Epithalamion," he particularly aims his scorn for convention and insistence on his own singularity at courtly poets:

> I am not of those *Heliconian* wits,
> Whose pleasing straines the *Courts* knowne humour fits.
> But a poore rurall *Shepheard* . . . (11.269–71)[15]

The embrace of a "rough" style and the life of a "poore rurall Shapheard" figures as a resistance to elite culture not merely because it is elite, but because it represents "knowne humour," i.e. tired literary convention. This iconoclastic stance dictates that a poet of originality embraces a "poore" identity.[16] In a Jonsonian formulation, Wither's proclaimed outsider status allows him to correct the court while fantasizing that they care enough about him to "hate" him:

> *I my selfe* though meanest stated,
> And in *Court* now almost hated,
> Will knit up my *Scourge*, and venter
> In the midst of them to enter;
> For I know, there's no disdaining,
> Where I looke for entertaining. (ll. 405–10)

The difference between Jonson and Wither, though, is that Wither envisions himself not as a gentle teacher of morals, but as a "Scourge," which is well in keeping with Wither's developing millenarian views.[17] His identity as a writer is thus infused with his larger political identity and his spiritual orientation – a radical one in which the conventional shepherd's pose is reconfigured as a rejection of conventional cultural constraints.

Conclusion: What Does It Mean to Be a Public Writer?

Wither's case also provides a fitting conclusion to this study because, like Milton, he is a border creature between the "Renaissance" – with its clear footing in patronage and manuscript-based literary systems – and the next period, where print authorship becomes fully installed as the vehicle for a nascent sense of professional authorship. I believe it is no coincidence that the period after the civil war witnessed a decline of the court's cultural authority (or at least its authority as a generator of fashionable literary forms) in favor of print culture, with its more populist literary forms like the magazine and the novel. The decreased political authority of the monarch no doubt had much to do with this change. However, I would argue that the decline of the manuscript coterie as a medium for the "private" exchange of writing between

[15] Quotes from "Epithalamion" are taken from Hunter's edition.

[16] I mean "iconoclastic" in both the general and particular senses of the term, since Wither (again, like Milton) hated idolatry and supported the destruction of images. See Christopher Hill, "George Wither and John Milton," *English Renaissance Studies Presented to Dame Helen Gardner in Honour of her Seventieth Birthday*, Oxford: Clarendon, 1980, 212–27, 216.

[17] No doubt prompted by the defeat of the Good Old Cause in 1660, Wither regarded the year 1666 as the date of the end of the world and the second coming. See Hill, "George Wither and John Milton," 219.

friends and the popularization of the "common" self make "public" writing possible. I shall conclude by reflecting briefly on how writing – and most especially "the poet" – becomes public domain, and how laboring authors fit into this history.

The terms "public" and "private" are open to a variety of definitions and applications. They could relate to, for example, domestic versus public space (or even different spaces *within* the domestic, such as different rooms), the state versus the home, or different forms of intimacy and interpersonal address. But I invoke the distinction as a means of talking about forms of writing. By public writing, I mean the kind in which writers – of common *or* elite status, but who profess to speak to everyone – have the opportunity to present their lives and their thoughts as *exempla* for a broad range of readers, often accompanied by descriptions of the process of writing itself. Moreover, what they expose is presented as initially "private" and fiercely individual, almost as though revealing the self were its own end – although the marketing context, with its focus on product and profit, shows that it is not. This is what it means to make writing "common" as well as a kind of "commons," where authors engage in exchange with a wide public. As laboring authors show in their varying ways, it takes the validation of both the "common" self – be this "common" status organic or constructed – and his or her experience in order to figure writing as an occupation to which one might commit.

Much critical attention has been paid to the construction of privacy in early modern Europe, particularly with respect to elite culture. Including such studies as Patricia Fumerton's work in *Cultural Aesthetics* on "the trivial selfhood of the aristocracy,"[18] work by Javitch, Orgel and Strong on courtly discourse and culture, and a robust body of criticism on domesticity and the private sphere, scholarship on the realms of the elite and/or the private has been necessary largely *because* these realms are private, and therefore murky and begging for elucidation. However, it is mainly among scholars of eighteenth-century Britain that we have seen fruitful discussions of the *public* as its own space and idea; scholars of the previous two centuries have given the public relatively little attention. It is insufficient to define the public simply in terms of that which it is not. The careers of laboring writers show that the public is not simply an antithesis of or a reaction against the private – it is a positive, deliberate stance that early modern changes in economic organization, social organization, and religion helped make possible. The excellent series *A History of Private Life*, edited by Roger Chartier, is an example of the critical scrutiny that notions of the private have received and how the public figures in comparison. Philippe Aries's introduction to the third volume, "Passions of the Renaissance," asks "How did the transition take place from a form of sociability in which private and public are confounded to one in which they are distinct, and in which the private may even subsume or curtail the public?"[19] While it is true in many respects that public and private witnessed a profound shift in the early modern period, I would

[18] Patricia Fumerton, *Cultural Aesthetics: Renaissance Literature and the Practice of Social Ornament*, Chicago: U of Chicago P, 1991, 1.

[19] Philippe Aries, "Introduction," *A History of Private Life, Vol. 3: Passions of the Renaissance*, ed. Roger Chartier, Cambridge, Mass.: Belknap Press of Harvard UP, 1989, 1–11, 9.

argue that the distinction between the two realms has been taken for granted, and that authorship is one area that significantly troubles this distinction.

In fact, it may be more appropriate to think of public and private as being permeable spheres, each incorporating degrees of the other, each realm fragmented into complex formulations rather than part of a unified "culture." For example, the writer's "community" – the group against which, in some accounts, the writer supposedly defines him or herself – itself is multifaceted, there are often more than one, and they might compete with each other. Just as culture is not a simple duality between "high" and "low," so can a bi-polar view of self vs. community and public vs. private be restrictive. Jean Marie Goulemot characterizes the medieval period as one in which "Writers belonged to the community: jongleurs, clerics, authors of sacred mysteries and profane plays existed only because a community – a convent, confraternity, or city – "commissioned" their works. The community, in which specific cultural practices were embodied, was the writer's *raison d'etre*; his work served its needs and brought it renown."[20] By contrast, it would follow that the early modern writer writes purely to gratify him or herself, particularly in a market context where, according to Marx's narrative, participants are isolated in their own self-interest. But as we have seen, the laboring writers I take as my examples – although they make much of their isolation – are also embedded in distinct occupational and social communities for which they serve as advocates. Moreover, the "right" readers form a community with authors by validating authors' efforts as self-representation. Readers enter the circle at the moment they purchase the book and read it. Goulemot writes that "The writer's subjectivity justifies and legitimates the writing, whether it be lyrical poetry or the knowledge-in-the-making that is the subject of [Montaigne's] *Essays*. The self, its freedom and its history, has become the justification for the act of writing."[21] While I agree that the self becomes paramount, in a *market* context, the self-as-justification is ultimately a strategic pose, one that attempts to engage the reader in a mutual contract of exchange. "Convent, confraternity, or city" do not authorize the writing – the "self" does, but ultimately with the readers' blessing. It would be disingenuous to suggest that presenting the self for publication, however much an author claims to defy public opinion, is *ever* an end in itself.

Much confusion can result from over-reliance on Habermas's notion of the "bourgeois public sphere." I find it useful to the extent that it charts a broad movement from courtly to common types of representation, both in forms of media and their contents. However, Habermas's description of this change has received criticism for its tendency toward abstraction, its neglect of material culture, and its lack of attention to the role of social struggle.[22] I hope to have made emergent ideas of the public more specific by highlighting the role of struggle and contradiction in

[20] Jean Marie Goulemot, "Literary Practices: Publicizing the Private," in Chartier, 363–95, 364.

[21] Goulemot, "Literary Practices," 370.

[22] See Craig Calhoun, "Introduction," *Habermas and the Public Sphere*, ed. Craig Calhoun, Cambridge: MIT Press, 1992, 1–48; Bruce Robbins, "The Public as Phantom," *The Phantom Public Sphere*, ed. Bruce Robbins, Minneapolis: U of Minnesota Press, 1993, vii–xxvi; and Michael Warner, "The Mass Public and the Mass Subject," in Calhoun, 234–56.

early modern representational shifts toward print and public culture. Most notably, the range of authors who experienced such difficulties shows that struggle was not felt only by the traditionally oppressed, but by those with access to privilege. The participation of a variety of different identities in representational change suggests the growth of a "public," if only because it is so diverse and inclusive. It also shows that ideas of the public emerged from different groups and subject positions – in conflict with *other* groups and subject positions – rather than involving a large-scale expansion of the whole of society all at once, as the lack of specificity in Habermas's account might lead one to believe.

Notably, despite the frequent presence of elitism, these authors seem to be moving toward increasingly egalitarian premises. Whitney does not know what to do with the loss of her household and family communities, thus she engages readers and the whole of London in her address. Furthermore, learning for her is clearly a privilege and writing a social risk. However, Nashe and Jonson, who feel entitled to more expectation, insist on writing as a special activity to be reserved only for those with "learning." In their specific contexts, these two writers are compelled to assert that writing is an exclusive "mystery" supported by adequate learning and a rejection of superficial social approval. Taylor and Wither maintain defenses of their own, but the revolutionary context in which they both operate prompts them to address "everybody," thus expanding their sense of audience outward to include, potentially, all members of society. In all cases, the creation of a reading public requires the careful rhetorical management of authors' defenses and anxieties; the reader is engaged in a complex game in which trust and esteem are alternately exchanged and withheld.

I do not argue that these authors successfully address the whole of society, nor do they represent it. But the *idea* of a public emerges out of these specific localities. Paradoxically, it is laboring writers' very individualism that prompts a sense of community between author and readers. The public is figured as a different kind of community than guild, household, or court. It is, theoretically, voluntary and open to everyone. While writers for the print market are certainly not without their elitism and prejudices, their writing is figured as "public" because, in theory, anyone can access it – if not right away, then eventually through publication, even in the case of Jonson's masques. This fact makes writing fundamentally distinct from self-mystifying forms of representation generated by closed circles, which adopt elite forms of representation whether they are truly elite or not. As the cases of Taylor and Wither especially show, writing publicly calls for a different style – an immediate, "transparent" self that seeks to engage readers directly, with no specific members in mind except for the "right" or "understanding" readers. Accounts of these authors' "honest" labor assure readers that their trust is justified.

The Schollers Purgatory is instructive in terms of understanding how the private experience of writing becomes public. Its title page makes Wither's private struggle into a matter or urgent public concern: "The Schollers Purgatory, Discovered in the Stationers Common-wealth, And Discribed in a Discourse Apologeticall, aswell for the publike advantage of the Church, the State & whole Common-wealth of *England*, as for the remedy of private injuries." Wither's private injuries become public matters, thus demonstrating one way in which the putatively "private" self becomes public by connecting through the medium of print. Wither makes a similar claim concerning his "private" injuries at the beginning of *Se Defendendo*, 1643: "Read; for, this Private Cause, if, rightly, tri'd, / The publike Wrongs hath, partly, typifi'd: / And, for himselfe, if You will heare Him, now, / Perhaps, ere long, Hee'l say as much, for You" (12: 1). By invoking a public/private distinction specifically, the story of an otherwise unremarkable self becomes indicative of larger social concerns. And, it must be admitted, the place Wither currently occupies in scholarship on the history of intellectual property shows that he in a way succeeded – his otherwise unremarkable poetry has attracted attention because of his efforts to make his private economic struggles matter, thereby gaining him status as an important figure in the history of professional authorship.

However, this is not to say that a critical legacy, past or present, makes one a successful author. Indeed, "success" as we define it today means "publication," an ambiguous achievement in early modern England. The story of how publication came to signify an author's excellence, instead of his or her material want or social stimgatization, is one in which notions of authorship-as-labor play a crucial part. Early modern authors who chose to embrace labor, in all the social complexity that the concept implied, took a first step toward the later installment of writing as a profession involving serious work and commitment – a process and a social stance that helps authors become publicly visible *as* authors, a role to be played in the shaping of culture.

Bibliography

Aers, David ,"A Whisper in the Ear of Early Modernists; or, Reflections on Literary Critics Writing the 'History of the Subject'," *Culture and History 1350–1600: Essays on English Communities, Identities, and Writing*, ed. David Aers, Detroit: Wayne State UP, 1992, 177–202.

Agnew, Jean-Christophe, *Worlds Apart: The Market and the Theater in Anglo-American Thought, 1550-1750*, Cambridge: Cambridge UP, 1986.

Aries, Philippe, "Introduction," in Chartier, 1–11.

Aubrey, John, *Brief Lives*, ed. Richard Barber, Totowa, NJ: Barnes and Noble, 1983.

Barish, Jonas A., "Jonson and the Loathed Stage," *A Celebration of Ben Jonson*, ed. William Blisset, Julian Patrick, and R.W. Van Fossen, Toronto: U of Toronto P, 1973, 27–53.

Barker, Francis, *The Tremulous Private Body: Essays on Subjection*, London: Methuen, 1984.

Barthes, Roland, "The Death of the Author," *Image, Music, Text*, trans. Stephen Heath, New York: Hill and Wang, 1977, 142–8.

Beaumont, Francis, *The Masque of the Inner Temple and Gray's Inn*, in Spencer and Wells.

Becker, Lucinda M., *Death and the Early Modern Englishwoman*, Aldershot, UK: Ashgate, 2003.

Bell, Walter George, *A Short History of the Worshipful Company of Tylers and Bricklayers of the City of London*, London: H.G. Montgomery, 1938.

Belsey, Catherine, *The Subject of Tragedy: Identity and Difference in Renaissance Drama*, London: Methuen, 1985.

Ben-Amos, Ilana Krausman, *Adolescence and Youth in Early Modern England*, New Haven: Yale UP, 1994.

Boehrer, Bruce, "The Poet of Labor: Authorship and Property in the Work of Ben Jonson," *Philological Quarterly* 72 (1993), 289–312.

Bulfinch's Complete Mythology, London: Spring Books, 1989.

Burke, Peter, *Popular Culture in Early Modern Europe*, London: Maurice Temple Smith, 1978.

Cahn, Susan, *Industry of Devotion: The Transformation of Women's Work in England, 1500–1660*, New York: Columbia Univ. Press, 1987.

Calhoun, Craig, "Introduction," *Habermas and the Public Sphere*, ed. Craig Calhoun, Cambridge: MIT Press, 1992, 1–48.

Capp, Bernard, "Arson, Threats of Arson, and Incivility in Early Modern England," *Civil Histories: Essays Presented to Sir Keith Thomas*, ed. Peter Burke, Brian Harrison, and Paul Slack, Oxford: Oxford UP, 2000, 197–213.

——, *The World of John Taylor the Water-Poet*, Oxford: Clarendon, 1994.

Certeau, Michel de, *The Practice of Everyday Life*, trans. Steven Rendall, Berkeley: U of California P, 1988.

Chapman, George, *The Memorable Masque*, in Lindley, 74–91.

Charles, Lindsey and Duffin, Lorna, eds, *Women and Work in Pre-Industrial England*, London: Croom Helm, 1985.

Chartier, Roger, ed., *A History of Private Life, Vol. 3: Passions of the Renaissance*, Cambridge, Mass.: Belknap Press of Harvard UP, 1989.

Child, Francis James, *English and Scottish Ballads*, London: Sampson Low, 1861.

Clark, Alice, *Working Life of Women in the Seventeenth Century*, London: Routledge, 1919.

Clark, Peter, *The English Alehouse, A Social History, 1200–1830*, New York: Longman, 1983, 79–80.

Clarke, Danielle, *The Politics of Early Modern Women's Writing*, London: Longman, 2001.

Craig, D. H., ed., *Ben Jonson: The Critical Heritage, 1599–1798*, London and New York: Routledge, 1990.

Cressy, David, "A Drudgery of Schoolmasters: The Teaching Profession in Elizabethan and Early Stuart England," *The Professions in Early Modern England*, ed. Wilfrid Prest, London: Croom Helm, 1987, 129–53.

Curtis, Mark, "The Alienated Intellectuals of Early Stuart England," *Past and Present* 23 (1962), 25–43.

——, *Oxford and Cambridge in Transition, 1558–1642*, Oxford: Clarendon, 1959.

Daniel, Samuel, *Tethys Festival*, in Lindley, 54–65.

Dekker, Thomas, *The Belman of London*, London, 1608.

——, *Lantern and Candle-light* (1608), reprinted in Arthur F. Kinney, ed., *Rogues, Vagabonds, and Sturdy Beggars*, Barre, Mass.: Imprint Society, 1973.

Dollimore, Jonathan, *Radical Tragedy: Religion, Ideology, and Power in the Drama of Shakespeare and His Contemporaries*, 2nd edn, Durham: Duke UP, 1993.

Evans, G. Blakemore, ed., *The Riverside Shakespeare*, 2nd edn, Boston and New York: Houghton Mifflin, 1997.

Fehrenbach, Robert J., "Isabella Whitney (fl. 1565–75) and the Popular Miscellanies of Richard Jones," *Cahiers elisabethains* (April 1981), 85–7.

——, "A Letter sent by Maydens of London," *English Literary Renaissance* 14, 3 (Autumn 1984), 285–304.

Felker, Michael, "The Poems of Isabella Whitney: A Critical Edition," diss. Texas Tech Univ., 1990.

Ferguson, Margaret, "Renaissance Concepts of the 'Woman Writer'," *Women and Literature in Britain*, ed. Helen Wilcox, Cambridge: Cambridge Univ. Press, 1996, 143–68.

Fletcher, Anthony and Stevenson, John, "Introduction," *Order and Disorder in Early Modern England*, ed. Fletcher and Stevenson, New York: Cambridge UP, 1985, 1–40.

Foucault, Michel, "What is an Author?", *The Foucault Reader*, Ed. Paul Rabinow, New York: Pantheon, 1984, 101–20.

Fumerton, Patricia, *Cultural Aesthetics: Renaissance Literature and the Practice of Social Ornament*, Chicago: U of Chicago P, 1991.

——, "London's Vagrant Economy: Making Space for 'Low' Subjectivity," in Orlin, 206–25.

Gardiner, John, *The Life and Times of George Chapman, 1559–1634*, Hitchin, UK: The Dogs of Tilehouse Street, 37.

Gardiner, Judith K. and Epp, Susanna S., "Ben Jonson's Social Attitudes: A Statistical Analysis," *Drama in the Renaissance: Comparative and Critical Essays*, ed. Clifford Davidson, C. J. Gianakaris, and John H. Stroupe, New York: AMS Press, 1986, 84–102.

Gay, David, "'Lawfull Charms' and 'Wars of Truth': Voice and Power in Writings by John Milton and George Wither," *Papers on Language and Literature* 36: 2 (Spring 2000), 177–97.

Gaze, W. Culling, *On and Along the Thames: James I, 1603–1625*, London: Jarrold and Sons, 1900.

Godfrey, Walter H., ed., "Inigo Jones and St. Paul's Cathedral," *London Topographical Record* 18, Cambridge: Cambridge UP, 1942, 41–6.

Gordon, D. J., "Poet and Architect: The Intellectual Setting of the Quarrel Between Ben Jonson and Inigo Jones," *Journal of the Warburg and Courtauld Institutes* 12 (1949), 152–78.

Goulemot, Jean Marie, "Literary Practices: Publicizing the Private," in Chartier, 363–95.

Greenblatt, Stephen, *Renaissance Self-Fashioning: From More to Shakespeare*, Chicago: U of Chicago P, 1980.

Griffiths, Paul, "The Structure of Prostitution in Elizabethan London," *Continuity and Change* 8, 1 (1993), 39–63.

Habermas, Jurgen, *The Structural Transformation of the Public Sphere: An Inquiry into a Category of Bourgeois Society*, trans. Thomas Burger, Cambridge: MIT Press, 1996.

Halasz, Alexandra, *The Marketplace of Print: Pamphlets and the Public Sphere in Early Modern England*, Cambridge: Cambridge UP, 1997.

Hall, Joseph, *Viridemiarum*, Edinburgh: Tait, 1824.

Halpern, Richard, *The Poetics of Primitive Acculmulation: English Renaissance Culture and the Genealogy of Capital*, Ithaca: Cornell UP, 1991.

Hanson, Elizabeth, *Discovering the Subject in Renaissance England*, Cambridge: Cambridge UP, 1998.

Harris, Tim, "Problematising Popular Culture," *Popular Culture in England, c. 1500–1850*, ed. Tim Harris, Hampshire, UK: Macmillan Press Ltd., 1995, 1–27.

Harrison, William, *The Description of England*, ed. Georges Edelen, Ithaca, NY: Cornell UP, 1968.

Hawkes, David, *Idols of the Marketplace: Idolatry and Commodity Fetishism in English Literature, 1580–1680*, New York: Palgrave, 2001.

Helgerson, Richard, *Self-Crowned Laureates: Spenser, Jonson, Milton and the Literary System*, Berkeley: U of California P, 1982.

Hensley, Charles S., *The Later Career of George Wither*. The Hague and Paris: Mouton, 1969.

Hereford, C. H. and Simpson, Percy and Evelyn, eds, *Ben Jonson*, 11 vols, Oxford: Clarendon, 1925–52.

Hill, Christopher, “A Bourgeois Revolution?”, *The Collected Essays of Christopher Hill*, Vol. 3, Sussex, UK: Harvester, 1986, 94–124.

——, *Change and Continuity in Seventeenth-Century England*, Cambridge, MA: Harvard UP, 1975.

——, “George Wither and John Milton,” *English Renaissance Studies Presented to Dame Helen Gardner in Honour of her Seventieth Birthday*, Oxford: Clarendon, 1980, 212–27.

Holbrook, Peter, *Literature and Degree in Renaissance England: Nashe, Bourgeois Tragedy, Shakespeare*, Newark: U of Delaware P, 1994.

Homer, *The Iliad*, trans. Robert Fagles, New York: Viking, 1990.

Hornblower, Simon and Spawforth, Anthony, eds, *Oxford Classical Dictionary*, rev. 3rd edn, New York: Oxford UP, 2003.

Humpherus, Henry, *History of the Origin and Progress of the Company of Watermen a Lightermen of the River Thames, with numerous historical notes*, 3 vols, Sudbury, UK.

Huntley, Frank Livingstone, “Joseph Hall, John Marston, and *The Returne from Parnassus*,” in *Illustrious Evidence: Approaches to English Literature of the Early Seventeenth Century*, ed. Earl Miner, Berkeley: U of California P, 1975, 3–22.

Jameson, Frederic, *The Political Unconscious: Narrative as a Socially Symbolic Act*, Ithaca: Cornell UP, 1981.

Javitch, Daniel, *Poetry and Courtliness in Renaissance England*, Princeton: Princeton UP, 1978.

Johnson, A. W., *Ben Jonson: Poetry and Architecture*, Oxford: Clarendon, 1994.

Jones, Ann Rosalind, *The Currency of Eros: Women's Love Lyric in Europe, 1540–1620*, Bloomington: Indiana Univ. Press, 1990.

——, ‘Maidservants of London: Sisterhoods of Kinship and Labor,” *Maids and Mistresses, Cousins and Queens*, ed. Susan Frye and Karen Robertson, New York: Oxford Univ. Press, 1999, 21–32.

——, “Nets and Bridles: Early Modern Conduct Books and Sixteenth-Century Women's Lyrics,” *The Ideology of Conduct*, eds Nancy Armstrong and Leonard Tennenhouse, New York: Methuen, 1987.

——, “Surprising Fame: Renaissance Gender Ideologies and Women's Lyric,” *The Poetics of Gender*, ed. Nancy K. Miller, New York: Columbia Univ. Press, 1986, 74–95.

Jones, Inigo and Davenant, William, *Salmacida Spolia*, in Spencer and Wells.

Jonson, Ben, *Q. Horatius Flaccus: His Art of Poetry, Englished by Ben Jonson*, London, 1640.

——, *The Workes of Benjamin Jonson, the Second Volume*, London, 1640.

Jordan, Constance, “Renaissance Women and the Question of Class,” *Sexuality and Gender in Early Modern Europe: Institutions, Texts, Images*, ed. James Grantham Turner, Cambridge: Cambridge Univ. Press, 1993, 90–106.

Keene, Derek, “Material London in Time and Space,” in Orlin, 55–74.

Kelso, Ruth, *The Institution of the Gentleman in English Literature of the Sixteenth Century: A Study in Renaissance Ideals*, Urbana, IL, 1926.

Kimbrough, Robert, ed., *Sir Philip Sidney: Selected Prose and Poetry*, 2nd edn, Madison, WI: U of Wisconsin P, 1983, 156.

Kinney, Arthur F., ed., *Rogues, Vagabonds & Sturdy Beggars: A New Gallery of Tudor and Early Stuart Rogue Literature*, Amherst: U of Massachusetts P, 1990.

Leapman, Michael, *Inigo: The Troubled Life of Inigo Jones, Architect of the English Renaissance*, London: Review, 2003, 274.

Leishmann, J.B., ed., *The Three Parnassus Plays (1598–1601)*, London: Ivor Nicholson and Watson Ltd., 1949, 26–34.

Lindley, David, ed., *Court Masques: Jacobean and Caroline Entertainments*, Oxford: Oxford UP, 1995.

Lloyd, Nathaniel, *A History of English Brickwork*, London: H. Greville Montgomery, 1928.

Loewenstein, Joseph, *The Author's Due: Printing and the Prehistory of Copyright*, Chicago: U of Chicago P, 2002.

——, *Ben Jonson and Possessive Authorship*, Cambridge: Cambridge UP, 2002.

——, "The Script in the Marketplace," *Representations* 12 (1985), 101–14.

——, "Wither and Professional Work," *Print, Manuscript, and Performance: The Changing Relations of the Media in Early Modern England*, ed. Arthur F. Marotti and Michael D. Bristol, Columbus: Ohio State UP, 2000, 103–24.

Lyne, Raphael, "A Case for Isabella Whitney," Cambridge University CERES Project, http://www.english.cam.ac.uk/ceres/aeneas/attrib.htm, last retrieved March 10, 2006.

Macray, William Dunn, ed., *The Pilgrimage to Parnassus: with the two parts of The Return from Parnassus; Three Comedies Performed in St. John's College, Cambridge*, Oxford: Clarendon, 1886.

Macrobius, *Commentary on the Dream of Scipio*, trans. William Harris Stahl, New York: Columbia UP, 1952.

Marx, Karl, *Grundrisse*, London: Penguin, 1993, 243–5.

Mascuch, Michael, *Origins of the Individualist Self: Autobiography and Self Identity in England, 1591–1791*, Stanford: Stanford UP, 1996.

Maus, Katherine Eisaman, "Facts of the Matter: Satiric and Ideal Economies in the Jonsonian Imagination," *English Literary Renaissance* 19 (1989), 42–64.

May, Steven, "Tudor Aristocrats and the Mythical 'Stigma of Print'," *Renaissance Papers* (1980), 11–18.

McKeon, Michael, *The Origins of the English Novel, 1600–1740*, Baltimore: Johns Hopkins UP, 1987.

McKerrow, Ronald B., ed., *The Works of Thomas Nashe*, 5 vols, Oxford: Basil Blackwell, 1958.

Mendelson, Sara and Crawford, Patricia, *Women in Early Modern England, 1550–1720*, Oxford: Oxford Univ. Press, 1998.

Meskill, Lynn Sermin, "Exorcising the Gorgon of Terror: Jonson's *Masque of Queens*," *ELH* 72:1 (2005), 181–207.

Mickel, Lesley, *Ben Jonson's Antimasques: A History of Growth and Decline*, Aldershot, UK: Ashgate, 1999.

Montrose, Louis, "Of Gentlemen and Shepherds: The Politics of Elizabethan Pastoral Form," *ELH* 50 (1983), 415–59.

Mulcaster, Richard, *Positions*, ed. Richard L. DeMolen, New York: Columbia UP, 1971.

Netzloff, Mark, "'Counterfeit Egyptians' and Imagined Borders: Jonson's *The Gypsies Metamorphosed*," *ELH* 68:4 (2001), 763–93.

Newcomb, Lori Humphrey, *Reading Popular Romance in Early Modern England*, New York: Columbia UP, 2002.

Norbrook, David, "Levelling Poetry: George Wither and the English Revolution, 1642–1649," *English Literary Renaissance* 21: 2 (Spring 1991), 217–56.

Notestein, Wallace, *Four Worthies: John Chamberlain, Anne Clifford, John Taylor, Oliver Heywood*, London: Jonathan Cape, 1956.

O'Day, Rosemary, *The Professions in Early Modern England, 1450–1800: Servants of the Commonweal*, Harlow, UK: Pearson, 2000.

Orgel, Stephen, ed., *The Complete Masques*, New Haven and London: Yale UP, 1975.

Orgel, Stephen and Strong, Roy, *Inigo Jones: The Theatre of the Stuart Court, Including the complete designs for productions at court for the most part in the collection of the Duke of Devonshire together with their texts and historical documentation*, 2 vols, Sotheby Parke Bernet for University of California Press, 1973.

O'Riordan, C., "The Democratic Revolution in the Company of Thames Watermen, 1641–2," *East London Record* 6 (1983), 17–27.

Orlin, Lena Cowen, ed., *Material London, ca. 1600*, Philadelphia: U of Pennsylvania P, 2000.

Orme, Nicholas, "Schoolmasters, 1307–1509," in *Profession, Vocation, and Culture in Later Medieval England: Essays Dedicated to the Memroy of A.R. Myers*, ed. Cecil H. Clough, Liverpool: Liverpool UP, 1982, 218–41.

Overbury, Thomas, *The Miscellaneous Works in Prose and Verse of Sir Thomas Overbury, Knt.*, ed. Edward F. Rimbault, London: John Russell Smith, 1856.

Panofsky, Richard J., ed., *The floures of philosophie (1572) / by Hugh Plat and A sweet nosgay (1573) and The copy of a letter (1567) / by Isabella Whitney, photoreproductions*, New York: Scholars' Facsimiles and Reprints, 1982.

Parker, Patricia, *Shakespeare from the Margins: Language, Culture, Context*, Chicago: U of Chicago P, 1996.

Paster, Gail Kern, Rowe, Katherine and Floyd-Wilson, Mary, eds, *Reading the Early Modern Passions: Essays in the Cultural History of Emotion*, Philadelphia: U of Pennsylvania P, 2004.

Patterson, Annabel, *Shakespeare and the Popular Voice*, Cambridge, Mass.: Basil Blackwell, 1989.

Paylor, W. J., ed., *The Overburian Characters*, Oxford: Basil Blackwell, 1936.

Phillippy, Patricia, "The Maid's Lawful Liberty: Service, the Household, and 'Mother B' in Isabella Whitney's A Sweet Nosgay," *Modern Philology* 95 (1998), 439–62.

Polanyi, Karl, *The Great Transformation*, Boston: Beacon, 1944.

Prescott, Anne Lake, *Imagining Rabelais in Renaissance England*, New Haven and London: Yale UP, 1998.

Puttenham, George, *The Arte of English Poesie*, ed. G.D. Wilcock and A. Walker, Cambridge: Cambridge UP, 1936.

Richards, Jennifer, *Rhetoric and Courtliness in Early Modern Literature*, Cambridge: Cambridge UP, 2003.
Riggs, David, *Ben Jonson: A Life*, Cambridge: Harvard UP, 1989.
Robbins, Bruce, "The Public as Phantom," *The Phantom Public Sphere*, ed. Bruce Robbins, Minneapolis: U of Minnesota Press, 1993, vii–xxvi.
Rollins, Hyder Edward, ed., *Tottel's Miscellany*, 2 vols, Cambridge: Harvard UP, 1928 1: 11. 1–8.
Rose, Mark, *Authors and Owners: The Invention of Copyright*, Cambridge: Harvard UP, 1995.
Rowlands, Samuel, *The Complete Works of Samuel Rowlands, 1598–1628*, Glasgow: Hunterian Club, 1880.
Russell, Elizabeth, "The Influx of Commoners into the University of Oxford Before 1581: An Optical Illusion?", *English Historical Review* 92 (1977), 721–45.
Santiago-Valles, Kelvin, "'Race,' Labor, 'Women's Proper Place,' and the Birth of Nations," *CR: The New Centennial Review* 3:3 (2003), 47–69.
Saunders, J. W., "The Stigma of Print: A Note on the Social Bases of Tudor Poetry," *Essays in Criticism* I (1951), 139–64.
Schleiner, Louise, *Tudor and Stuart Women Writers*, Bloomington: Indiana Univ. Press, 1994.
Schofield, John, "The Topography and Buildings of London, ca. 1600," in Orlin, 296–321.
Siskin, Clifford, *The Work of Writing: Literature and Social Change in Britain, 1700–1830*, Baltimore: Johns Hopkins UP, 1998.
Smith, Thomas, *De Republica Anglorum*, London, 1583.
Soens, Lewis, ed., *Sir Philip Sidney's Defense of Poesy*, Lincoln: U of Nebraska P, 1970.
Southey, Robert, *Lives and Works of the Uneducated Poets*, ed. J.S. Childers, London: Humphrey Milford, 1925.
Spencer, T. J. B. and Wells, S., *A Book of Masques in Honour of Allardyce Nicoll*, Cambridge: Cambridge UP, 1967.
Stevenson, Laura Caroline, *Praise and Paradox: Merchants and Craftsmen in Elizabethan Popular Literature*, Cambridge: Cambridge UP, 1984.
Stone, Lawrence, "The Educational Revolution in England, 1560–1640," *Past and Present* 28 (1964), 41–80.
Tawney, R.H. and Power, Eileen, *Tudor Economic Documents*, 3 vols, London: Longmans, 1951.
Taylor, Charles, *Sources of the Self: The Making of Modern Identity*, Cambridge: Harvard UP, 1989.
Taylor, John, *Works of John Taylor, The Water-Poet, Comprised in the Folio Edition of 1630*, 5 vols, Manchester: Spenser Society, 1869.
Works of John Taylor, The Water Poet, Not Included in the Folio Volume of 1630, 5 vols, Manchester: Spenser Society, 1870–8.
Taylors Farewell to the Tower-Bottles, London, 1622.
Thirsk, Joan and Cooper, J.P., eds, *Seventeenth Century Economic Documents*, Oxford: Clarendon, 1972.
Thompson, Lloyd A., *Romans and Blacks*, Norman, OK: U of Oklahoma P, 1989.

Travitsky, Betty, ed., "The Maner of Her Wyll'," *ELR* 10, 4 (Winter 1980), 76–95.

Turner, Jennifer, "Jack Wilton and the Art of Travel," in *Critical Approaches to English Prose Fiction 1520–1640*, ed. Donald Beecher, Ottawa: Dovehouse, 1998, 123–56.

Unwin, George, *The Gilds and Companies of London*, New York: Barnes and Noble, 1964.

Walker, Kim, *Women Writers of the English Renaissance*, New York: Twayne Publishers, 1996.

Wall, Wendy, *The Imprint of Gender: Authorship and Publication in the English Renaissance*, Ithaca: Cornell UP, 1993.

Ward, Joseph P., *Metropolitan Communities: Trade Guilds, Identity, and Change in Early Modern London*, Stanford, CA: Stanford UP, 1997.

Warner, Michael, "The Mass Public and the Mass Subject," *Habermas and the Public Sphere*, ed. Craig Calhoun, Cambridge: MIT Press, 1992, 234–56.

Weber, Max, *The Protestant Ethic and the Spirit of Capitalism*, trans. Talcott Parsons, London: Routledge, 1992.

Whyman, Susan, "Gentle Companions: Single Women and their Letters in Late Stuart England," *Early Modern Women's Letter Writing, 1450–1700*, ed. James Daybell, London: Palgrave, 2001, 177–93.

Wild, Robert, *Alas poore scholler, wither wilt thou goe: or Strange altrations which at this time be; there's many did thinke they never should see. To the tune of, Halloo my fancy, &c*, London, 1641.

Williams, Raymond, "The Writer: Commitment and Alignment," *Marxism Today* (June 1980): 22–5.

Wither, George, *A Collection of Emblemes, Ancient and Moderne*, London, 1635.

——, *The hymnes and songes of the church*, London, 1623.

——, *Miscellaneous Works*, 20 vols, Manchester: Spenser Society, 1871–1882, New York: Burt Franklin, 1967.

——, *Vox Pacifica*, London, 1645.

Woodmansee, Martha, "The Genius and the Copyright: Economic and Legal Conditions of the Emergence of the 'Author'," *Eighteenth Century Studies* 17 (4) (Summer 1984), 425–48.

Woodward, Donald, *Labourers and Building Craftsmen in the Towns of Northern England, 1450–1750*, Cambridge: Cambridge UP, 1995.

Wright, Louis B. , *Middle-Class Culture in Elizabethan England*, Chapel Hill: U of North Carolina P, 1935.

Wrightson, Keith, *English Society, 1580–1680*, London: Hutchinson, 1982.

——, "Estates, Degrees, and Sorts: Changing Perceptions of Society in Tudor and Stuart England," *Language, History, and Class*, ed. Penelope J. Corfield, Oxford: Basil Blackwell, 1991, 30–52.

Zagorin, Perez, *Ways of Lying: Dissimulation, Persecution, and Conformity in Early Modern Europe*, Cambridge, MA: Harvard UP, 1990.

Index

For Product Safety Concerns and Information please contact our EU representative GPSR@taylorandfrancis.com
Taylor & Francis Verlag GmbH, Kaufingerstraße 24, 80331 München, Germany

www.ingramcontent.com/pod-product-compliance
Ingram Content Group UK Ltd.
Pitfield, Milton Keynes, MK11 3LW, UK
UKHW021438080625
459435UK00011B/296

* 9 7 8 0 3 6 7 8 9 3 0 1 9 *